FAMILY ALBUM

FAMILY ALBUM

More Glorious Knits for Children and Adults

KAFFE FASSETT & ZOË HUNT

PHOTOGRAPHY BY STEVE LOVI

CLARKSON N. POTTER, INC./PUBLISHERS

SQUARES AND PLAIDS

For years I've been attracted to simple squares. Every part of the world has variations on this eternal shape, whether tiled floors or intricate basketweaves, craftsmen have arranged squares into handsome patterns. I stumbled across this idea for bright jumbles of squares in an exhibition of Italian shoes. Small, bright strips of coloured leather had been woven to create squares of multicolours on an elegant shoe. I rushed home and knitted the Squares bright colourway which we nicknamed 'Hopscotch' (page 12). Steve suggested the black and white chequerboard to give a crisp edge to the pattern.

This concept of five stitches across and six rows up each square can be applied to dozens of colour schemes from burnished dark tones of maroon, bottle green and bean brown, to mother-of-pearl pastel. Soft spring greens and pinks work too (page 18) and I took the deep bright palette from the autumn shawl for another lively alternative (page 30). My favourite is Zoë's soft, finely knitted Battenburg colouring (page 22) which we named after the party cake. The crisp squares contrast beautifully with the faded elegance of the close tones. You can, of course, change scale easily as we have done in the Battenburg and autumn colourways.

Squares is worked in the intarsia method throughout. The trick here is to work out as accurately as possible how long a piece of yarn is needed to complete one square. Then you can cut each piece roughly to that length, thus avoiding tangles.

There is something so refreshing about the uncompromising order of plaids – covering a garment shape with a tidy grid. All over the world, in Africa, Japan, South America and probably most famously, in Scotland, plaids have contributed to these grid patterns. I have used a simple technique here – which I hope will be the starting point for many of your variations – of outlining stripes of colour in a deeper or lighter tone of the background. You could introduce another single line of colour between these colour stripes; much more colour could be used of course.

When knitting these Plaids, the two main colours are worked in fairisle. The single stitch vertical lines are worked by the intarsia method, each with a separate piece of yarn which is left attached to the work throughout and carried loosely up across the horizontal stripes on the back of the work. These yarns should each be twisted round the two main colours before working the stitch.

One of the most interesting uses of plaid is in combination with other patterns. You could use bands of plaid alternately with bands of other patterns in this book or make up your own to create a sort of patchwork.

RIGHT AND OVERLEAF *The Child's Squares Button Shoulder Sweater, page 12 – we named it 'Hopscotch' – was inspired by Italian shoes of woven leather. I hope you can find sharp little buttons to match the chequerboard border.*

PREVIOUS PAGE *In a heavenly Moroccan field, the children are wearing Bright Squares Trousers, and the Diagonal Stripe Dress and Hat, page 60. I am wearing the Split Diamond Crewneck in cotton, page 172. This pattern is also available in kit form.*

Inc row (ws) With H, rib 6[3,5], make 1, * rib 4[4,3], make 1; rep from * to last 6[3,6] sts, rib to end. 48[52,56] sts.

Change to larger needles and work border patt as foll:

1st row (rs) K (2J, 2L) to end.
2nd row P (2L, 2J) to end.
3rd row K (2L, 2J) to end.
4th row P (2J, 2L) to end.

Rep these 4 rows twice more AND AT THE SAME TIME, inc one st at each end of next and foll 4th row, working inc sts into patt. 52[56,60] sts.

Cont in patt as foll:

Beg with a K row and working in st st throughout cont in patt from Chart, beginning and ending rows as indicated (noting that first row on Chart shows st inc at each end of row) AND AT THE SAME TIME, inc one st at each end of next and every foll 4th row, working inc sts into patt until there are 88[94,100] sts. Cont without shaping until 72[78,84] rows in all have been worked from Chart. Cast(bind) off *loosely*.

Make a 2nd sleeve in the same way.

FINISHING

Press work lightly on ws according to instructions on bands, omitting ribbing.

BACK NECKBAND

Using smaller needles, E and with rs facing, K across 20[24,28] sts of right shoulder, pick up and K 44[46,48] sts evenly around back neck, then K

Baby's Bright Squares Trousers

omit for 1st size — omit for 2nd size

M	N	T	U	J	E	A	L	S	F	T	D	G	R	M
D	G	H	C	Q	T	R	M	B	G	N	C	F	A	D
S	R	J	L	G	F	S	H	C	U	M	E	T	N	S
E	M	B	S	R	M	E	T	N	A	Q	J	H	G	E
J	L	C	N	A	U	C	D	G	E	S	R	M	Q	J
H	T	E	M	D	J	L	M	R	T	F	A	N	S	H
A	N	G	R	C	F	T	B	J	H	M	D	T	E	A
M	D	C	U	T	N	G	H	C	D	S	B	J	R	C	D	M
L	S	E	A	Q	M	D	S	F	T	L	G	H	M	N	S	L
C	H	J	L	C	U	T	R	M	B	A	F	S	Q	T	H	C
D	M	Q	G	E	J	B	A	N	C	H	T	U	G	R	M	D
G	N	C	R	M	H	S	F	T	Q	J	D	M	E	A	N	G
U	T	L	S	D	C	N	M	H	G	R	A	F	C	Q	T	U
C	D	M	Q	T	R	A	B	J	E	M	L	S	H	J	D	C
B	G	H	J	F	S	Q	C	U	A	B	T	R	M	E	G	B
A	R	S	D	M	L	G	E	T	N	S	H	J	Q	C	R	A

omit for 2nd size
omit for 1st size

across 20[24,28] sts of left shoulder. 84[94,104] sts.
Work 5 rows in K1, P1 rib in stripes as foll:
2 rows E, 2 rows d, 1 row W.
Using W, cast (bind) off *loosely* in rib.

FRONT NECKBAND

Using smaller needles, E and with rs facing, K across 20[24,28] sts of left shoulder, pick up and K 23 sts evenly down left front neck, 16[18,20] sts across centre front and 23 sts up right front neck, then K across 20[24,28] sts of right shoulder. 102[112,122] sts.
Work 2 rows in K1, P1 rib using E.
<u>3rd row</u> With d, rib 3[5,7], cast(bind) off 2 sts, * rib 5[6,7] including st already on needle, cast(bind) off 2 sts *; rep from * to * once more, rib 64[66,68] including st already on needle, cast(bind) off 2 sts; rep from * to * twice more, rib to end.
<u>4th row</u> With d, rib to end, casting on 2 sts over each 2 cast(bound) off.
<u>5th row</u> With W, rib to end.
Using W, cast (bind) off *loosely* in rib.
Overlap front neckband on to back neckband and oversew at armhole edges. Mark back and front at side edge 18.5[19.5,20.5]cm/7¼[7¾,8¼]in down from shoulder. Using backstitch, join cast-(bound-)off edge of sleeves to back and front between markers, matching centre of top of sleeve to shoulder.
Press seams.
Using backstitch on main knitting and an edge to edge st on rib, join side and sleeve seams.
Press all seams. Sew on buttons.

BABY'S BRIGHT SQUARES TROUSERS

MATERIALS

General yarn weight used – lightweight cotton
Rowan *Soft Cotton* (50g/1¾oz balls) in the foll 11 colours:
  A (546) strawberry ice – 1[1,1] ball
  B (539) bermuda – 1[1,1] ball
  C (533) antique pink – 1[1,1] ball
  D (547) mermaid – 1[1,1] ball
  E (548) eau de nil – 1[1,1] ball
  F (528) rain cloud – 1[1,1] ball
  G (534) frolic – 1[1,1] ball
  H (531) fiord – 1[1,1] ball
  J (544) lilac – 1[1,1] ball
  L (542) bluebell – 1[1,1] ball
  M (545) sugar pink – 1[1,1] ball
Rowan *Knobbly Cotton* (50g/1¾oz balls) in the foll colour:
  N (566) hyacinth – 1[1,1] ball
Rowan *Cabled Mercerised Cotton* (50g/1¾oz balls) in the foll 5 colours:
  Q (323) hydro – 1[1,1] ball
  R (324) sky high – 1[1,1] ball
  S (322) blush – 1[1,1] ball
  T (312) old rose – 1[1,1] ball
  U (307) spode – 1[1,1] ball
One pair each 2¼mm (US size 1) and 3mm (US size 3) knitting needles *or size to obtain correct tension (gauge)*
4 buttons
Elastic thread (optional)

SIZES

To fit 3-6[9-12,18-24]months or 42-45[46-48, 51-53]cm/16½-18[18¼-19,20-21]in chest.
Figures for larger sizes are given in square brackets; where there is only one set of figures, it applies to all sizes.
For finished measurements see diagram.

TENSION(GAUGE)

29 sts and 37 rows to 10cm/4in over patt on 3mm (US size 3) needles.
Check your tension(gauge) before beginning.

NOTES

When working rib, carry yarn not in use up the side of work.

RIGHT LEG

Using smaller needles and A, cast on 64[74,84] sts.
Work 33 rows in K1, P1 rib, working in stripes of (2 rows B, 2 rows A) 8 times, 1 row B.
<u>Inc row</u> (ws) With B, (rib 1, make 1) 1[2,3] times, (rib 2, make 1) to last 1[2,3] sts, (rib 1, make 1) 0[1,2] times, rib 1. 96[112,128] sts.
Change to larger needles and cont in patt as foll:
Beg with a K row and working in st st throughout, cont in patt from Chart as foll:
<u>1st row</u> 4A, 8R, 8C, 0[0,8]Q, 0[0,8]J, 0[8,8]H, 0[8,8]S, 8N, 8T, 8E, 8G, 8L, 8M, 8D, 8S, 8R, 4A, thus omitting 4 squares for first size and 2 squares for 2nd size.
Work 9 more rows in colours as set.
<u>11th row</u> 4B, 8G, 8E, 0[0,8]M, 0[0,8]R, 0[8,8]T, 0[8,8]B, 8A, 8U, 8C, 8Q, 8S, 8F, 8J, 8H, 8G, 4B.
Cont to work in coloured squares of 8 sts by 10 rows throughout, omitting squares for first and 2nd sizes as shown on Chart until 70[80,90] rows in all have been worked in patt, so ending with a ws row.

Crotch Shaping

Keeping patt correct, cast(bind) off 3 sts at beg of next 2 rows, 2 sts at beg of foll 2 rows, then one st at beg of next 6 rows.
Leave rem 80[96,112] sts on a spare needle.
Make Left Leg in the same way.

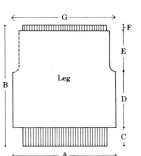

BABY'S BRIGHT SQUARES TROUSERS
A = 33[38.5,44]cm/ 13¼[15½,17½]in
B = 45[49.5,54]cm/ 18[19½,21½]in
C = 8cm/3¼in
D = 19[21.5,24.5]cm/ 7½[8½,9¾]in
E = 15.5[17.5,19]cm/ 6¼[6¾,7½]in
F = 2.5cm/1in
G = 50[57,65]cm/ 20[23,26]in all round

LEFT *A Moroccan grandmother sits before her blue door. The children are wearing the Diagonal Stripe Dress, page 60, and Bright Squares Trousers.*

OVERLEAF *These are the adult's and child's versions of a spring green-and-pink Squares confection. We have played with scale on these garments. A simple all-over pattern like Squares is not difficult to scale up or down, page 6.*

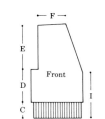

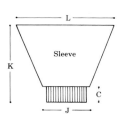

ADULT'S SQUARES JACKET
A = 53.5[59,65]cm/
21¼[23¾,26]in
B = 55[58,60.5]cm/22[23,24]in
C = 10cm/4in
D =
16[19,21.5]cm/6½[7½,8½]in
E = 29cm/11½in
F = 12[15,17.5]cm/4¾[6,7]in
G = 20[20.5,21.5]cm/
8[8¼,8½]in
H = 25[28,31]cm/
10[11¼,12½]in
I = 24.5[27,30]cm/
9¾[11,12]in
J = 29cm/11½in
K = 50.5cm/20¼in
L = 58cm/23in

PREVIOUS PAGE AND BELOW
Adult's Squares Jacket,
and the child is wearing
the Flags Jumpsuit,
page 135.

Body
Join legs to beg body as foll:
Using larger needles and with rs facing, beg
with left leg and keeping colours correct, patt
80[96,112] sts of left leg, then cont across
80[96,112] sts of right leg. 160[192,224] sts.
Cont until 128[144,160] rows in all have been
worked in patt.

Waistband
Change to smaller needles.
Dec row (rs) With B, K 14[7,6], (K2 tog, K 8[5,4]) to
last 6[3,2] sts, K to end. 146[166,188] sts.
Work 14 rows in K1, P1 rib, working in stripes as
foll: 1 row B, (2 rows A, 2 rows B) 3 times, 1 row A.
Using A, cast(bind) off *loosely* in rib.

STRAPS
Using smaller needles and A, cast on 15 sts.
Working throughout in stripes of 2 rows B, 2 rows
A, cont in rib as foll:
1st row (rs) K2, (P1, K1) to last st, K1.
2nd row K1, (P1, K1) to end.
Rep these 2 rows until 126[142,158] rows in all
have been worked.
Keeping stripe patt correct divide as foll:
Next row (rs) K2, (P1, K1) twice, P1, cast (bind) off
one st, (P1, K1) to last st, K1.
Cont on last set of 7 sts only:
Beg 2nd row, work 15 rows more in rib as before.
Buttonhole row (rs) K2, P1, cast(bind) off one st,
P1, K2.
Next row K1, P1, K1, yfwd, K1, P1, K1.
Next row K2, P1, K1, P1, K2.
Work 6 rows more in rib as set.
Using A, cast(bind) off in rib. Return to sts which
were left; with ws facing rejoin yarn, K1, (P1, K1)
to end.
Complete to match first side.
Make a 2nd strap in the same way.

FINISHING
Press work lightly on ws according to instructions
on ball bands, omitting ribbing. Using an edge to
edge st, join leg seams as far as crotch shaping.
Using an edge to edge st, join short crotch seam at
front and entire centre seam at back. Press seams.
Mark sides and centre front and back of waistband, then put markers half way between these
points. Sew on buttons 2cm/¾in either side of
these last markers, halfway up the front waist-

band. Attach straps to buttons at front, then sl st
them on the inside at back, centred on halfway
markers, when you are sure of lengths, crossing
straps over at back. If desired run elastic thread
along ws of work through every rib row at waistband and ankles, catching in on every other st.
Turn up rib at ankle and hold in place with a st at
inside leg seam.

ADULT'S SQUARES
JACKET

MATERIALS
General yarn weight used – 4 ply (fingering)
Rowan *Botany* (25g/1oz hanks) in the foll 16
colours:
  A (1) white – 2[2,2] hanks
  B (4) cream – 2[2,2] hanks
  C (6) custard – 2[2,2] hanks
  D (12) sunshine – 1[1,1] hank
  E (89) light emerald – 2[2,2] hanks
  F (416) almond – 2[2,2] hanks
  G (76) pistachio – 2[2,2] hanks
  H (49) sky blue – 2[2,2] hanks
  J (123) duck egg – 2[2,2] hanks
  L (48) cloud blue – 2[2,2] hanks
  M (103) flesh – 2[2,2] hanks
  N (121) mauve – 2[2,2] hanks
  Q (120) platinum – 2[2,2] hanks
  R (68) sugar pink – 2[2,2] hanks
  S (621) shocking pink – 2[2,2] hanks
  T (83) powder – 2[2,2] hanks
One pair each 2¼mm (US size 1) and 3mm (US size
3) knitting needles *or size to obtain correct ten-*
sion(gauge)
2¼mm (US size 1) circular needle, 100cm or 40in
long
6[5,7] buttons

SIZES
To fit 81-86[91-96,102-107]cm/32-34[36-38, 40-
42]in bust.
Figures for larger sizes are given in square
brackets; where there is only one set of figures, it
applies to all sizes.
For finished measurements see diagram.

TENSION(GAUGE)
27 sts and 37 rows to 10cm/4in over patt on 3mm
(US size 3) needles.
Check your tension(gauge) before beginning.

NOTES
Each 'square' is 8 sts by 10 rows, the diagram shows
the layout of the colours. The cardigan has an
unusual rib for the front band, 2 colours are used in
every row making it less stretchy than normal rib.
It is an ordinary K3, P3 rib but the K sts are worked
in one colour and the P sts in another. Take care not
to pull yarns too tightly across ws of work and
always take both colours right to end of row.

BACK
Using smaller needles and R, cast on 144[160,176]
sts.
Work 50 rows in K1, P1 rib in stripes as foll:
3 rows E, 2 rows A, 3 rows S, 2 rows G, 3 rows H, 2
rows T, 3 rows D, 2 rows F, 3 rows N, 2 rows A, 3
rows C, 2 rows Q, 3 rows J, 2 rows B, 3 rows R, 2
rows G, 3 rows H, 2 rows M, 3 rows F, 2 rows B.
Change to larger needles.
Beg with a K row and working in st st throughout

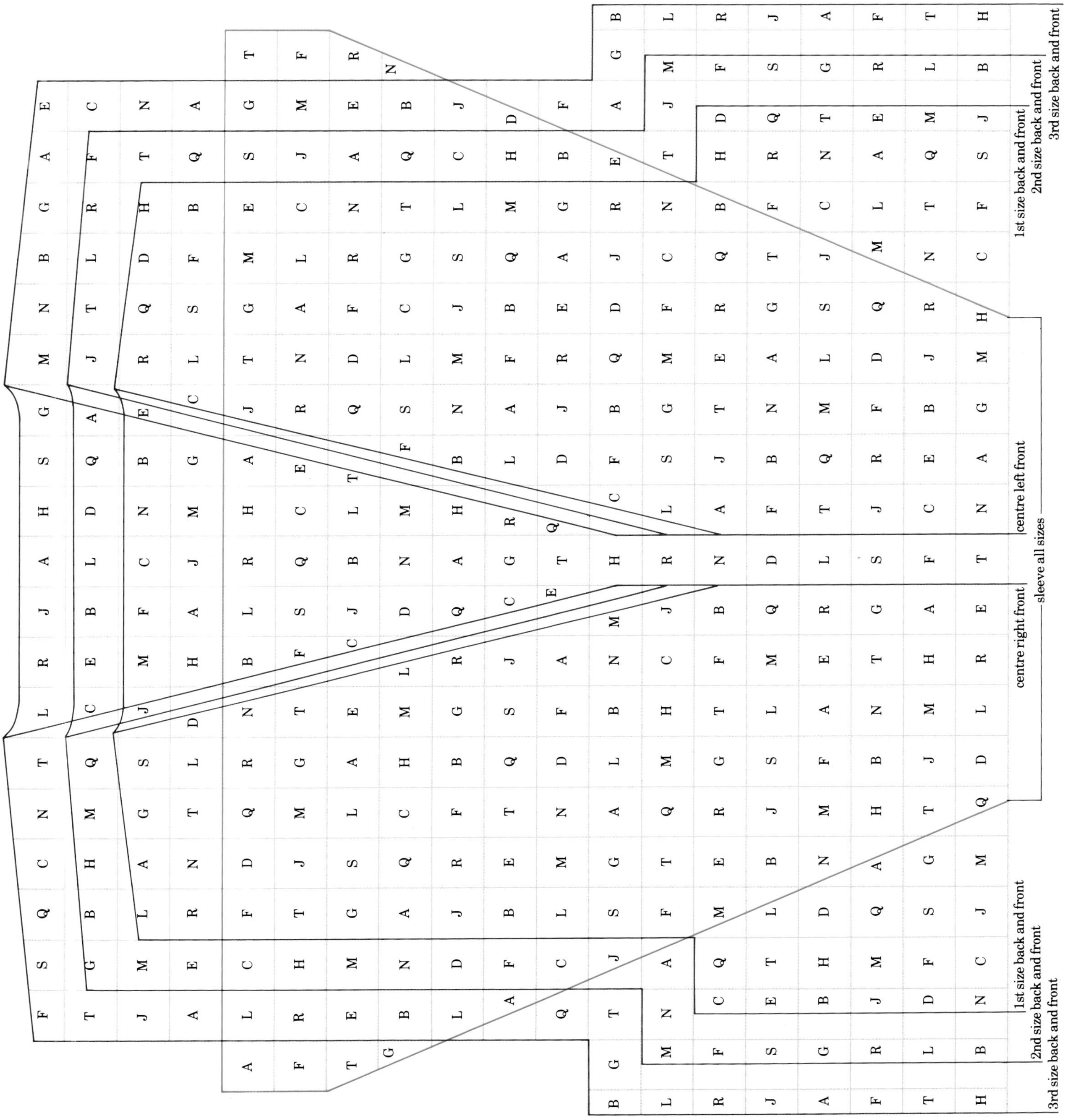

1st size back and front
2nd size back and front
3rd size back and front

1st size back and front
2nd size back and front
3rd size back and front

centre left front

centre right front

sleeve all sizes

cont in patt as foll:

<u>1st row</u> K 0[0,4]H, 0[4,8]B, 4[8,8]J, 8S, 8F, 8C, 8H, 8M, 8G, 8A, 8N, 8T, 8E, 8R, 8L, 8D, 8Q, 8M, 8J, 8C, 4[8,8]N, 0[4,8]B, 0[0,4]H.

Cont in patt as set, changing colours of squares on every foll 10th row until 60[70,80] rows in all have been worked in patt, so ending with a ws row.

Armhole Shaping

Keeping patt correct, cast(bind) off 12 sts at beg of next 2 rows. 120[136,152] sts.

Cont without shaping until 166[176,186] rows in all have been worked in patt, so ending with a ws row.

Shoulder and Neck Shaping

Keeping patt correct, cast(bind) off 11[14,16] sts at beg of next 2 rows.

<u>Next row</u> (rs) Cast(bind) off 11[13,16] sts, patt 19[21,23] including st already on needle, cast(bind) off 38[40,42] sts, patt to end.

Cont on last set of sts only for left back:

Cast(bind) off 11[13,16] sts at beg of next row, then 8 sts at beg of foll row.

Cast(bind) off rem 11[13,15] sts.

BELOW *Adult's Squares Jacket.*

Return to sts which were left; with ws facing rejoin yarn to neck edge, cast(bind) off 8 sts and patt to end. Cast(bind) off rem 11[13,15] sts.

LEFT FRONT

Using smaller needles and R, cast on 68[76,84] sts and work 50 rows in striped rib as for Back. Change to larger needles.

Beg with a K row and working in st st throughout cont in patt as foll: **

<u>1st row</u> K 0[0,4]H, 0[4,8]B, 4[8,8]J, 8S, 8F, 8C, 8H, 8M, 8G, 8A, 8N.

Cont in patt as set, changing colours of squares as for Back until 54[64,74] rows in all have been worked in patt, so ending with a ws row.

Front Edge and Armhole Shaping

Keeping patt correct, dec one st at end of next and foll 4th row. Work 1 row without shaping.

Cast(bind) off 12 sts at beg of next row.

Keeping armhole edge straight, cont to dec at front edge only on every 4th row as set until 33[40,47] sts rem.

Cont without shaping until 166[176,186] rows in all have been worked in patt, so ending with a ws row.

Shoulder Shaping

Keeping patt correct, cast(bind) off 11[14,16] sts at beg of next row, then 11[13,16] sts at beg of foll alt row. Work 1 row without shaping.

Cast(bind) off rem 11[13,15] sts.

RIGHT FRONT

Work as given for Left Front to **.

<u>1st row</u> K 8E, 8R, 8L, 8D, 8Q, 8M, 8J, 8C, 4[8,8]N, 0[4,8]B, 0[0,4]H.

Cont in patt as set, changing colours of squares as for Back until 54[64,74] rows in all have been worked in patt, so ending with a ws row.

Front Edge and Armhole Shaping

Keeping patt correct, dec one st at beg of next and foll 4th row. Work 2 rows without shaping.

Cast(bind) off 12 sts at beg of next row.

Cont to match Left Front, reversing all shaping.

SLEEVES

Using smaller needles and R, cast on 78 sts and work 50 rows in striped rib as for Back. Change to larger needles.

Beg with a K row and working in st st throughout cont in patt as foll:

<u>1st row</u> K 1H, with H, make 1, 2H, 8M, 8G, 8A, 8N, 8T, 8E, 8R, 8L, 8D, 2Q, with Q, make 1, 1Q. 80 sts.

Cont in patt as set, changing colours of squares on every foll 10th row AND AT THE SAME TIME, inc one st at each end of the 4th and every foll 3rd row, working inc sts into patt until there are 168 sts.

Cont without shaping until 150 rows in all have been worked in patt, so ending with a ws row.

Cast(bind) off *loosely*.

Make a 2nd sleeve in the same way.

FINISHING

Press work lightly on ws according to instructions on bands, omitting ribbing.

Using backstitch, join shoulder seams. Press seams.

FRONT BAND

Using circular needle, Q and with rs facing, pick up and K 42 sts evenly up right front welt (2 sts at beg then approximately 4 sts for every 5 rows),

170[180,190] sts to shoulder seam (one st for every row), 59[63,67] sts around back neck, then 170[180,190] sts down left front edge to top of welt and 42 sts to lower edge. 483[507,531] sts. Working backwards and forwards in rows, cont in 2 colour rib as foll:

<u>1st row</u> (ws) P3E, (take R to rs, K3R, take R to ws, P3E) to end.

<u>2nd row</u> K3J, (take R to rs, P3R, take R to ws, K3J) to end.

<u>3rd row</u> As first row, but using J and T instead of E and R.

<u>4th row</u> As 2nd row, but using T instead of R.

<u>Buttonhole row</u> P3F, (take T to rs, K3T, take T to ws, P3F) to last 96[102,114] sts, * take T to rs, K1T, cast (bind) off 1T, K1T, take T to ws, (P3F, take T to rs, K3T, take T to ws) 2[3,2] times, P3F; rep from * 4[3,5] times more, (take T to rs, K1T, cast(bind) off 1T, K1T, take T to ws) P3F.

<u>6th row</u> * K3F, take A to rs, P1A, with A, yrn, P1A, take A to ws, (K3F, take A to rs, P3A, take A to ws) 2[3,2] times; rep from * 4[3,5] times, K3F, take A to rs, P1A, with A, yrn, P1A, take A to ws, (K3F, take A to rs, P3A, take A to ws) to last 3 sts, K3F.

<u>7th row</u> As first row, but using F and A instead of E and R.

<u>8th row</u> As 2nd row, but using G and A instead of J and R.

<u>9th row</u> As first row, but using G and A instead of E and R.

<u>10th row</u> As 8th row.

Cast(bind) off in 2 colour rib as foll:

Cast(bind) off 3G, * take A to rs, cast(bind) off 3A, take A to ws, cast(bind) off 3G; rep from * to end.

Press front band lightly so that it lies flat. Using backstitch, join cast-(bound-)off edge of sleeves to back and front armholes, matching centre of top of sleeve to shoulder and making sure that 'squares' match exactly, easing to fit. Sew last few rows of sleeve to cast-(bound-)off sts at underarm. Press seams. Using backstitch on main knitting and an edge to edge st on rib, join side and sleeve seams. Press all seams. Sew on buttons.

BABY'S YELLOW PLAID SHORTS

MATERIALS

General yarn weight used – lightweight cotton
Rowan *Soft Cotton* (50g/1¾oz balls) in the foll 4 colours:

A (551) lemon ice – 2[2,2,2,2] balls
B (537) apple – 2[2,2,2,2] balls
C (534) frolic – 1[1,1,1,1] ball
D (539) bermuda – 1[1,1,1,1] ball

Rowan *Cabled Mercerised Cotton* (50g/1¾oz balls) in the foll 2 colours:

E (307) spode – 1[1,1,1,1] ball
F (312) old rose – 1[1,1,1,1] ball

Rowan *Knobbly Cotton* (50g/1¾oz balls) in the foll colour:

G (566) hyacinth – 1[1,1,1,1] ball

One pair each 2¼mm (US size 1) and 3mm (US size 3) knitting needles *or size to obtain the correct tension(gauge)*
4 buttons
11 pairs of small press fasteners (snaps)
Elastic thread (optional)

SIZES

To fit 3[6,9,12,18]months or 42[45,48,51,53]cm/16[18,19,20,21]in chest.

Figures for larger sizes are given in square brackets; where there is only one set of figures, it applies to all sizes.
For finished measurements see diagram.

ABOVE *Baby's Yellow Plaid Shorts, and the Adult's Orange Plaid V-neck Sweater.*

TENSION(GAUGE)

32 sts and 36 rows to 10cm/4in over patt on 3mm (US size 3) needles.
Check your tension(gauge) before beginning.

NOTES

When working in patt from Chart (pages 28-29), read odd rows (K) from right to left and even rows (P) from left to right.

BACK RIGHT LEG

Using smaller needles and A, cast on 35[37,39, 41,43] sts.
Work 30 rows in K1, P1 rib, working in stripes of (2 rows B, 2 rows A) 7 times, 2 rows B.
<u>Inc row</u> (ws) With A, * (rib 1, make 1) 3 times, rib 1; rep from * to last 3[1,3,5,3] sts, (make 1, rib 1) 1[0,2,4,3] times, rib 2[1,1,1,0]. 60[64,68,72,76] sts.
Change to larger needles and cont in patt as foll:
Beg with a K row and working in st st throughout,

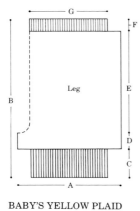

BABY'S YELLOW PLAID SHORTS
A = 18.5[20,21,22.5,23.5]cm/
7½[8,8½,9,9½]in
B = 32[33.5,35.5,37,38.5]cm/
12¾[13¼,14,14¾,15¼]in
C = 7cm/2¾in
D = 4.5cm/1¾in
E = 18[19.5,21.5,23,24.5]cm/
7¼[7¾,8½,9¼,9¾]in
F = 2.5cm/1in
G = 44[47.5,51,54,57.5]cm/
17¾[19,20½,21¾,23]in all round

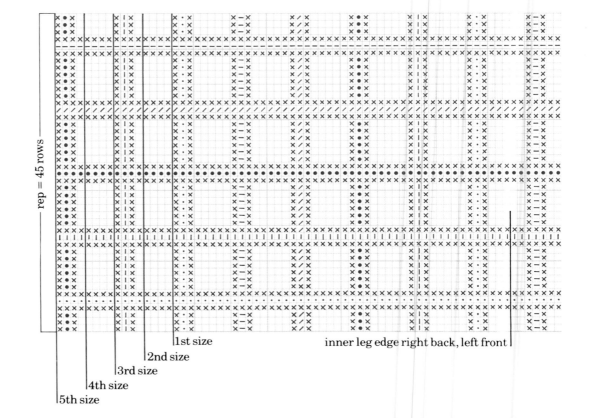

rep = 45 rows

1st size
2nd size
3rd size
4th size
5th size

inner leg edge right back, left front

PREVIOUS PAGE *Against a background of the Adult's Orange Plaid V-neck Sweater, the boy wears Yellow Plaid Shorts, page 25, the girl wears Brushstrokes Scoopneck Sweater, page 72, and her friend wears a pink Brushstrokes Skirt made in the same way as the Child's Circle Square Skirt on page 176. The woman is wearing a cotton sleeveless sweater which is knitted using the border from the Adult's Tweedy Diagonal Box Stripe Crewneck Sweater on page 56.*

cont in patt from Chart starting and ending rows as indicated for right back.
Cont until 17 rows in all have been worked in patt, so ending with rs row. Cut yarns.
Leave these sts on a spare needle.

BACK LEFT LEG
Work as given for Right Leg, *but* starting and ending Chart as indicated for left back.
Do not cut yarns.

Body
Join legs to beg body as foll:
Using larger needles and with ws facing, beg with Left Leg and keeping colours correct, patt 60[64,68,72,76] sts of Left Leg, then cont across 60[64,68, 72, 76] sts of Right Leg. 120[128, 136,144,152] sts.

Crotch Shaping
Next row (rs) Patt 57[61,65,69,73], with B, K3 tog tbl, with D, K3 tog, patt to end.
Next row Patt to end as now set.
Next row Patt 55[59,63,67,71], with B, K3 tog tbl, with A, K3 tog, patt to end.
Next row Patt to end as now set.
Next row Patt 54[58,62,66,70], with G, K2 tog tbl, with G, K2 tog, patt to end.
Next row Patt to end as now set.
Next row Patt 53[57,61,65,69], with A, K2 tog tbl, with A, K2 tog, patt to end.
Next row Patt to end as now set.
Next row Patt 52[56,60,64,68], with A, K2 tog tbl, with A, K2 tog, patt to end.
106[114,122,130,138] sts.
Cont in patt from row 28 as now set, rep rows 1-45 until 81[87,93,99,105] rows in all have been worked in patt.

Waistband
Change to smaller needles.
Dec row (ws) With A, * P1, P2 tog; rep from * to last

1[0,2,1,0] sts, P 1[0,2,1,0]. 71[76,82,87,92] sts.
Work 11 rows in K1, P1 rib, working in stripes as foll:
(2 rows B, 2 rows A) twice, 2 rows B, 1 row A. Using A, cast (bind) off *loosely* in rib.

FRONT
Work exactly as given for Back, BUT noting that right back becomes left front and left back becomes right front.

FRONT INSIDE LEG BORDERS
Using smaller needles, A, and with rs facing, pick up and K 24 sts (approximately 3 sts for every 4 rows) along side edge of rib, 18 sts from top of rib to crotch (approximately one st for every row), 18 sts from crotch to top of rib, then 24 sts along side edge of rib. 84 sts.
Work 4 rows in K1, P1 rib.
Cast(bind) off in rib.

BACK INSIDE LEG BORDERS
Work exactly as given for Front.

BRACES
Using smaller needles and A, cast on 15 sts.
Working throughout in stripes of 2 rows B, 2 rows A, cont in rib as foll:
1st row (rs) K2, (P1, K1) to last st, K1.
2nd row K1, (P1, K1) to end.
Rep these 2 rows until 94[102,110,118,134] rows in all have been worked.
Keeping stripe patt correct, divide as foll:
Next row (rs) K2, (P1, K1) twice, P1, cast (bind) off one st, (P1, K1) to last st, K1.
Cont on last set of 7 sts only:
Beg 2nd rib row, work 13[13,15,15,15] rows more in rib as before.
Buttonhole row (rs) K2, P1, cast (bind) off one st, P1, K2.
Next row K1, P1, K1, yfwd, K1, P1, K1.
Next row K2, P1, K1, P1, K2.

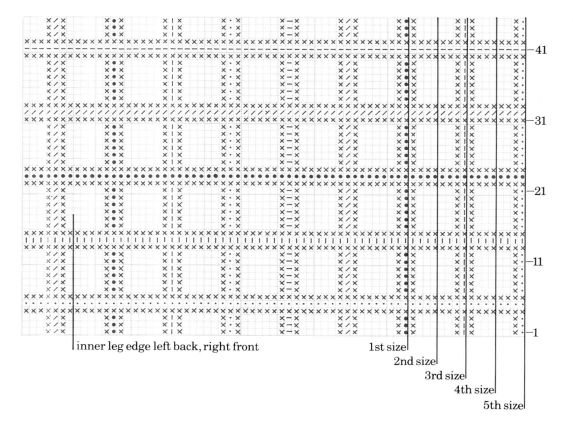

□ = A
☒ = B
⊟ = C
⊡ = D
⊡ = E
⊞ = F
⊡ = G

—41

—31

—21

—11

—1

inner leg edge left back, right front

1st size
2nd size
3rd size
4th size
5th size

Work 6 rows more in rib as set.
Using A, cast(bind) off in rib.
Return to sts which were left; with ws facing rejoin yarn, K1, (P1, K1) to end.
Beg 1st rib row complete to match first side. Make a 2nd strap in the same way.

FINISHING
Press work lightly on ws according to instructions on ball bands, omitting ribbing. Using an edge to

edge st on rib and backstitch on main knitting, join side seams, reversing seam on cuffs to allow for turning. Press seams. Sew on press fasteners (snaps) to inside leg borders, placing one at centre of crotch and others at equal intervals along borders. Sew one button 3cm/1¼in either side of centre front half way up the waistband, then sew another button 3[3,4,4,5]cm/1¼[1¼,1½,1½,2]in to outside edge of each of these 2 buttons. Attach straps to buttons at front, then sl st other end on to the inside of waistband with centres about 5cm/2in either side of centre back, when you are sure of lengths. If desired, run elastic thread along ws of work through every rib row at waistband, catching in on every other st. Turn up rib at lower edge and hold in place with a st at inside leg seam.

ADULT'S ORANGE PLAID V-NECK SWEATER

MATERIALS
General yarn weight used – Aran (heavy worsted)
Rowan *Soft Cotton* (50g/1¾oz balls) in the foll 3 colours:
  A (534) frolic – 7[8] balls
  B (545) sugar pink – 1[1] ball
  C (537) apple – 1[1] ball
Rowan *Handknit DK Cotton* (50g/1¾oz balls) in the foll 4 colours:
  D (261) sunflower – 1[1] ball
  E (256) violet – 1[1] ball
  F (281) hastings green – 1[1] ball
  G (280) pastel – 1[1] ball
Rowan *Knobbly Cotton* (50g/1¾oz balls) in the foll colour:
  H (568) bright pink – 7[8] balls
One pair each 3¾mm (US size 5) and 4½mm (US size 7) knitting needles *or size to obtain correct tension(gauge)*

LEFT *Baby's Yellow Plaid Shorts, seen here with the Adult's Orange Plaid V-neck Sweater.*

OVERLEAF *The triangular Autumn Shawl, lying amongst the leaves of New Hampshire, was knitted while travelling through Morocco, using every autumnal shade I could lay hands on and the Squares sweater worn by the girl was made with leftover yarns. I shaded each scale of the shawl from light to bright to deeper tone, carrying the outline colour across the rows. The woman is wearing the Adult's Orange Plaid V-neck Sweater.*

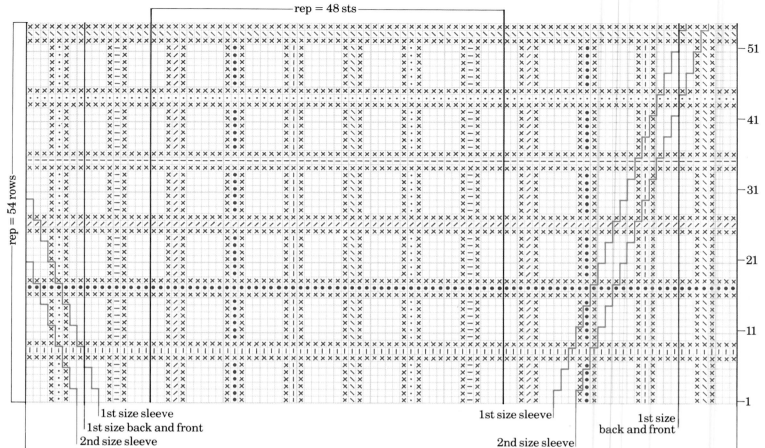

rep = 48 sts

rep = 54 rows

—51
—41
—31
—21
—11
—1

1st size sleeve
1st size back and front
2nd size sleeve
2nd size back and front

1st size sleeve
2nd size sleeve

1st size back and front
2nd size back and front

□ = A
Ⅱ = B
◺ = C
⊟ = D
◉ = E
◪ = F
· = G
⊠ = H

SIZES
To fit 96-102[107-112]cm/38-40[42-44]in bust/chest.
Figures for larger size are given in square brackets; where there is only one set of figures, it applies to both sizes.
For finished measurements see diagram.

TENSION(GAUGE)
23 sts and 26 rows to 10cm/4in over patt on 4½mm (US size 7) needles.
Check your tension(gauge) before beginning.

NOTES
Yarns A, B, C and H are used double throughout.
When working in patt from Chart (page 32), read odd rows (K) from right to left and even rows (P) from left to right.

BACK
Using smaller needles and D, cast on 110[122] sts.
Work 15 rows in K1, P1 rib in stripes as foll:
(2 rows A, 2 rows H) 3 times, 2 rows A, 1 row H.
<u>Inc row</u> (ws) With H, rib 1[6], make 1, * rib 6[5], make 1; rep from * to last 1[6] sts, rib to end. 129[145] sts.
Change to larger needles and cont in patt as foll:
Beg with a K row and working in st st throughout cont in patt from Chart, starting and ending rows as indicated rep rows 1-54 to form patt.
Cont until 134[150] rows in all have been worked in patt, so ending with a ws row.

Shoulder Shaping
Keeping patt correct, cast(bind) off 15[17] sts at beg of next 2 rows, 14[17] sts at beg of foll 2 rows, then 14[16] sts at beg of next 2 rows.

Leave rem 43[45] sts on a spare needle.

FRONT
Work as given for Back until 90[104] rows in all have been worked in patt.

Neck Shaping
<u>Next row</u> (rs) Patt 65[73] and leave these sts on a spare needle, patt to end.
Cont on last set of sts only for right front as foll:
<u>Next row</u> Patt to end.
Keeping patt correct, dec one st at beg of next and every foll alt row until 43[50] sts rem.
Work 2 rows without shaping, 135[151] rows in all have been worked in patt, so ending with a rs row.

Shoulder Shaping
** Cast(bind) off 15[17] sts at beg of next row, then 14[17] sts at beg of foll alt row.
Work 1 row without shaping.
Cast(bind) off rem 14[16] sts.
Return to sts which were left; with ws facing slip first st on to a st holder, rejoin yarns to neck edge and patt to end. 64[72] sts.
Keeping patt correct, dec one st at end of next and every foll alt row until 43[50] sts rem.
Work 1 row without shaping, 134[150] rows in all have been worked in patt, so ending with a ws row.

Shoulder Shaping
Work as given for first side from ** to end.

SLEEVES
Using smaller needles and D, cast on 42[46] sts and work 15 rows in striped rib as for Back.
<u>Inc row</u> (ws) With H, rib 2, * make 1, rib 2; rep from * to end. 62[68] sts.

32

ADULT'S ORANGE PLAID
V-NECK SWEATER
A = 56[63]cm/22¼[25¼]in
B = 56.5[62.5]cm/
22½[25]in
C = 5cm/2in
D = 18.5[21.5]cm/
7½[8½]in
E = 19[20]cm/7¼[8¼]in
F = 27[29.5]cm/
10¾[11¾]in
G = 41cm/16½in
H = 54[56.5]cm/
21½[22½]in

LEFT *The Adult's Orange
Plaid V-neck Sweater
and a Child's Blue Plaid
Jacket – two examples of
our basic plaid. This
simple formula lends
itself to many different
colour schemes.*

Change to larger needles and cont in patt as foll:
Beg with a K row and working in st st throughout
cont in patt from Chart, starting and ending rows
as indicated rep rows 1-54 to form patt AND AT THE
SAME TIME, inc one st at each end of the 3rd and
every foll 3rd row, working inc sts into patt until
there are 124[130] sts.
Work 1 row without shaping. 94 rows in all have
been worked in patt.
Cast(bind) off *loosely.*
Make a 2nd sleeve in the same way.

FINISHING
Press work lightly on ws according to instructions
on ball bands, omitting ribbing. Using backstitch,
join left shoulder seam. Press seam.

NECKBAND
Using smaller needles, H and with rs facing, K
43[45] sts of back neck, pick up and K 48 [50] sts
evenly down left front neck, K one st from centre
front, then pick up and K 48 [50] sts evenly up

right front neck.
140[146] sts.
Work 7 rows in K1, P1 rib in stripes as foll:
1 row H, 2 rows A, 2 rows H, 2 rows A AND AT THE
SAME TIME, dec at centre front as foll:
<u>1st row</u> (ws) (P1, K1) 23[24] times, P2 tog, P1,
P2 tog tbl, K1, (P1, K1) 44[46] times.
<u>2nd row</u> (rs) Rib 88[92], K2 tog tbl, K1, K2 tog, rib
to end.
Cont to dec at centre front in this way on every
row, always working decs knitwise on rs rows and
purlwise on ws rows.
Using D, cast(bind) off in rib.
Using backstitch on main knitting and an edge to
edge st on rib, join right shoulder and neckband
seam. Press seam. Mark back and front at side
edges 27[28.5]cm/10¾[11¼]in from shoulders.
Using backstitch, join cast-(bound-)off edge of
sleeves to back and front between markers,
matching centre of top of sleeve to shoulder seam.
Press seams. Using backstitch, join side and
sleeve seams. Press all seams.

CIRCLES AND DOTS

Circles are one of the most satisfying and soothing shapes in our lives. Flowers, fruits, stones, shells and most of the dishes we eat from all come in circular form. Floating Circles is a pattern from my first book and it seemed such a natural for a child that we reworked it and did a black and a green version of the original pattern with a button shoulder (pages 38 and 42). The adult's cotton version is slightly more complicated in that the background is a mixture of about 10 shades of one colour. This gives a richer effect than our all-over colour backgrounds. These yarns must be very close in colour and tone so that one fades into the next like a watercolour wash. The different textures help to give it this soft painterly feel.

The idea of motifs on a solid ground can be easily explored by knitters eager to have a go at variations on the theme. Rows of little diamonds, squares or spade shapes could create a similar effect. Playing with colours can be very satisfying; I've seen even inexperienced knitters produce lively versions of complex knitting patterns. Changing the formula slightly gives a new look as the version on a white background (page 37) shows. We kept the background and circle solid and used bright changing colours on the outlines.

To work Floating Circles, we used the fairisle method throughout. The outline colour can be carried up the side of the work if it is needed for the next row of circles.

Spots and dots are another universal theme, recurring constantly in the fashion world because of their intrinsic freshness. Zoë's Dot Stripe is borrowed from a Japanese 'komon' or small pattern design on printed fabric. For anything from simple to dizzy-making complexity, patterns in Japanese textiles are a goldmine for the inventive knitter.

The original of Dot Stripe was more irregular but Zoë wanted to produce a pattern that was quick and simple to knit so we devised this repeating pattern. You can break up the regularity quite easily by introducing more shades to the dot colours. You could also work with groups of similar shades for the background and the stripes so that each section of background or stripe was slightly different from the last, giving the design a less regular look. Perhaps try the simple one first and then, once you have the feel of it, try something more demanding. The occasional motif in the row can be done with a separate piece of yarn, or you can Swiss darn (duplicate stitch) your variations in later. This design is worked in the fairisle method throughout. The two main colours should be carried up the side of the work and caught into the first stitch of every second row when not in use to avoid large loops down the side seam of the finished garment.

RIGHT *These are the adult's and child's versions of Black Floating Circles, page 38. I love seeing this old favourite of mine scaled down for a child.*

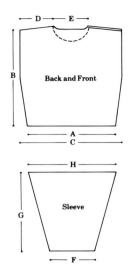

CHILD'S BLACK FLOATING CIRCLES BUTTON SHOULDER SWEATER

A = 28[30.5,33,35.5,38,40.5]cm/
11¼[12¼,13¼,14,15,16]in
B = 33[35.5,38.5,41,44,46.5]cm/
13[14¼,15¼,16½,17½,18½]in
C = 34[36.5,39,41.5,44,46.5]cm/
13½[14¾,15½,16¾,17½,18¾]in
D = 10[11,12,13,14,15]cm/
4[4½,4¾,5¼,5½,6]in
E = 14[14.5,15,15.5,16,16.5]cm/
5½[5¾,6,6¼,6½,6¾]in
F = 18.5[19,19.5,20.5,21,21.5]cm/
7¼[7½,7¾,8,8¼,8½]in
G = 27[29.5,31.5,34,36,38.5]cm/
10¾[11¾,12½,13½,14½,15¼]in
H = 29[31,34,36,39,41]cm/
11½[12½,13½,14½,15¼,16¼]in

Chart One

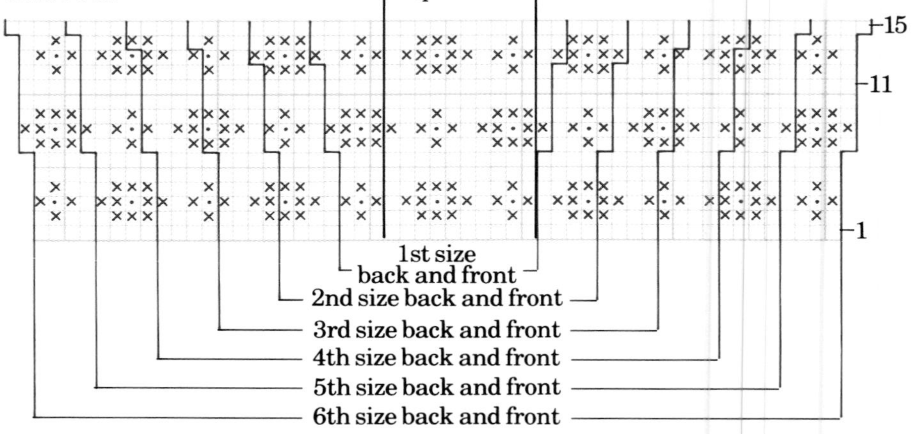

rep = 10 sts

—15
—11

—1

1st size
back and front
2nd size back and front
3rd size back and front
4th size back and front
5th size back and front
6th size back and front

Chart Two

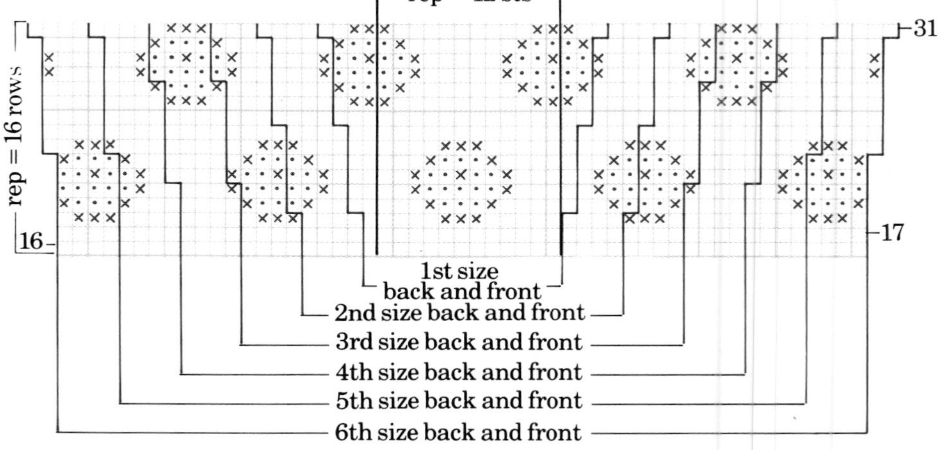

rep = 12 sts

rep = 16 rows

—31

16—

—17

1st size
back and front
2nd size back and front
3rd size back and front
4th size back and front
5th size back and front
6th size back and front

Chart Three

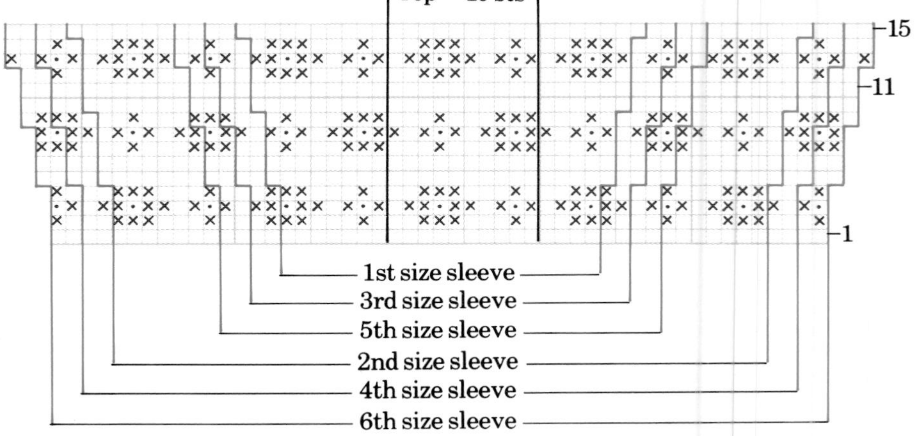

rep = 10 sts

—15
—11

—1

1st size sleeve
3rd size sleeve
5th size sleeve
2nd size sleeve
4th size sleeve
6th size sleeve

Chart Four

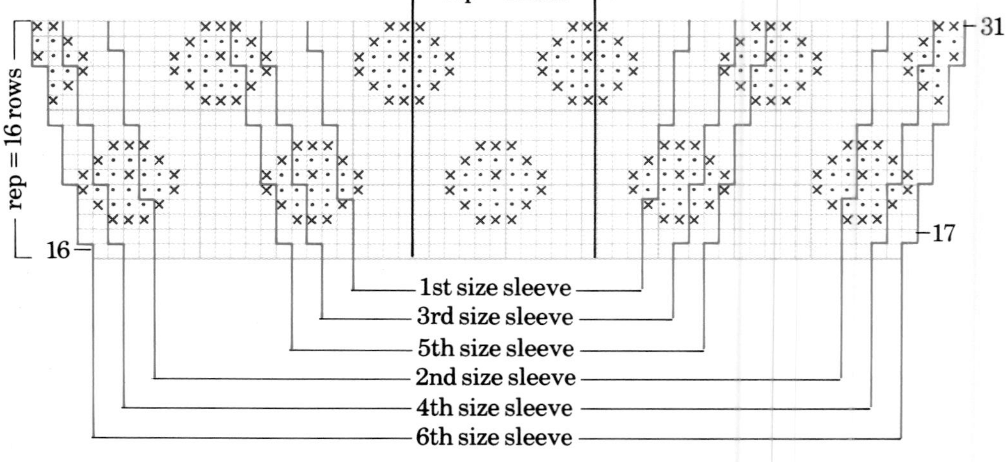

rep = 12 sts

rep = 16 rows

—31

16—

—17

1st size sleeve
3rd size sleeve
5th size sleeve
2nd size sleeve
4th size sleeve
6th size sleeve

PREVIOUS PAGE *The white version of Floating Circles, seen here with the two black versions, simply uses bright jewel colours as outlines for the black circles.*

CHILD'S BLACK FLOATING CIRCLES BUTTON SHOULDER SWEATER

MATERIALS

General yarn weight used – 4 ply (fingering)
Rowan *Botany* (25g/1oz hanks) in the foll 9 colours:
A (62) black – 5[5,6,6,7,8] hanks
B (55) lobelia – 1[1,1,2,2,2] hanks
C (632) plum – 1[1,1,1,1,1] hank
D (126) purple – 1[1,1,1,1,1] hank
E (501) lavender – 1[1,1,1,1,1] hank
F (51) cornflower – 1[1,1,1,1,1] hank
G (45) pillar box – 1[1,1,1,2,2] hanks
H (630) straw – 2[2,2,3,3,3] hanks
J (95) orchid – 1[1,1,1,1,1] hank
Rowan *Fine Fleck Tweed* (25g/1oz hanks) in the foll 2 colours:
L (21) apricot – 1[1,1,1,1,1] hank
M (94) blackcurrant – 1[1,1,1,1,1] hank
One pair each 2¼mm (US size 1) and 3mm (US size 3) knitting needles *or size to obtain correct tension (gauge)*
3[4,4,4,4,4] buttons

SIZES

To fit 2[4,6,8,10,12]yrs or 53[56,61,66,71,76]cm/
21[22,24,26,28,30]in chest.
Figures for larger sizes are given in square brackets; where there is only one set of figures, it applies to all sizes.
For finished measurements see diagram.

TENSION(GAUGE)

33 sts and 36 rows to 10cm/4in over patt on 3 mm (US size 3) needles.
Check your tension(gauge) before beginning.

NOTES

When working in patt from Chart, read odd rows (K) from right to left and even rows (P) from left to right.

BACK

Using smaller needles and B, cast on 93[101,109,117,125,133] sts.
Beg with a K row, work 5 rows in st st to form hem.
<u>Next row</u> (ws) K to end, to form fold line.
Change to larger needles and cont in patt as foll:
Beg with a K row and working in st st throughout cont in patt from Chart 1 then Chart 2, beginning and ending rows as indicated. Rows 16-31 of Chart 2 form the rep of circle patt *but* work and change colours as given in colour sequence table AND AT THE SAME TIME, inc one st at each end of the 7th and every foll 6th[6th,7th,7th, 8th,8th] row, working inc sts into patt until there are 113[121,129,137,145,153] sts. Cont without shaping until 118[128,138,148,158,168] rows in all have been worked from Charts, so ending with a ws row.

Shoulder and Neck Shaping

Keeping patt correct, cast(bind) off 12[13,14, 15,16,17] sts at beg of next 2 rows.
89[95,101,107,113,119] sts.
<u>Next row</u> (rs) Cast(bind) off 11[12,13,14,15,16] sts, patt 18[19,20,21,22,23] including st already on needle, cast(bind) off 31[33,35,37,39,41] sts, patt to end. Cont on last set of sts only for left back:
Cast(bind) off 11[12,13,14,15,16] sts at beg of next

COLOUR SEQUENCE TABLE

Rows	□	⊠	·
1-5	L	D	H
6-10	A	M	H
11-15	F	G	H
16-20	A	H	G
21-23	A	H	J
24-31	A	H	C
32-39	A	H	G
40-45	A	H	D
46-47	A	H	J
48-55	A	H	M
56-63	A	L	G
64-69	A	H	G
70-75	A	H	J
76-79	A	H	E
80-87	A	L	M
88-95	A	H	C
96-111	A	H	G
112-119	A	H	D

Repeat for circle colours beginning with row 16.

LEFT *The man and the boy are both wearing Black Floating Circles sweaters.*

OVERLEAF *The Floating Circles in vivid pastels look brilliant against the rich blues of a Moroccan village wall. You can see here how Zoë has made subtle changes in the ground of the orange version to give more depth of tone. See page 42 for the pattern of the child's version.*

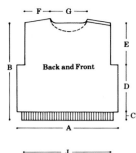

Back and Front

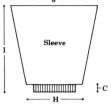

Sleeve

CHILD'S GREEN FLOATING CIRCLES BUTTON SHOULDER SWEATER
A = 34[36.5,39,41.5,44,46.5]cm/ 13½[14½,15½,16½,17½,18½]in
B = 33[36,39,42,45,48]cm/ 13[14¼,15½,16¾,18,19¼]in
C = 4cm/1½in
D = 14.5[16.5,18,20,22,23.5]cm/ 5¾[6½,7¼,8,8¾,9½]in
E = 14.5[15.5,17,18,19.5,20.5]cm/ 5¾[6¼,6¾,7¼,7¾,8¼]in
F = 7.5[8,9,9.5,10.5,11.5]cm/ 3[3¼,3½,3¾,4¼,4½]in
G = 13.5[14,15,15.5,16,16.5]cm/ 5½[5¾,6,6¼,6½,6¾]in
H = 19[20.5,21.5,22.5,24,25]cm/ 7½[8,8½,9,9½,10]in
I = 30.5[33,35.5,38,40.5,43]cm/ 12[13,14,15,16,17]in
J = 29[31,34,36,39,41]cm/ 11½[12½,13½,14½,15½,16½]in

row and 7 sts at beg of foll row. Cast(bind) off rem 11[12,13,14,15,16] sts.
Return to sts which were left; with ws facing rejoin yarns to neck edge, cast(bind) off 7 sts and patt to end. Cast(bind) off rem 11[12,13,14,15,16] sts.

FRONT

Work as given for Back until 100[110,120,130, 140,150] rows in all have been worked from Charts, so ending with a ws row.

Neck Shaping

Next row (rs) Patt 47[50,53,56,59,62], cast (bind) off 19[21,23,25,27,29] sts, patt to end.
Cont on last set of sts only for right front:
Next row Patt to end.
Keeping patt correct, cast(bind) off 3 sts at beg of next row, 2 sts at beg of foll 3 alt rows, then one st at beg of foll 4 alt rows. 34[37,40,43,46,49] sts.
Work 2 rows without shaping.

Shoulder Shaping

Keeping patt correct, cast(bind) off 12[13,14,15, 16,17] sts at beg of next row, then 11[12,13,14,15,16] sts at beg of foll alt row. Work 1 row without shaping, then cast(bind) off rem 11[12,13,14,15,16] sts.
Return to sts which were left; with ws facing rejoin yarns to neck edge, cast(bind) off 3 sts and patt to end. Work 1 row without shaping.
Keeping patt correct, cast(bind) off 2 sts at beg of next and foll 2 alt rows, then one st at beg of foll 2 alt rows.
36[39,42,45,48,51] sts.

Shoulder and Neck Shaping

Cast(bind) off 12[13,14,15,16,17] sts at beg of next row, one st at beg of foll row, 11[12,13,14,15,16] sts at beg of next row, then one st at beg of foll row. Cast(bind) off rem 11[12,13,14,15,16] sts.

SLEEVES

Using smaller needles and B, cast on 61[63,65, 67,69,71] sts.
Beg with a K row, work 5 rows in st st to form hem.
Next row (ws) K to end, to form fold line.
Change to larger needles and cont in patt as foll:
Beg with a K row and working in st st throughout cont in patt from Chart 3 then Chart 4, beginning and ending rows as indicated and working Chart 4 in same colour sequence as for Back AND AT THE SAME TIME, inc one st at each end of the 5th and every foll 5th[5th,4th,4th,4th,4th] row, working inc sts into patt until there are 95[103,111,119,127, 135] sts.
Cont without shaping until 98[106,114,122,130, 138] rows in all have been worked from Charts, so ending with a ws row.
Cast(bind) off loosely.
Make a 2nd sleeve in the same way.

FINISHING

Press work lightly on ws according to instructions on bands.
Using backstitch, join right shoulder seam.

NECKBAND

Using larger needles, A and with rs facing, pick up and K 64[66,68,70,72,74] sts evenly around front neck and 49[51,53,55,57,59] sts evenly around back neck. 113[117,121,125,129,133] sts.
1st row (ws) P – first size: 1M, 2A[2nd size: 1M, 3A, 1M, 2A,3rd size: 1A,4th size: 2A, 1M, 2A,5th size: 3M, 3A, 1M, 2A,6th size: 1M, 2A], on all sizes: (1A, 3M, 3A, 1M, 2A) to end.

2nd row K to end in patt as now set, working to match row 8 as for Back.
3rd row As first row.
4th row With A, K to end.
Change to smaller needles and cont in B only as foll:
5th row P to end.
6th row P to end, to form fold line.
Beg with a P row, work 7 rows in st st to form hem. Cast(bind) off loosely.
Turn in and press neckband on fold line and sl st lightly on ws.

BUTTON BAND

Using smaller needles, A and with rs facing, pick up and K 5 sts along edge of neckband and 34[37,40,43,46,49] sts evenly across left back shoulder. 39[42,45,48,51,54] sts.
Work 6 rows in K1, P1 rib.
Cast(bind) off in rib.

BUTTONHOLE BAND

Using smaller needles, A and with rs facing, pick up and K 34[37,40,43,46,49] sts evenly across left front shoulder and 5 sts along edge of neckband. 39[42,45,48,51,54] sts.
Work 2 rows in K1, P1 rib.
Next row (ws) Rib 3, cast(bind) off 2 sts, * rib 10[9,9,10,10,11] including st already on needle, cast(bind) off 2 sts; rep from * to last 10[4,7,7,10,10] sts, rib to end.
Next row Rib to end, casting on 2 sts over each 2 cast(bound) off.
Work 2 more rows, then cast(bind) off in rib as set.
Lap buttonhole band over button band and oversew at armhole edge. Mark back and front at side edges 14.5[15.5,17,18,19,20.5]cm/5¾[6¼,6¾,7¼, 7¾,8]in down from shoulder line. Using backstitch, join cast-(bound-) off edge of sleeves to back and front between markers, matching centre of top of sleeve to shoulder. Press all seams. Using backstitch, join side and sleeve seams including hems. Turn up and press hems along fold line and sl st loosely on ws. Press all seams. Sew on buttons.

CHILD'S GREEN FLOATING CIRCLES BUTTON SHOULDER SWEATER

MATERIALS
General yarn weight used – lightweight cotton
Rowan *Soft Cotton* (50g/1¾oz balls) in the foll 7 colours:
  A (539) bermuda – 4[4,4,5,5,5] balls
  B (523) wheat – 1[1,1,1,1,1] ball
  C (551) lemon ice – 1[1,1,1,1,1] ball
  D (545) sugar pink – 1[1,1,1,1,1] ball
  E (533) antique pink – 1[1,1,1,1,1] ball
  F (544) lilac – 1[1,1,1,1,1] ball
  G (534) frolic – 1[1,1,1,1,1] ball
Rowan *Knobbly Cotton* (50g/1¾oz balls) in the foll colour:
  H (561) ecru – 1[1,1,2,2,2] balls
Rowan *Cabled Mercerised Cotton* (50g/1¾oz balls) in the foll colour:
  J (322) blush – 1[1,1,1,1,1] ball
One pair each 2¼mm (US size 1) and 3mm (US size 3) knitting needles *or size to obtain correct tension(gauge)*
3[3,3,4,4,4] buttons

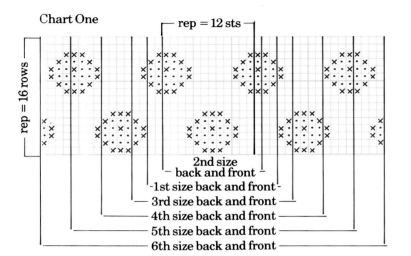

Chart One rep = 12 sts

rep = 16 rows

- 2nd size back and front -
- 1st size back and front -
- 3rd size back and front -
- 4th size back and front -
- 5th size back and front -
- 6th size back and front -

Chart Two rep = 12 sts

rep = 16 rows

- 1st size sleeve -
- 2nd size sleeve -
- 3rd size sleeve -
- 4th size sleeve -
- 5th size sleeve -
- 6th size sleeve -

SIZES

To fit 2[4,6,8,10,12]yrs or 53[56,61,66,71,76]cm/ 21[22,24,26,28,30]in chest. *Figures for larger sizes are given in square brackets; where there is only one set of figures, it applies to all sizes. For finished measurements see diagram.*

TENSION(GAUGE)

33 sts and 33 rows to 10cm/4in over patt on 3mm (US size 3) needles.
Check your tension(gauge) before beginning.

NOTES

The sweater has an unusual rib at the waist, cuffs and neckband, 2 colours are used in every row making it less stretchy than normal rib. It is an ordinary K2, P2 rib but the K sts are worked in one colour and the P sts in another. Take care not to pull yarns too tightly across ws of work and always take both colours right to end of row. When working in patt from Chart, read odd rows (K) from right to left and even rows (P) from left to right.

BACK

Using smaller needles and *two* yarns A and H, cast on 100[108,116,124,132,140] sts as foll:
With H, put a sl st on to left hand needle to make first st, cast on (2A, 2H) until there are 97[105,113,121,129,137] sts, then 2A, 1H. (Keep tension as you would if casting on in the normal way, by carrying the yarn not in use across the back of work). Break off H.
<u>1st row</u> (rs) K1C, (take A to rs, P2A, take A to ws, K2C) to last 3 sts, take A to rs, P2A, take A to ws, K1C.
<u>2nd row</u> P1D, (take A to rs, K2A, take A to ws, P2D) to last 3 sts, take A to rs, K2A, take A to ws, P1D.
<u>3rd row</u> As first row, *but* using J instead of C.
<u>4th row</u> As 2nd row.
<u>5th row</u> As first row, *but* using B instead of C.
<u>6th row</u> As 2nd row.
<u>7th row</u> As first row, *but* using F instead of C.
<u>8th row</u> As 2nd row, *but* using G instead of D.
<u>9th row</u> As first row, *but* using E instead of C.
<u>10th row</u> As 2nd row, *but* using E instead of D.
<u>11th row</u> As first row, *but* using D instead of C.
<u>12th row</u> As 2nd row.
<u>13th–16th rows</u> As 11th and 12th rows twice.
Change to larger needles.
<u>Next row</u> (rs) With A, K to end.
<u>Inc row</u> (ws) With A, P 2[6,4,2,6,4], make 1, * P 8[8,9,10,10,11], make 1; rep from * to last 2[6,4,2,6, 4] sts, P to end.

113[121,129,137,145,153] sts.
Cont in patt as foll:
Beg with a K row and working in st st throughout cont in patt from Chart 1, beginning and ending rows as indicated, working background in A throughout and changing colour of circles as given in colour sequence table.
Cont until 48[54,60,66,72,78] rows in all have been worked in patt, so ending with a ws row.

Armhole Shaping

Keeping patt correct, cast(bind) off 9[10,10,11,11, 11] sts at beg of next 2 rows.
95[101,109,115,123,131] sts.
Cont without shaping until 96[106,116,126, 136,146] rows in all have been worked in patt

OVERLEAF A Child's Dot Stripe Button Shoulder Sweater is shown with the Adult's Dot Stripe Turtleneck Sweater and the Child's Dot Stripe Jacket, page 48, in front of a Key West mural. The father is wearing Tumbling Blocks in dark silks and tweed; this pattern is available in kit form.

COLOUR SEQUENCE TABLE

Rows	☒	⋅
1-6	H	D
9-14	H	G
17-22	B	F
25-30	H	E
33-38	H	J
41-46	C	D
49-54	H	F
57-62	B	G
65-70	H	D
73-78	H	E
81-86	C	J
89-94	B	F
97-102	H	G
105-110	H	D
113-118	C	E
121-126	H	J
129-134	H	F
137-142	B	D
145-150	H	G

STRIPES AND BOXES

My first real awareness of diagonal stripes was seeing barber's poles and rock candy when I was young. As my taste for the exotic grew, I became aware of the dramatic and beautiful use of the diagonal stripe on the shaded borders of Chinese robes. The exquisitely toned stripes seemed to give a wonderful sense of movement.

Zoë has used bold, easy-to-knit diagonals in her childrens' dresses (pages 60, 65, 103). I particularly like them topped off with the large diamond pattern on the yoke. Working with manageable lengths of yarn encourages the changes of tone as you progress up the diagonal; if you also pick a different tone or texture of yarn you create an even richer sense of movement. Diagonal Stripe is worked in intarsia. It is possible to work the Diagonal Stripe Dress (page 60) with the balls attached but they tend to tangle. Try cutting off lengths of yarn for the colours at the right-hand side of the work, i.e. those that will disappear off the side of the work first, and use balls for the new colours being introduced at the left side (see page 195).

Zoë bought an old carpet in the fleamarket that really haunted me. Its bold, simple diagonal stripes were in cream, two blues and a red. It was always fresh and alive to my eye and this started me looking at other diagonal striped textiles. I noticed that the most lively diagonals always had little motifs dotted up them.

My first attempt at Diagonal Box was the bright chevron with pointed borders (page 55). It is worked by the intarsia method, except for the border where it is partly fairisle. Steve suggested we take a few of the contrasting colours from Diagonal Boxes to create an easy-to-knit child's version. The boxes are repeated in fairisle across the rows and you can leave balls attached for the solid diagonal stripes.

Bright astounding colours are wonderful but there is always a place for the cool, neutral classics. There is so much in our environment that contains beiges and greys that my tweedy version blends in beautifully. Like the children's versions (page 61), it employs a definite sequence in the diagonal stripes and the boxes are knitted in fairisle.

We have given you a good basic diagonal and a slightly embellished one in the Diagonal Box pattern but you could go on and on playing with this basic concept – for instance, outlining each stripe in a bright colour, or studding the Diagonal Stripe with different shaped motifs, such as flowers, circles or stars.

RIGHT *Two Bright Diagonal Box Stripe Sweaters. The simplified child's version has a slash neck opening and, if you want to experiment, the border on the bright adult version, page 55, can be adapted to almost any oriental-type pattern.*

Shoulder and Neck Shaping

Next row (rs) Cast(bind) off 8[9,10,11,12,13] sts, patt 24[25,27,28,30,32] including st already on needle, cast(bind) off 31[33,35,37,39,41] sts, patt to end. Cont on last set of sts only for left back:
Keeping patt correct, cast(bind) off 8[9,10,11,12,13] sts at beg of next row, 4 sts at beg of foll row, 8[9,10,11,12,13] sts at beg of next row, then 3 sts at beg of foll row. Cast(bind) off rem 9[9,10,10,11,12] sts. Return to sts which were left; with ws facing rejoin yarns to neck edge, cast(bind) off 4 sts and patt to end.
Complete to match first side, reversing all shaping.

FRONT

Work as given for Back until 80[90,100,110, 120,130] rows in all have been worked in patt.

Neck Shaping

Next row (rs) Patt 42[44,47,49,52,55], cast(bind) off 11[13,15,17,19,21] sts, patt to end.
Cont on last set of sts only for right front:
Next row Patt to end.
Keeping patt correct, cast(bind) off 5 sts at beg of next row, 3 sts at beg of foll alt row, 2 sts at beg of foll 3 alt rows, then one st at beg of foll 3 alt rows. 25[27,30,32,35,38] sts.

Shoulder Shaping

Cast(bind) off 8[9,10,11,12,13] sts at beg of next and foll alt row. Work 1 row without shaping, then cast(bind) off rem 9[9,10,10,11,12] sts.
Return to sts which were left; with ws facing rejoin yarns to neck edge, cast(bind) off 5 sts and patt to end. Work 1 row without shaping.
Cast(bind) off 3 sts at beg of next row, 2 sts at beg of foll 3 alt rows, then one st at beg of foll alt row. 27[29,32,34,37,40] sts.

Shoulder Shaping

Cast(bind) off 8[9,10,11,12,13] sts at beg of next row, one st at beg of foll row, 8[9,10,11,12,13] sts at beg of next row, then one st at beg of foll row. Cast(bind) off rem 9[9,10,10,11,12] sts.

SLEEVES

Using smaller needles and A and H, cast on 48[52,56,60,64,68] sts using the same method as for Back. Break off H.
Work 16 rows in striped rib as for Back.
Change to larger needles.
Next row (rs) With A, K to end.
Inc row (ws) With A, P 3[5,7,2,4,6], make 1, * P 3[3,3,4,4,4], make 1; rep from * to last 3[5,7,2,4,6] sts, P to end. 63[67,71,75,79,83] sts.
Cont in patt as foll:
Beg with a K row and working in st st throughout cont in patt from Chart 2, beginning and ending rows as indicated and working in same colour sequence as for Back AND AT THE SAME TIME, inc one st at each end of the 5th and every foll 4th row, working inc sts into patt until there are 95[103, 111,119,127,135] sts.
Cont without shaping until 88[96,104,112,120,128] rows in all have been worked in patt, so ending with a ws row.
Cast(bind) off loosely.
Make a 2nd sleeve in the same way.

FINISHING

Press work lightly on ws according to instructions on ball bands, omitting ribbing. Using backstitch, join right shoulder seam.

NECKBAND

Using smaller needles, A and with rs facing, pick up and K 66[68,70,72,74,76] sts evenly around front neck and 50[52,54,56,58,60] sts evenly around back neck. 116[120,124,128,132,136] sts.
1st row (ws) P1F, (take A to rs, K2A, take A to ws, P2F) to last 3 sts, take A to rs, K2A, take A to ws, P1F.
2nd row K1D, (take A to rs, P2A, take A to ws, K2D) to last 3 sts, take A to rs, P2A, take A to ws, K1D.
3rd row As first row, but using B instead of F.
4th row As 2nd row.
5th row As first row, but using J instead of F.
6th row As 2nd row.
7th row As first row, but using C instead of F.
8th row As 2nd row, but using H instead of D.
Cast(bind) off in rib in two colours, A and H, working each st in its own colour.

BUTTON BAND

Using smaller needles, A and with rs facing, pick up and K 9 sts along edge of neckband and 25[27,30,32,35,38] sts evenly across back left shoulder. 34[36,39,41,44,47] sts.
Work 6 rows in K1, P1 rib. Cast(bind) off in rib.

BUTTONHOLE BAND

Using smaller needles, A and with rs facing, pick up and K 25[27,30,32,35,38] sts evenly across front left shoulder and 9 sts along edge of neckband. 34[36,39,41,44,47] sts.
Work 2 rows in K1, P1 rib.
Next row (ws) Rib 3, cast(bind) off 2 sts, * rib 8[9,10,8,9,10] including st already on needle, cast(bind) off 2 sts; rep from * to last 9[9,10,6,6,6] sts, rib to end.
Next row Rib to end, casting on 2 sts over each 2 cast(bound) off.
Work 2 more rows, then cast(bind) off in rib as set.
Lap buttonhole band over button band and over-sew at armhole edge. Using backstitch, join cast-(bound-)off edge of sleeves to armhole edge, matching centre of top of sleeve to shoulder seam and sewing last few rows of sleeves to cast-(bound-)off sts at underarm. Press all seams. Using backstitch on main knitting and an edge to edge st on rib, join side and sleeve seams. Press seams. Sew on buttons.

ADULT'S DOT STRIPE TURTLENECK SWEATER

MATERIALS

General yarn weight used – chunky (bulky)
2 strands of yarn are used together throughout.
Rowan *Grainy Silks* (50g/1¾oz hanks) in the foll colour:
  A (805) mousse – 6[7,7] hanks
Rowan *Silkstones* (50g/1¾oz hanks) in the foll colour:
  B (836) mulberry – 5[5,6] hanks
Rowan *Lightweight DK* (25g/1oz hanks) in the foll 6 colours:
  C (417) grey green – 2[2,2] hanks
  D (89) light emerald – 2[2,3] hanks
  E (49) sky blue – 2[2,2] hanks
  F (48) cloud blue – 2[2,3] hanks
  G (122) pale blue – 2[2,3] hanks
  H (63) eau de nil – 2[3,3] hanks
Rowan *Light Tweed* (25g/1oz hanks) in the foll colour:

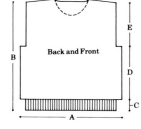

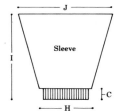

ADULT'S DOT STRIPE
TURTLENECK SWEATER
A = 55[59.5,64]cm/
22[23¾,25½]in
B = 62[66.5,71]cm/
24¾[26¼,28¼]in
C = 6.5cm/2½in
D = 30[33,35.5]cm/12[13,14]in
E =
25.5[27,29]cm/10¼[10¾,11¾]in
F = 15[16.5,18]cm/5¾[6½,7]in
G = 18.5[19.5,20.5]cm/
7½[7¾,8¼]in
H = 29[31,33]cm/
11½[12½,13¼]in
I = 50[53,55.5]cm/
20[21,22]in
J = 51[54,58]cm/
20½[21½,23½]in

J (220) jade – 2[2,2] hanks
Rowan *Fine Cotton Chenille* (50g/1¾oz balls) in
the foll colour:
 L (390) aqua – 1[1,1] ball
One pair each 4mm (US size 6) and 5mm (US size
8) knitting needles *or size to obtain correct tension(gauge)*

SIZES
To fit 86-91[96-102,107-112]cm/34-36[38-40,42-
44]in bust/chest.
*Figures for larger sizes are given in square
brackets; where there is only one set of figures, it
applies to all sizes.*
For finished measurements see diagram.

TENSION(GAUGE)
19 sts and 22 rows to 10cm/4in over patt on 5mm
(US size 8) needles.
Check your tension(gauge) before beginning.

NOTES
*Yarn B should be carried up side of work and
caught in at the edge of work on every 2nd row,
when not in use.*
*When working in patt from Chart, read odd rows
(K) from right to left and even rows (P) from left to
right.*

BACK
Using smaller needles and B, cast on 86[90,94] sts.
Work 17 rows in K1, P1 rib in stripes as foll:
4 rows A, (2 rows B, 4 rows A) twice, 1 row B.
Inc row (ws) With B, rib 7[1,8], make 1, * rib 4[4,3],
make 1; rep from * to last 7[1,8] sts, rib to end.
105[113,121] sts.
Change to larger needles and cont in patt as foll:
Beg with a K row and working in st st throughout
cont in patt from Chart, beginning and ending
rows as indicated, rep rows 1-12 to form patt, *but
work rows of spots in different colours as shown in
key.*
Cont until 66[72,78] rows in all have been worked
in patt, so ending with a ws row.

Armhole Shaping
Keeping patt correct, cast(bind) off 7 sts at beg of
next 2 rows. 91[99,107] sts.
Cont without shaping until 122[132,142] rows in
all have been worked in patt, so ending with a ws
row.

Shoulder and Neck Shaping
Keeping patt correct, cast(bind) off 10[11,12] sts at
beg of next 2 rows.
Next row Cast(bind) off 9[10,11] sts, patt 17[18,19]
including st already on needle, cast(bind) off

19[21,23] sts, patt to end.
Cont on last set of sts only for left back:
Cast(bind) off 9[10,11] sts at beg of next row, then 8
sts at beg of foll row. Cast(bind) off rem 9[10,11] sts.
Return to sts which were left; with ws facing rejoin
yarns to neck edge, cast(bind) off 8 sts and patt to
end. Cast(bind) off rem 9[10,11] sts.

FRONT
Work as given for Back until 104[114,124] rows in
all have been worked in patt.

Neck Shaping
Next row (rs) Patt 41[44,47], cast(bind) off 9[11,13]
sts, patt to end.
Cont on last set of sts only for right front:
Next row Patt to end.
Keeping patt correct, cast(bind) off 3 sts at beg of
next row, 2 sts at beg of foll 3 alt rows, then one st
at beg of foll 4 alt rows. 28[31,34] sts.
Work 2 rows without shaping.

Shoulder Shaping
Cast(bind) off 10[11,12] sts at beg of next row, then
9[10,11] sts at beg of foll alt row. Work 1 row without shaping, then cast off rem 9[10,11] sts.
Return to sts which were left; with ws facing rejoin
yarns to neck edge, cast(bind) off 3 sts and patt to
end.
Complete to match first side, reversing all
shaping.

SLEEVES
Using smaller needles and B, cast on 42[44,46] sts
and work 17 rows in striped rib as for Back.
Inc row (ws) With B, rib 3[1,7], make 1, * rib 3[3,2],
make 1; rep from * to last 3[1,7] sts, rib to end.
55[59,63] sts.
Change to larger needles and cont in patt as foll:
Beg with a K row and working in st st throughout
cont in patt from Chart, beginning and ending
rows as indicated work spots in same sequence as
for Back AND AT THE SAME TIME, inc one st at each
end of the 3rd and every foll 4th row, working inc
sts into patt until there are 97[103,111] sts.
Cont without shaping until 96[102,108] rows in all
have been worked in patt, so ending with a ws row.
Cast(bind) off *loosely.*
Make a 2nd sleeve in the same way.

FINISHING
Press work lightly on ws according to instructions
on bands, omitting ribbing.
Using backstitch, join left shoulder seam.

COLLAR
Using smaller needles, A and with rs facing, pick

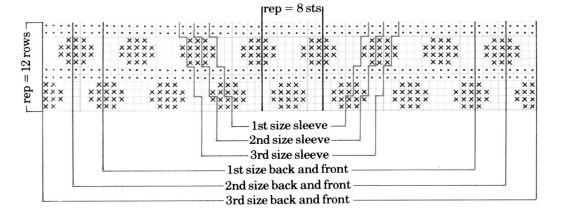

□ = A
⊡ = B
⊠ = H Rows 1-4
      L Rows 7-10
      G Rows 13-16
      J Rows 19-22
      F Rows 25-28
      D Rows 31-34
      E Rows 37-40
      C Rows 43-46
Repeat as necessary

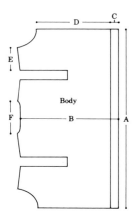

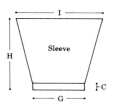

CHILD'S DOT STRIPE JACKET
A = 57.5[60,63,66,72,77.5]cm/
23[24,25¼,26½,28¾,31]in
B =
27[29.5,32,34.5,37.5,40.5]cm/
10½[11½,12½,13½,14¾,15¾]in
C = 3.5cm/1¼in
D =
19.5[22,23.5,26,28.5,31.5]cm/
7¾[8¾,9½,10½,11½,12¾]in
E = 7.5[8,8,8.5,9,10]cm/
3[3,3,3¼,3½,4]in
F = 11[12,12.5,13,14,14.5]cm/
4½[4¾,5,5¼,5½,5¾]in
G = 18[19.5,21,21,22.5,22.5]cm/
7¼[7¾,8½,8½,9,9]in
H =
20[21.5,23.5,27,29,30.5]cm/
7¾[8½,9¼,10¾,11½,12¼]in
I = 26[28,30,32.5,34.5,36.5]cm/
10½[11¼,12,13,13¾,14½]in

ABOVE RIGHT *Child's Dot Stripe Jacket and the Adult's Dot Stripe Turtleneck Sweater.*

up and K 38[40,42] sts around back neck and 66[68,70] sts around front neck. 104[108,112] sts. Work 34 rows in K1, P1 rib in stripes as foll: 3 rows A, (2 rows B, 4 rows A) 5 times, 1 row B. Using B, cast(bind) off *loosely* in rib.
Join right shoulder and collar seam, taking care to reverse seam on collar to allow for turning. Using backstitch, join cast-(bound-)off edge of sleeves to back and front armholes, matching centre of top of sleeve to shoulder seam and sewing last few rows of sleeve to cast-(bound-)off sts at underarm. Press all seams. Using backstitch, join side and sleeve seams. Press seams. Fold collar in half to outside.

CHILD'S DOT STRIPE JACKET

MATERIALS
General yarn weight used – lightweight double knitting (sport)
Rowan *Grainy Silks* (50g/1¾oz hanks) in the foll colour:
  A (805) mousse – 1[2,2,2,3,3] hanks
Rowan *Silkstones* (50g/1¾oz hanks) in the foll colour:
  B (836) mulberry – 1[1,1,2,2,2] hanks
Rowan *Lightweight DK* (25g/1oz hanks) in the foll 6 colours:
  C (417) grey green – 2[2,3,3,3,4] hanks
  D (89) light emerald – 1[1,1,1,1,1] hank
  E (49) sky blue – 1[1,1,1,1,1] hank
  F (48) cloud blue – 1[1,1,1,1,1] hank
  G (122) pale blue – 1[1,1,1,1,1] hank
  H (63) eau de nil – 1[1,1,1,2,2] hanks
Rowan *Light Tweed* (25g/1oz hanks) in the foll colour:
  J (220) jade – 1[1,1,1,1,1] hank
Rowan *Fine Cotton Chenille* (50g/1¾oz balls) in the foll colour:
  L (390) aqua – 1[1,1,1,1,1] ball
One pair each 2¾mm (US size 2) and 3¼mm (US size 3) knitting needles *or size to obtain correct tension(gauge)*
6[6,6,6,7,7] buttons

SIZES
To fit 6months[12months,18months,2yrs,4yrs, 6yrs] or 45[48,51,53,56,61]cm/18[19,20,21,22,24]in chest.
Figures for larger sizes are given in square brackets; where there is only one set of figures, it applies to all sizes.
For finished measurements see diagram.

TENSION(GAUGE)
28 sts and 33 rows to 10cm/4in over patt on 3¼mm (US size 3) needles.
Check your tension(gauge) before beginning.

NOTES
The body is worked in one piece to armholes. Yarn B should be carried up side of work and caught in at the edge of work on every 2nd row, when not in use. When working in patt from Chart, read odd rows (K) from right to left and even rows (P) from left to right.

BODY
Using smaller needles and C, cast on 143[151,159, 167,183,199] sts. ** Beg with a K row, work 4 rows in st st to form hem.
Picot edge row (rs) (K2 tog, yfwd) to last st, K1.

6th row P to end.
Change to larger needles and work border patt as foll:
1st row (rs) K 1C, (1B, 1C) to end.
2nd row P 1G, (1B, 1G) to end.
3rd row K 1L, (1B, 1L) to end.
4th row P 1J, (1A, 1J) to end.
5th row K 1E, (1B, 1E) to end.
6th row P 1H, (1A, 1H) to end.
7th row K 1F, (1A, 1F) to end.
8th row As 6th row. **
Inc row With B, K 4[8,3,7,6,6], make 1, * K8[8,9,9, 10,11], make 1; rep from * to last 3[7,3,7,7,6] sts. K to end. 161[169,177,185,201,217] sts.
Next row With B, P to end.
Cont in patt as foll:
Beg with a K row and working in st st throughout cont in patt from Chart, beginning and ending rows as indicated, rep rows 1-12 to form patt, *but* work rows of spots in different colours as shown in key. Cont until 34[38,42,46,52,58] rows in all have been worked from Chart.

Armhole Shaping
Next row (rs) Patt 36[38,39,41,44,48], cast(bind) off 8[8,10,10,12,12] sts, patt 73[77,79,83,89,97] including st already on needle, cast(bind) off 8[8,10,10,12,12] sts, patt to end.
Cont on last set of sts only for left front:
Keeping patt correct, cont without shaping until 65[73,79,87,95,105] rows in all have been worked from Chart, so ending with a rs row.

Neck Shaping
Keeping patt correct, cast(bind) off 4 sts at beg of next row, 3 sts at beg of foll 2[3,2,3,3,3] alt rows, 2 sts at beg of foll 2[1,3,2,2,3] alt rows, then one st at beg of foll 1[1,1,1,2,1] alt rows. 21[22,22,23,25,28] sts. 76[84,92,100,110,120] rows in all have been worked from Chart.

Shoulder Shaping
Cast(bind) off 7[8,8,8,9,10] sts at beg of next row, then 7[7,7,8,8,9] sts at beg of foll alt row. Work 1 row without shaping, then cast(bind) off rem 7[7,7,7,8,9] sts.
Return to sts which were left; with ws facing rejoin yarns to next 73[77,79,83,89,97] sts and patt to end. Cont on these sts only for Back.
Keeping patt correct, cont without shaping until 76[84,92,100,110,120] rows in all have been

worked from Chart, so ending with a ws row.

Shoulder and Neck Shaping

Keeping patt correct, cast(bind) off 7[8,8,8,9,10] sts at beg of next 2 rows. 59[61,63,67,71,77] sts.
Next row Cast(bind) off 7[7,7,8,8,9] sts, patt 11[11,11,11,12,13] including st already on needle, cast(bind) off 23[25,27,29,31,33] sts, patt to end.
Cont on last set of sts only for left back:
Cast(bind) off 7[7,7,8,8,9] sts at beg of next row, then 4 sts at beg of foll row.
Cast(bind) off rem 7[7,7,7,8,9] sts.
Return to sts for right back; with ws facing rejoin yarns to neck edge, cast(bind) off 4 sts and patt to end. Cast(bind) off rem 7[7,7,7,8,9] sts.
Return to sts which were left; with ws facing rejoin yarns to armhole edge of right front and cont as foll:
Keeping patt correct, cont without shaping until 64[72,78,86,94,104] rows in all have been worked from Chart, so ending with a ws row.

Neck Shaping

Keeping patt correct, cast(bind) off 4 sts at beg of next row, 3 sts at beg of foll 2[3,2,3,3,3] alt rows, 2 sts at beg of foll 2[1,3,2,2,3] alt rows, then one st at beg of foll 1[1,1,1,2,1] alt rows.
21[22,22,23,25,28] sts. Work 2 rows without shaping, so ending with a rs row.

Shoulder Shaping

Keeping patt correct, cast(bind) off 7[8,8,8,9,10] sts at beg of next row, then 7[7,7,8,8,9] sts at beg of foll alt row. Work 1 row without shaping, then cast(bind) off rem 7[7,7,7,8,9] sts.

SLEEVES

Using smaller needles and C, cast on 39[41,43,43,45,45] sts and work as given for Body from ** to **.
Inc row (rs) With B, K 3[1,6,6,5,5], make 1, * K 3[3,2,2,2,2], make 1; rep from * to last 3[1,7,7,6,6] sts, K to end. 51[55,59,59,63,63] sts.
Next row With B, P to end.
Beg with a K row and working in st st throughout cont in patt from Chart, beginning and ending rows as indicated work spots in same sequence as for Body AND AT THE SAME TIME, inc one st at each end of the 5th and every foll 4th row, working inc sts into patt until there are 73[79,85,91,97,103] sts. Cont without shaping until 54[60,66,78,84,90] rows in all have been worked from Chart, so ending with a ws row. Using B, cast(bind) off *loosely*.
Make a 2nd sleeve in the same way.

FINISHING

Press work lightly on ws according to instructions on bands. Using backstitch, join shoulder seams. Using backstitch, join cast-(bound-)off edge of sleeves to back and front armholes, matching centre of top of sleeve to shoulder seam and sewing last few rows of sleeve to cast-(bound-)off sts at underarm. Using backstitch, join sleeve seams. Press all seams. Turn up and press hems at picot edge on cuffs and lower edge of Body and sl st lightly on ws.

BUTTON BAND

Work on left for girls and right for boys.
Using smaller needles and A and with rs facing, pick up and K 59[65,69,75,81,89] sts evenly along front edge (picking up 10 sts from picot edge to inc row, 3 sts to every 4 rows, plus one extra st at neck). Change to larger needles and cont as foll:

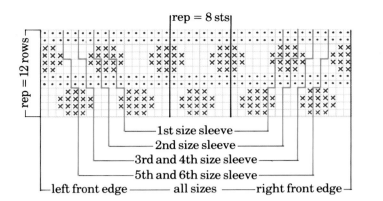

rep = 8 sts

rep = 12 rows

———1st size sleeve———
———2nd size sleeve———
———3rd and 4th size sleeve———
———5th and 6th size sleeve———
left front edge——— all sizes ———right front edge

1st row (ws) P 1F, (1A, 1F) to end. ***
2nd row K 1G, (1A, 1G) to end.
3rd row P 1C, (1B, 1C) to end.
Change to smaller needles and cont in C only as foll:
4th row K to end.
Picot edge row P1, (P2 tog, yrn) to last 2 sts, P2.
Beg with a K row, work 6 rows in st st to form hem. Cast(bind) off *loosely*.

BUTTONHOLE BAND

Work on right for girls and left for boys.
Work as given for Button Band to ***.
2nd row Work in same colour sequence as 2nd row of Button Band AND AT THE SAME TIME, patt 3[4,3,4,3,5], cast(bind) off 2 sts, * patt 8[9,10,11,10,11] including st already on needle, cast(bind) off 2 sts; rep from * 4[4,4,4,5,5] times more, patt to end.
3rd row Work in same colour sequence as 3rd row of Button Band AND AT THE SAME TIME, cast on 2 sts over each 2 cast(bound) off.
Change to smaller needles and cont in C only:
4th row K to end.
Picot edge row P1, (P2 tog, yrn) to last 2 sts, P2.
6th row K to end.
7th row P4, cast(bind) off 2 sts, * P 8[9,10,11,10,11] including st already on needle, cast(bind) off 2 sts; rep from * 4[4,4,4,5,5] times more, P to end.
8th row K to end, casting on 2 sts over each 2 cast(bound) off.
Beg with a P row, work 3 rows in st st. Cast(bind) off *loosely*. Turn up and press hems to inside and sl st lightly on ws. Sew round double buttonholes.

COLLAR

Using smaller needles, A and with ws facing, pick up and K 31[32,35,36,39,40] sts evenly up left front neck, 37[39,41,43,45,47] sts around back neck and 31[32,35,36,39,40] sts down right front neck. 99[103,111,115,123,127] sts.
Beg with a P row, work 3 rows in st st.
4th row K 1H, (1A, 1H) to end.
5th row P 1F, (1A, 1F) to end.
6th row As 4th row.
7th row P 1E, (1B, 1E) to end.
8th row K 1J, (1A, 1J) to end.
9th row P 1L, (1B, 1L) to end.
10th row K 1G, (1A, 1G) to end.
11th row P 1C, (1B, 1C) to end.
Cont in C only as foll:
12th row K to end.
Picot edge row P1, (P2 tog, yrn) to last 2 sts, P2.
Beg with a K row, work 6 rows in st st to form hem. Cast(bind) off *loosely*. Press collar, turn up and press hem at picot edge to inside and sl st lightly on ws. Oversew hem and collar tog at centre front edges. Sew on buttons.

□ = A
⊡ = B
⊠ = H Rows 1-4
L Rows 7-10
G Rows 13-16
J Rows 19-22
F Rows 25-28
D Rows 31-34
E Rows 37-40
C Rows 43-46
Repeat as necessary

STRIPES AND BOXES

My first real awareness of diagonal stripes was seeing barber's poles and rock candy when I was young. As my taste for the exotic grew, I became aware of the dramatic and beautiful use of the diagonal stripe on the shaded borders of Chinese robes. The exquisitely toned stripes seemed to give a wonderful sense of movement.

Zoë has used bold, easy-to-knit diagonals in her childrens' dresses (pages 60, 65, 103). I particularly like them topped off with the large diamond pattern on the yoke.

Working with manageable lengths of yarn encourages the changes of tone as you progress up the diagonal; if you also pick a different tone or texture of yarn you create an even richer sense of movement. Diagonal Stripe is worked in intarsia. It is possible to work the Diagonal Stripe Dress (page 60) with the balls attached but they tend to tangle. Try cutting off lengths of yarn for the colours at the right-hand side of the work, i.e. those that will disappear off the side of the work first, and use balls for the new colours being introduced at the left side (see page 195).

Zoë bought an old carpet in the fleamarket that really haunted me. Its bold, simple diagonal stripes were in cream, two blues and a red. It was always fresh and alive to my eye and this started me looking at other diagonal striped textiles. I noticed that the most lively diagonals always had little motifs dotted up them.

My first attempt at Diagonal Box was the bright chevron with pointed borders (page 55). It is worked by the intarsia method, except for the border where it is partly fairisle. Steve suggested we take a few of the contrasting colours from Diagonal Boxes to create an easy-to-knit child's version. The boxes are repeated in fairisle across the rows and you can leave balls attached for the solid diagonal stripes.

Bright astounding colours are wonderful but there is always a place for the cool, neutral classics. There is so much in our environment that contains beiges and greys that my tweedy version blends in beautifully. Like the children's versions (page 61), it employs a definite sequence in the diagonal stripes and the boxes are knitted in fairisle.

We have given you a good basic diagonal and a slightly embellished one in the Diagonal Box pattern but you could go on and on playing with this basic concept – for instance, outlining each stripe in a bright colour, or studding the Diagonal Stripe with different shaped motifs, such as flowers, circles or stars.

RIGHT *Two Bright Diagonal Box Stripe Sweaters. The simplified child's version has a slash neck opening and, if you want to experiment, the border on the bright adult version, page 55, can be adapted to almost any oriental-type pattern.*

⊠ = H for outline rows 1-19 only

□ each square 'box' has a single st of the colour it is sitting on
in the middle i.e. in rows 20-22 box 'C' a st of J in the centre

ADULT'S BRIGHT DIAGONAL BOX STRIPE CREWNECK SWEATER

MATERIALS

General yarn weight used – lightweight double knitting (sport)
Rowan *Lightweight DK* (25g/1oz hanks) in the foll 19 colours:

A (115) flame – 4[4] hanks
B (125) turquoise – 1[1] hank
C (25) tangerine – 2[2] hanks
D (44) scarlet – 1[2] hanks
E (46) maroon – 3[3] hanks
F (66) salmon – 2[3] hanks
G (14) sweetcorn – 2[2] hanks
H (50) china blue – 3[4] hanks
J (90) emerald – 2[2] hanks
L (124) kelly green – 1[1] hank
M (406) olive – 4[4] hanks
N (75) pale green – 1[1] hank
Q (74) green – 1[1] hank
R (103) flesh – 1[2] hanks
S (34) bright green – 1[1] hank
T (43) cerise – 2[2] hanks
U (95) orchid – 1[1] hank
V (93) buddleia – 1[1] hank
W (8) mustard – 1[1] hank

Rowan *Fine Fleck Tweed* (25g/1oz hanks) in the foll 2 colours:

X (44) red – 2[2] hanks
Y (12) yellow – 3[3] hanks

Rowan *Light Tweed* (25g/1oz hanks) in the foll 2 colours:

Z (214) blossom – 1[2] hanks
a (220) jade – 1[1] hank

One pair each 3mm (US size 3) and 3¾mm (US size 5) knitting needles *or size to obtain correct tension(gauge)*

SIZES

To fit 91-96[102-107]cm/36-38[40-42]in chest.
Figures for larger size are given in square brackets; where there is only one set of figures, it applies to both sizes.
For finished measurements see diagram (page 56).

TENSION(GAUGE)

23.5 sts and 30 rows to 10cm/4in over patt on 3¾mm (US size 5) needles.
Check your tension(gauge) before beginning.

NOTES

Yarns X and Y are used double throughout.
On every 'box' the centre st is worked in the same colour as that surrounding the 'box' – this cannot be shown on Chart due to lack of space.
When working rows 1-19, yarn H is carried to the end of every row. To obtain a neat finish, twist the yarn that forms each 'house' around the yarn that forms the 'house' just worked and yarn H tog, thus linking the 2 'house' yarns.
When working in patt from Chart, read odd rows (K) from right to left and even rows (P) from left to right.

BACK

Using smaller needles and E, cast on 122[132] sts.
Work 21 rows in K1, P1 rib in stripes as foll:
1 row E, 1 row A, 2 rows Q, 1 row H, 1 row E, 1 row Q, 1 row H, 2 rows A, 2 rows Y, 1 row H, 1 row Q, 1 row A, 3 rows E, 1 row H, 1 row Q, 1 row E.

Inc row (ws) With E, rib 11[6], make 1, * rib 10, make 1, rep from * to last 11[6] sts, rib to end. 133[145] sts.
Change to larger needles and cont in patt as foll:
Beg with a K row and working in st st throughout cont in patt from Chart, beginning and ending rows as indicated (please note that the 'boxes' are in a different position within each stripe on the left half of the garment than they are on the right).
Cont until 164[178] rows in all have been worked in patt, so ending with a ws row.

Shoulder and Neck Shaping

Keeping patt correct, cast(bind) off 15[17] sts at beg of next 2 rows.
Next row Cast(bind) off 15[17] sts, patt 24[25] including st already on needle, cast (bind) off 25[27] sts, patt to end.
Cont on last set of sts only for left back:
Keeping patt correct, cast(bind) off 15[17] sts at beg of next row, then 9 sts at beg of foll row.
Cast(bind) off rem 15[16] sts.
Return to sts which were left; with ws facing rejoin yarns to neck edge, cast(bind) off 9 sts and patt to end. Cast(bind) off rem 15[16] sts.

PAGES *52-53 A Child's Bright Diagonal Box Stripe Crewneck Sweater. The inset picture shows both the man and the boy wearing Bright Diagonal Box Stripe Crewneck Sweaters. The adult's version is available in kit form.*

BELOW *The Adult's Bright Diagonal Box Stripe Crewneck Sweater is photographed in Key West with a yellow version of a Flags Crewneck Sweater.*

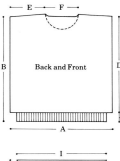

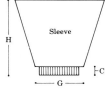

ADULT'S BRIGHT
DIAGONAL BOX STRIPE
CREWNECK SWEATER
A = 56.5[61.5]cm/22¼[24½]in
B = 60[65]cm/24[26]in
C = 5.5cm/2¼in
D = 54.5[59.5]cm/21¾[23¾]in
E = 19[21]cm/7½[8½]in
F = 18.5[19.5]cm/7¼[7½]in
G = 25[28.5]cm/10[11½]in
H = 45.5[47.5]cm/18¼[19¼]in
I = 50[54]cm/19¾[21½]in

BELOW *The Adult's
Bright Diagonal Box
Stripe Crewneck
Sweater and a Flags
Crewneck.*

FRONT

Work as given for Back until 142[156] rows in all
have been worked in st st.

Neck Shaping

<u>Next row</u> (rs) Patt 61[66], cast(bind) off 11[13] sts,
patt to end.
Cont on last set of sts only for right front:
<u>Next row</u> Patt to end.
Keeping patt correct, cast(bind) off 3 sts at beg of
next and foll alt row, 2 sts at beg of foll 3 alt rows,
then one st at beg of foll 4 alt rows. 45[50] sts.
Work 4 rows without shaping.

Shoulder Shaping

Cast(bind) off 15[17] sts at beg of next and foll alt
row. Work 1 row without shaping, then cast(bind)
off rem 15[16] sts. Return to sts which were left;
with ws facing rejoin yarns to neck edge,
cast(bind) off 3 sts and patt to end. Complete to
match first side, reversing all shaping.

SLEEVES

Using smaller needles and E, cast on 48[52] sts
and work 21 rows in striped rib as for Back.
<u>Inc row</u> (ws) With E, rib 4[5], make 1, * rib 4[3],
make 1; rep from * to last 4[5] sts, rib to end.
59[67] sts.
Change to larger needles and cont in patt as foll:
Beg with a K row and working in st st throughout
cont in patt from Chart, beginning and ending
rows as indicated AND AT THE SAME TIME, inc one
st at each end of the 5th and every foll 4th row,
working inc sts into patt until there are 117[127]
sts. Cont without shaping until 120[126] rows in
all have been worked in st st, so ending with a ws
row. Cast(bind) off *loosely*.
Make a 2nd sleeve in the same way.

FINISHING

Press work lightly on ws according to instructions
on bands, omitting ribbing.
Using backstitch, join left shoulder seam.

NECKBAND

Using smaller needles, E and with rs facing, pick
up and K 45[47] sts around back neck and 77[79]
sts around front neck. 122[126] sts.
Work 11 rows in K1, P1 rib in stripes as foll:
1 row E, 1 row A, 2 rows Q, 1 row H, 1 row E, 1 row A,
2 rows Y, 1 row Q, 1 row E.

Using E, cast(bind) off *loosely* in rib.
Using backstitch on main knitting and an edge to
edge st on rib, join right shoulder and neckband
seam. Press seams. Mark back and front at side
edge 25[27]cm/10[10¾]in down from shoulder
seam. Using backstitch, join cast-(bound-)off edge
of sleeves to back and front between markers,
matching centre of top of sleeve to shoulder seam.
Press all seams. Using backstitch on main knitting and an edge to edge st on rib, join side and
sleeve seams. Press seams.

ADULT'S TWEEDY DIAGONAL BOX STRIPE CREWNECK SWEATER

MATERIALS

General yarn weight used – lightweight double
knitting (sport)
Rowan *Grainy Silks* (50g/1¾oz hanks) in the foll 3
colours:
  A (812) blackcurrant – 1[1,1,1] hank
  B (808) branch – 1[1,1,1] hank
  C (805) mousse – 1[1,1,1] hank
Rowan *Silkstones* (50g/1¾oz hanks) in the foll 6
colours:
  D (829) woad – 2[2,2,2] hanks
  E (831) orchid – 1[1,1,1] hank
  F (832) blue mist – 2[3,3,3] hanks
  G (834) beetle – 1[1,1,1] hank
  H (826) chilli – 1[1,1,1] hank
  J (835) eau de nil – 1[1,1,1] hank
Rowan *Light Tweed* (25g/1oz hanks) in the foll 3
colours:
  L (203) pebble – 5[6,7,7] hanks
  M (208) silver – 2[3,3,3] hanks
  N (213) lavender – 1[1,1,1] hank
One pair each of 2¾mm (US size 2) and 3¼mm
(US size 3) knitting needles *or size to obtain correct
tension(gauge)*

SIZES

To fit 96[102,107,112]cm/38[40,42,44]in bust/
chest.
*Figures for larger sizes are given in square
brackets; where there is only one set of figures, it
applies to all sizes.*
For finished measurements see diagram (page 60).

TENSION(GAUGE)

24 sts and 33 rows to 10cm/4in over patt on 3¼mm
(US size 3) needles.
Check your tension(gauge) before beginning.

NOTES

*When you have completed the Chart cont in diago-
nal stripe and box patt as before, introducing new
colours at the right hand edge (when the previous
stripe has 12 sts) in the foll order: D, F, L, D, L, F,
M, D, F, L, D, L, F AND AT THE SAME TIME, beg on
the 81st row, work the boxes in the same sequence as
before, ie. rows 81-83 box is worked in A, rows
87-89 box is worked in N, etc. When working in patt
from Chart, read odd rows (K) from right to left and
even rows (P) from left to right.*

BACK

Using smaller needles and A, cast on
100[108,116,124] sts.
* Beg with a K row, work 9 rows in st st to form
hem.

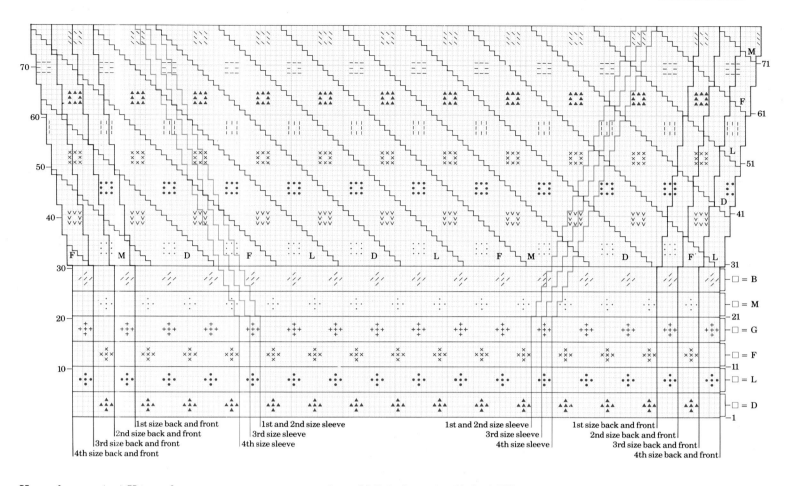

1st size back and front
2nd size back and front
3rd size back and front
4th size back and front

1st and 2nd size sleeve
3rd size sleeve
4th size sleeve

1st and 2nd size sleeve
3rd size sleeve
4th size sleeve

1st size back and front
2nd size back and front
3rd size back and front
4th size back and front

□ = B
□ = M
□ = G
□ = F
□ = L
□ = D

Hem edge row (ws) K to end.

Change to larger needles and cont in patt as foll: *
Beg with a K row and working in st st throughout
cont in patt from Chart, starting and ending rows
as indicated AND AT THE SAME TIME, inc one st at
each end of the 31st and every foll 6th row, working inc sts into patt until there are 128[136,
144,152] sts.

Cont without shaping until 200[208,216,224] rows
in all have been worked from Chart, so ending
with a ws row.

Shoulder and Neck Shaping

Keeping patt correct, cast(bind) off 14[16,17,17] sts
at beg of next 2 rows.

Next row (rs) Cast(bind) off 14[15,16,18] sts, patt
19[20,21,23] including st already on needle,
cast(bind) off 34[34,36,36] sts, patt to end.

Cont on last set of sts only for left back as foll:
Keeping patt correct, cast(bind) off 14[15,16,18] sts
at beg of next row, then 5 sts at beg of foll row.
Cast(bind) off rem 14[15,16,18] sts.

Return to sts which were left; with ws facing rejoin
yarns to neck edge, cast(bind) off 5 sts and patt to
end.

Cast(bind) off rem 14[15,16,18] sts.

FRONT

Work as given for Back until 180[188,196,204]
rows in all have been worked from Chart.

Neck Shaping

Next row (rs) Patt 55[59,62,66], cast(bind) off
18[18,20,20] sts, patt to end.

Cont on last set of sts only for right front as foll:
Next row Patt to end.

Keeping patt correct, cast(bind) off 3 sts at beg of
next row, 2 sts at beg of foll 2 alt rows, then one st

at beg of foll 6 alt rows. 42[46,49,53] sts.
Work 2 rows without shaping.

Shoulder Shaping

** Cast(bind) off 14[16,17,17] sts at beg of next row,
then 14[15,16,18] sts at beg of foll alt row. Work 1
row without shaping.

Cast(bind) off rem 14[15,16,18] sts.

Return to sts which were left; with ws facing rejoin
yarns to neck edge, cast(bind) off 3 sts and patt to
end.

Next row Patt to end.

Keeping patt correct, cast(bind) off 2 sts at beg of
foll 2 alt rows, then one st at beg of foll 6 alt rows.
42[46,49,53] sts.

Work 2 rows without shaping.

Shoulder Shaping

Work as given for first side from ** to end.

SLEEVES

Using smaller needles and A, cast on 52[52,56,60]
sts and work as given for Back from * to *.

Beg with a K row and working in st st throughout
cont in patt from Chart, starting and ending rows
as indicated AND AT THE SAME TIME, inc one st at
each end of the 21st and every foll 3rd row, working inc sts into patt until there are 130[134,
138,142] sts.

Cont without shaping until 140[146,152,158] rows
in all have been worked from Chart.

Cast(bind) off loosely.

Make a 2nd sleeve in the same way.

FINISHING

Press work lightly on ws according to instructions
on bands. Turn up and press hems to inside. Using
backstitch, join left shoulder seam. Press seam.

⊡ = A
▲ = B
⊠ = C
⊙ = E
⊘ = F
⊞ = G
⊟ = H
⊠ = J
⊞ = L
⊻ = N

OVERLEAF *The Adult's
Tweedy Diagonal Box
Stripe Crewneck
Sweater is knitted up in
textured yarns and some
silk/wool mix. This
pattern is available in
kit form. The child and
mother are wearing
Circle Square Crewneck
Sweaters. The pattern
for the adult's version is
on page 188 and is also
available in kit form.*

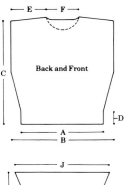

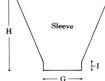

ADULT'S TWEEDY DIAGONAL BOX STRIPE CREWNECK SWEATER
A = 41.5[45,48.5,51.5]cm/
16½[18,19¼,20½]in
B = 53.5[56.5,60,63]cm/
21½[22½,24,25½]in
C = 60.5[63,65.5,68]cm/
24¼[25¼,26,27]in
D = 9cm/3½in
E = 17.5[19,20.5,22]cm/
7[7½,8,8¾]in
F = 18.5[18.5,19,19]cm/
7½[7½,8,8]in
G = 21.5[21.5,23.5,25]cm/
8½[8½,9¼,10]in
H = 42.5[44,46,48]cm/
17[17½,18¼,19]in
I = 6cm/2¼in
J = 54[56,57.5,59]cm/
21½[22¼,23,23½]in

RIGHT *In a rich jumble of stripes, the finely knitted Child's Diagonal Box Stripe Sweater, available in kit form, is shown here with an Adult's Diagonal Stripe Shawl Collar Sweater, also available in kit form, and a Child's Diagonal Stripe Sleeveless Sweater.*

NECKBAND
Using smaller needles, B and with rs facing, pick up and K 44[44,46,46] sts around back neck and 56[56,58,58] sts around front neck.
100[100,104,104] sts.
<u>1st row</u> (ws) With D, P to end.
<u>2nd row</u> K 6[6,4,4]D, * 1B, 7D; rep from * to last 6[6,4,4] sts, 1B, 5[5,3,3]D.
<u>3rd row</u> P 4[4,2,2]D, * 3B, 5D; rep from * to last 8[8,6,6] sts, 3B, 5[5,3,3]D.
<u>4th row</u> As 2nd row.
<u>5th row</u> With D, P to end.
Change to smaller needles and cont in B only as foll:
<u>6th row</u> K to end.
<u>Hem edge row</u> (ws) K to end.
Beg with a K row, work 7 rows in st st to form hem. Cast(bind) off *very loosely* using larger needle.
Using backstitch, join right shoulder and neckband seam. Turn up and press hem to inside. Mark back and front at side edges 27[28,29,29.5]cm/10¾[11,11½,11¾]in from shoulders. Using backstitch, join cast- (bound-)off edge of sleeves to back and front between markers, matching centre of top of sleeve to shoulder seam.
Press seams. Using backstitch, join side and sleeve seams.
Press all seams. Fold hems to inside on hem edge row and sl st lightly on ws.

BABY'S DIAGONAL STRIPE DRESS AND HAT

MATERIALS
General yarn weight used – lightweight cotton
Rowan *Soft Cotton* (50g/1¾oz balls) in the foll 12 colours:
  A (545) sugar pink – 1[1,2,2] balls
  B (547) mermaid – 1[1,1,1] ball
  C (546) strawberry ice – 1[1,1,1] ball
  D (521) bleached – 1[1,1,1] ball
  E (539) bermuda – 1[1,1,1] ball
  F (533) antique pink – 1[1,1,1] ball
  G (542) bluebell – 1[1,1,1] ball
  H (534) frolic – 1[1,1,1] ball
  J (548) eau de nil – 1[1,1,1] ball
  L (528) rain cloud – 1[1,1,1] ball
  M (544) lilac – 1[1,1,1] ball
  N (531) fiord – 1[1,1,1] ball
Rowan *Knobbly Cotton* (50g/1¾oz balls) in the foll colour:
  Q (570) electric blue – 1[1,1,1] ball
One pair each 2¼mm (US size 1) and 3mm (US size 3) knitting needles *or size to obtain correct tension(gauge)*
4 buttons
Elastic thread (optional)

SIZES
To fit 6[12,18,24]months or 45[48,51,53]cm/18[19,20,21]in chest.
Figures for larger sizes are given in square brackets; where there is only one set of figures, it applies to all sizes.
For finished measurements see diagram (page 63).

TENSION(GAUGE)
28 sts and 36 rows to 10cm/4in over patt on 3mm (US size 3) needles.
40 sts and 36 rows to 10cm/4in over single rib on 3mm (US size 3) needles.
Check your tension(gauge) before beginning.

NOTES
There are 3 charts for this dress (page 63), Chart 1 for the skirt and Charts 2 and 3 for the bodice. Bodice 1st and 3rd sizes are on Chart 2 and 2nd and 4th sizes are on Chart 3.
When working in patt from Chart 2 or 3, read odd rows (K) from right to left and even rows (P) from left to right.
SK2P=slip 1 knitwise, K2 tog, psso.

FRONT
Using smaller needles and A, cast on 132[144, 156,168] sts.
Beg with a K row, work 4 rows in st st to form hem.
<u>Picot edge row</u> (rs) K1, (K2 tog, yfwd) to last st, K1.
<u>Next row</u> P to end.
Change to larger needles and cont in border patt as foll:
<u>1st row</u> With B, K to end.
<u>2nd row</u> With B, P to end.
<u>3rd row</u> With C, K to end.
<u>4th row</u> P 1D, (2Q, 2D) to last 3 sts, 2Q, 1D.
<u>5th row</u> K to end in colour sequence as set.
<u>6th and 7th rows</u> As 4th and 5th rows.
<u>8th row</u> With C, P to end.
Cont in diagonal stripe patt as foll:
<u>1st row</u> K 12M, 12E, 12F, 12G, 12A, 12J, 12H, 12L, 12C, 12B, 12A, 0[12,12,12]N, 0[0,12,12]M, 0[0,0,12]E.
<u>2nd row</u> P 0[0,0,1]F, 0[0,1,12]E, 0[1,12,12]M, 1[12,12,12]N, 12A, 12B, 12C, 12L, 12H, 12J, 12A, 12G, 12F, 12E, 11M.
Working in st st throughout as set, move stripes over one st to the right on every row in this way, introducing new colours to left side edge of work at beg of every foll 12th row, keep 12 sts in each stripe and use Chart 1 as a guide.
Cont until 77[89,101,113] rows in all have been worked in stripe patt, so ending with a rs row.

Waistband
Change to smaller needles.
Working in colours as set:
<u>Dec row</u> (ws) P4, (P2 tog) to last 4 sts, P4. 70[76,82,88] sts.
Work 4 rows in K1, P1 rib in stripe sequence as set, twisting yarns tog as you go. **
Change to larger needles. Beg with a K row and working in st st throughout cont in patt from Chart 2, beginning and ending rows as indicated. Work 6 rows.

Armhole Shaping
Keeping patt correct as on Chart 2 or 3, cast (bind) off 2[2,2,3] sts at beg of next 2 rows, 2 sts at beg of next 2 rows, 1[1,2,2] sts at beg of next 2 rows, then one st at beg of next 4[6,6,6] rows. 56[60,64,68] sts. Work 12[12,14,16] rows without shaping.

Neck Shaping
<u>Next row</u> (rs) Patt 25[26,27,28], cast (bind) off 6[8,10,12] sts, patt to end.
Cont on last set of sts only for right front:
Work 1 row without shaping.
Keeping patt correct, cast(bind) off 2 sts at beg of next and foll 2 alt rows, then one st at beg of foll 4 alt rows. 15[16,17,18] sts.
Cont without shaping until 53[55,57,59] rows in all have been worked from Chart 2 or 3, so ending with a rs row. Leave sts on a spare needle.
Return to sts which were left; with ws facing rejoin yarns to neck edge, cast(bind) off 2 sts and patt to end.
Cast(bind) off 2 sts at beg of foll 2 alt rows, then

one st at beg of foll 4 alt rows.
15[16,17,18] sts.
Cont without shaping until 53[55,57,59] rows in all have been worked from Chart 2 or 3, so ending with a rs row.
Leave sts on a spare needle.

BACK

Work as given for Front to **.
Change to larger needles.
Beg with a K row and working in st st throughout cont in patt from Chart 2 or 3, beginning and ending rows as indicated and dividing for back open-ing as foll:

Next row (rs) Patt 34[37,40,43], cast (bind) off 2 sts, patt to end.
Cont on last set of sts only for left back:
Work 6 rows without shaping.

Armhole Shaping

Keeping patt correct as on Chart 2 or 3, cast(bind) off 2[2,2,3] sts at beg of next row, 2 sts at beg of foll alt row, 1[1,2,2] sts at beg of foll alt row, then one st at beg of foll 2[3,3,3] alt rows. 27[29,31,33] sts.
Cont without shaping until 36[38,40,42] rows in all have been worked from Chart 2 or 3.

RIGHT *Here are the Baby's Diagonal Stripe Dress and Hat, and the Baby's Bright Squares Trousers, page 17, in a Moroccan meadow. I am wearing the Adult's Split Diamond Crewneck Sweater, page 172; this pattern is also available in kit form.*

Chart One

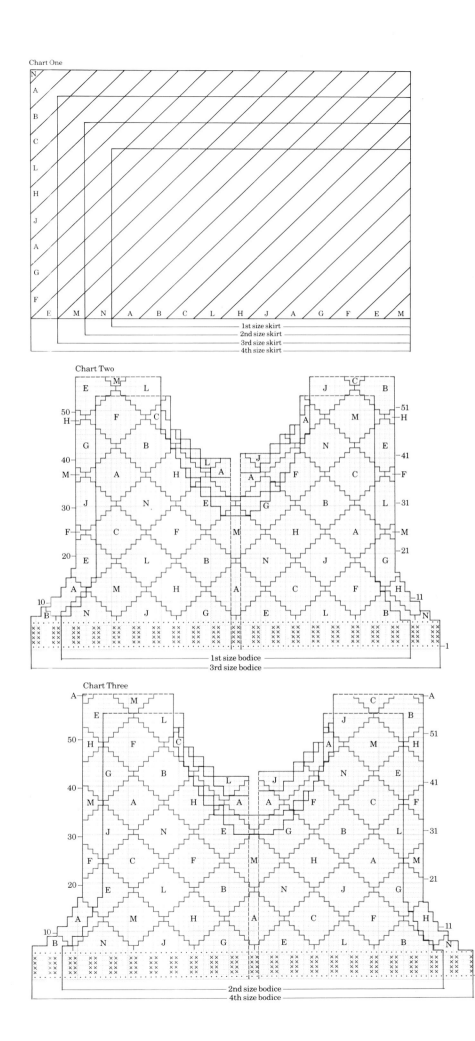

1st size skirt
2nd size skirt
3rd size skirt
4th size skirt

Chart Two

1st size bodice
3rd size bodice

Chart Three

2nd size bodice
4th size bodice

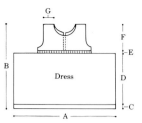

G

Dress

BABY'S DIAGONAL STRIPE
DRESS AND HAT
A = 47[51.5,55.5,60]cm/
18¾[20½,22¼,24]in
B = 39.5[43.5,47.5,51.5]cm/
15½[17,18¾,20¼]in
C = 2.5cm/1in
D = 21[24.5,28,31.5]cm/
8½[9¾,11¼,12½]in
E = 1cm/¼in
F = 15[15.5,16,16.5]cm/
5¾[6,6¼,6½]in
G = 5[5.5,6,6.5]cm/
2[2¼,2½,2½]in

RIGHT *London's Kew Gardens in spring is a perfect setting for a Flags Crewneck Sweater and a soft pastel version of Diagonal Stripe Dress and Hat on the baby. Over the girl's shoulder is a stunning blanket by Zoë. It is seen in greater detail as the background.*

Neck Shaping

Keeping patt correct, cast(bind) off 4[5,6,7] sts at beg of next row, 2 sts at beg of foll 3 alt rows, then one st at beg of foll 2 alt rows. 15[16,17,18] sts.
Cont without shaping until 53[55,57,59] rows in all have been worked from Chart 2 or 3.
Leave sts on a spare needle.
Return to sts which were left; with ws facing rejoin yarns to centre back and work 5 rows without shaping.

Armhole Shaping

Keeping patt correct as on Chart 2 or 3, cast(bind) off 2[2,2,3] sts at beg of next row, 2 sts at beg of foll alt row, 1[1,2,2] sts at beg of foll alt row, then one st at beg of foll 2[3,3,3] alt rows. 27[29,31,33] sts.
Cont without shaping until 37[39,41,43] rows in all have been worked from Chart 2 or 3.
Complete as given for first side.

FINISHING

Press work lightly on ws according to instructions on ball bands. Join shoulders as foll:
Place both sets of sts for right shoulder on 2 needles with points to armhole edge, with rs tog cast(bind) off all sts knitting tog one st from each needle as you go. Beg at neck edge, work in the same way for left shoulder.

ARMHOLE BORDERS

With smaller needles and C and with rs facing, pick up and K 88[92,96,100] sts around armhole edge (13[14,15,16] sts round curve, approximately 8 sts for every 9 rows along straight edge, then 13[14,15,16] sts round curve).
* Beg with a P row, work in st st as foll:
1st and 2nd rows 1D, (2Q, 2D) to last 3 sts, 2Q, 1D.
Cont in A only.
3rd row P to end.
Picot edge row K1, (K2 tog, yfwd) to last st, K1.
5th row P to end.
Work 4 rows in st st to form hem.
Cast(bind) off *loosely*.

NECKBAND

Using smaller needles, C and with rs facing, pick up and K 23[24,25,26] sts evenly along left back neck, 62[64,66,68] sts around front neck and 23[24,25,26] sts along right back neck. 108[112,116,120] sts.
Work as given for Armhole Borders from * to end.
Turn up and press hems at picot edge of skirt, neck and armholes. Using an edge to edge st, join side seams and ends of armhole borders. Sl st hems lightly on ws. Press all seams.

BUTTON BAND

Using smaller needles and A and with rs facing, pick up and K 42[44,46,48] sts evenly along left back opening, including neckband (one st for every row). ** Work 3 rows in K1, P1 rib.
Cast(bind) off *loosely* in rib.

BUTTONHOLE BAND

Work along right back opening as given for Button Band to **.
1st row Rib 5[7,9,8], cast(bind) off 2 sts, * rib 9[9,9,10] including st already on needle, cast(bind) off 2 sts, rep from * twice more, rib to end.
2nd row Rib to end, casting on 2 sts over each 2 cast(bound) off.
Work 1 more row, then cast(bind) off *loosely* in rib.
Join ends of bands to cast-(bound)-off sts at centre back, overlapping bands. Sew on buttons. If

desired thread elastic through rib at waistband on ws of work, catching in on every other st.

HAT

Using smaller needles and A, cast on 110[120,130,140] sts. Beg with a K row, work 4 rows in st st to form hem.
Picot edge row (rs) K1, (K2 tog, yfwd) to last st, K1.
Next row P to end.
Change to larger needles and cont in border patt as foll:
1st row With B, K to end.
2nd row With B, P to end.
3rd row With C, K to end.
4th row P 0[1,0,1]D, 2Q, (2D, 2Q) to last 0[1,0,1] st, 0[1,0,1]D.
5th row K to end in colour sequence as set.
6th and 7th rows As 4th and 5th rows.
8th row With C, P to end.
Cont in stripe patt as foll:
1st row (rs) K 11[12,13,14]M, 11[12,13,14]N, 11[12,13,14]F, 11[12,13,14]J, 11[12,13,14]C, 11[12,13,14]B, 11[12,13,14]A, 11[12,13,14]G, 11[12,13,14]H, 11[12,13,14]E, twisting yarns tog as you go on ws.
Working in colours as set cont in K1, P1 rib, twisting yarns tog as you go. Work 5 rows.
Next row (rs) Rib 11[12,13,14], ** bring yarn to rs of work, bring next colour to rs, twist on rs, rib 11[12,13,14]; rep from ** to end. From now on always twist yarns tog on this side of work, thus allowing for brim to be turned up.
Cont without shaping until 43[47,51,55] rows in all have been worked in stripe patt.

Crown Shaping

Keeping colours as set throughout:
Next row * Rib 4[4,5,6], SK2P[SK2P,P3 tog, SK2P], rib 8[9,10,11], P3 tog[SK2P,SK2P,SK2P], rib 4[5,5,5]; rep from * 4 times more. 90[100,110,120] sts.
Work 3 rows in K1, P1 rib.
Next row * Rib 3[3,4,5], P3 tog[P3 tog,SK2P, P3 tog], rib 6[7,8,9], SK2P[P3 tog,P3 tog,P3 tog], rib 3[4,4,4]; rep from * 4 times more. 70[80,90,100] sts.
Work 3 rows in K1, P1 rib.
Next row * Rib 2[2,3,4], SK2P[SK2P, P3 tog,SK2P], rib 4[5,6,7], P3 tog[SK2P, SK2P,SK2P], rib 2[3,3,3]; rep from * 4 times more. 50[60,70,80] sts.
Work 1 row in K1, P1 rib.
Next row * Rib 1[1,2,3], P3 tog[P3 tog,SK2P, P3 tog], rib 2[3,4,5], SK2P[P3 tog,P3 tog,P3 tog], rib 1[2,2,2]; rep from * 4 times more. 30[40,50,60] sts.
Work 1 row in K1, P1 rib.
Next row * Rib 0[0,1,2], SK2P[SK2P,P3 tog, SK2P], rib 0[1,2,3], P3 tog[SK2P,SK2P,SK2P], rib 0[1,1,1]; rep from * 4 times more. 10[20,30,40] sts.
Work 1 row in K1, P1 rib.
On 3rd and 4th sizes only: * Rib 0[1], SK2P [P3 tog], rib 0[1], P3 tog; rep from * 4 times more. 10[20] sts.
On 2nd and 4th sizes only: (K2 tog tbl) to end. 10 sts.
On all sizes: thread M through all sts, pull tight, fasten then leave a long end to join seam. Yarn ends may be finished off in 2 ways: either tie them in a knot as a group on rs or ws (making a tassel) and cut off at desired length, OR fasten off each yarn separately on ws of work so that they are invisible. Press border, then turn up hem at picot edge and press. Join seam, then sl st hem lightly on ws of work. Fold back brim.

BRUSHES AND COMBS

 Brushstrokes was one of Zoë's earliest successes; she found the idea in a wonderful costume book by Max Tilke entitled *Costume Patterns and Designs*. A medieval leather doublet with fabric revealed through slashes was the inspiration for her first peplum jacket. The wide vertical bands allow gentle changes of tone which give such a quality to the design. The adult sweaters (pages 71, 75) are knitted in doubled yarns, making it even easier to shade colours subtly. When you work with two yarns of different tones together, break off only one when changing yarn to avoid sudden contrasts. The secret with this one is to collect as many shades of yarn in your background as possible. Do have a go at a version of your own; it is a natural for personal interpretation. I could see it working well in ochery browns like the original leather, or in deep wine reds. With the brushstrokes, make sure that you never use the same colour on two strokes which are adjacent in any direction. This helps to give the design movement and balance. Also, try to avoid changing colours in two adjacent vertical bands in the same row as this will create a horizontal line cutting across the design which might look ugly.

Brushstrokes is worked mostly by the intarsia method. For the vertical lines, break off long lengths of yarn. These will be easier to pull through the inevitable tangle. The background colours can be worked with the balls attached because they are constantly changing, but if you get into a tangle, cut them off. The brushstrokes themselves should be worked with short lengths of yarn; you will soon work out how long they need to be.

Being a born knitter, Zoë is brilliant at inventing patterns that are effective, yet easy and rhythmic to knit. The bold two-colours-in-a-row pattern of Combs gives a sense of rippling colour when seen at a distance. The idea was taken from a book of Japanese fabric prints. Have a go with your own colourings by picking many different tones of two colours.

You may find that it's not as easy as it looks to get the colours to read against one another. As there is only one stitch of colour in the vertical striped sections, they tend to fade miraculously into each other so that two colours that looked quite different in balls, are disastrously similar when knitted in the same design. But if you persevere, you will see what sort of colours are called for.

Keep trying different combinations and don't rip out your swatches – you may like one section from one swatch and one from another. Once you've done the designing, this is one of the easiest motifs to knit and your sweater will grow very fast. Combs is worked in fairisle throughout.

RIGHT *The glory of Kew Gardens is the backdrop to the Adult's Brushstrokes Crewneck Sweater, page 71, available in kit form, and the Baby's Shorts, which are the same shape as the Yellow Plaid Shorts on page 25.*

160 · 150 · 140 · 130 · 120 · 110 · 100 · 90 · 80 · 70 · 60 · 50 · 40 · 30 · 20 · 10

161 · 151 · 141 · 131 · 121 · 111 · 101 · 91 · 81 · 71 · 61 · 51 · 41 · 31 · 21 · 11 · 1

A A — back and front A A A A — sleeve A A A A A A — sleeve A A A A — back and front

· work in colour written in red

ADULT'S BRUSHSTROKES CREWNECK SWEATER

MATERIALS

General yarn weight used – Aran (heavy worsted)
2 strands of yarn are used together throughout, except for yarn Z which is used single, unless otherwise stated.
Rowan Botany (25g/1oz hanks) in the foll 16 colours:
  A (97) navy – 5 hanks
  B (634) midnight – 2 hanks
  C (56) royal – 3 hanks
  D (55) lobelia – 3 hanks
  E (108) indigo – 2 hanks
  F (501) lavender – 1 hank
  G (45) pillar box – 1 hank
  H (125) turquoise – 2 hanks
  J (633) peacock – 5 hanks
  L (91) pine forest – 2 hanks
  M (25) tangerine – 1 hank
  N (26) rust – 1 hank
  Q (41) pink – 1 hank
  R (115) flame – 1 hank
  S (9) brass – 1 hank
  T (405) pale olive – 1 hank
Rowan Fine Fleck Tweed (25g/1oz hanks) in the foll 5 colours:
  U (56) royal – 2 hanks
  V (90) emerald – 2 hanks
  W (100) sage – 2 hanks
  X (44) ruby – 1 hank
  Y (412) brick – 1 hank
Rowan Handknit DK Cotton (50g/1¾oz balls) in the foll colour:
  Z (279) bayou – 2 balls
One pair each 3¾mm (US size 5) and 4½mm (US size 7) knitting needles *or size to obtain correct tension(gauge)*

SIZE

To fit up to 102cm/40in chest.
For finished measurements see diagram.

TENSION(GAUGE)

21 sts and 27 rows to 10cm/4in over patt on 4½mm (US size 7) needles.
Check your tension(gauge) before beginning.

NOTES

The 'brushstroke' colours are marked in red on Chart. When working in patt from Chart, read odd rows (K) from right to left and even rows (P) from left to right.

BACK

Using smaller needles and QQ, cast on 86 sts.
Work 19 rows in K1, P1 rib in stripes as foll:
4 rows Z, 1 row SS, 4 rows EE, 1 row GG, 4 rows Z, 1 row SS, 4 rows EE.
Inc row (ws) With GG, * rib 3, make 1; rep from * to last 2 sts, rib 2. 114 sts.
Change to larger needles and cont in patt as foll:
Beg with a K row and working in st st throughout cont in patt from Chart, beginning and ending rows as indicated until 90 rows in all have been worked in patt, so ending with a ws row.

Armhole Shaping

Keeping patt correct, cast(bind) off 7 sts at beg of next 2 rows. 100 sts.
Cont without shaping until 160 rows in all have been worked in patt.

Shoulder and Neck Shaping

Next row (rs) Cast(bind) off 11 sts, patt 31 including st already on needle, cast(bind) off 16 sts, patt to end.
Cont on last set of sts only for left back:
Keeping patt correct, cast(bind) off 11 sts at beg of next row, then 5 sts at beg of foll row, cast(bind) off 11 sts at beg of next row, then 4 sts at beg of foll row. Cast(bind) off rem 11 sts.
Return to sts which were left; with ws facing rejoin yarns to neck edge, cast(bind) off 5 sts and patt to end.
Cast(bind) off 11 sts at beg of next row, then 4 sts at beg of foll row.
Cast(bind) off rem 11 sts.

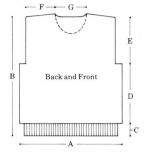
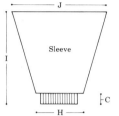

ADULT'S BRUSHSTROKES
CREWNECK SWEATER
A = 54.5cm/21½in
B = 66cm/26in
C = 6.5cm/2½in
D = 33.5cm/13¼in
E = 26cm/10¼in
F = 15.5cm/6¼in
G = 16cm/6½in
H = 25.5cm/10¼in
I = 52.5cm/20¾in
J = 52cm/20½in

PREVIOUS PAGE AND LEFT
The Adult's Brushstrokes Crewneck Sweater, available in kit form, and a pair of Baby's Brushstrokes Shorts.

71

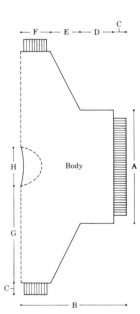

CHILD'S BRUSHSTROKES SCOOPNECK SWEATER
A = 42cm/16¾in
B = 37cm/14¾in
C = 4.5cm/1¾in
D = 12cm/4¾in
E = 10.5cm/4¼in
F = 10cm/4in
G = 35cm/14in
H = 15.5cm/6¼in

72

FRONT

Work as given for Back until 136 rows in all have been worked in patt.

Neck Shaping

Next row (rs) Patt 45, cast(bind) off 10 sts, patt to end. Cont on last set of sts only for right front:
Next row Patt to end.
Keeping patt correct, cast(bind) off 3 sts at beg of next row, 2 sts at beg of foll 2 alt rows, then one st at beg of foll 5 alt rows. 33 sts.
Cont without shaping until 161 rows in all have been worked in patt, so ending with a rs row.

Shoulder Shaping

Cast(bind) off 11 sts at beg of next and foll alt row. Work 1 row without shaping, then cast(bind) off rem 11 sts. Return to sts which were left; with ws facing rejoin yarns to neck edge, cast(bind) off 3 sts and patt to end.
Complete to match first side, reversing all shaping.

SLEEVES

Using smaller needles and QQ, cast on 42 sts. Work 19 rows in striped rib as for Back.
Inc row (ws) With GG, rib 4, make 1, * rib 3, make 1; rep from * to last 5 sts, rib 5. 54 sts.
Change to larger needles and cont in patt as foll: Beg with a K row and working in st st throughout cont in patt from Chart, beginning and ending rows as indicated AND AT THE SAME TIME, inc one st at each end of the 3rd and every foll 4th row, working inc sts into patt until there are 108 sts. Cont without shaping until 124 rows in all have been worked in patt, so ending with a ws row.
Cast(bind) off *loosely*.
Make a 2nd sleeve in the same way.

FINISHING

Press work lightly on ws according to instructions on bands, omitting ribbing.
Using backstitch, join left shoulder seam.

NECKBAND

Using smaller needles and GG and with rs facing, pick up and K 38 sts around back neck and 66 sts around front neck. 104 sts.
Beg with a P row, cont in st st working in colours as foll:
1st row With HJ, P to end.
2nd row K (2AA, 2CC) to end.
3rd row P 1CC, (2AA, 2CC) to last 3 sts, 2AA, 1CC.
4th row K (2CC, 2AA) to end.
5th row P 1AA, (2CC, 2AA) to last 3 sts, 2CC, 1AA.
6th row As 2nd row.
7th row With QQ, P to end.
8th row With JL, K to end.
Picot edge row With JL, P1, (P2 tog, yrn) to last st, P1.
10th row As 8th row.
With *one* strand only of J, beg with a P row work 7 rows in st st to form hem. Cast(bind) off *loosely*. Press neckband and fold in hem at picot edge. Using backstitch, join right shoulder and neckband seam and sl st hem loosely on ws. Press seams. Using backstitch, join cast-(bound-) off edge of sleeves to back and front armholes, matching centre of top of sleeve to shoulder seam and sewing last few rows of sleeve to cast(bound) off sts at underarm. Press all seams. Using backstitch on main knitting and an edge to edge st on rib, join side and sleeve seams. Press seams.

CHILD'S BRUSHSTROKES SCOOPNECK SWEATER

MATERIALS

General yarn weight used – 4 ply (fingering)
Approximately 100g/4oz of mixed yarns in each of two groups of colours, A (yellow) and B (orange)
Approximately 75g/3oz in yarn C (raspberry)
Approximately 25g/1oz of mixed yarns in group D (blue)
One pair 2¼mm (US size 1) knitting needles, 3mm (US size 3) circular needle 100cm or 40in long *or size to obtain correct tension(gauge)*
One 2.50mm (US size B1) crochet hook

SIZE

To fit 4-6yrs or 56-61cm/22-24in chest.
For finished measurements see diagram.

TENSION(GAUGE)

27 sts and 36 rows to 10cm/4in over patt on 3mm (US size 3) needles.
Check your tension(gauge) before beginning.

NOTES

The sweater is worked in one piece with cuffs added afterwards.
All yarns in group A or B should be similar to each other, both in colour and weight so that one fades gently into the next, but the textures should be as varied as possible.
Yarn C is worked in one colour throughout, although if you run out simply choose another yarn that is similar.
Group D consists of 8 different shades of the same colour, varied in texture and tone. Try to avoid changing colour in 2 adjacent panels on the same row as this would give straight lines across the work which would jump out and look ugly. If you look at the Chart on page 70 it will give you some idea of how to tackle the problem.
When working in patt from Chart (page 78), read odd rows (K) from right to left and even rows (P) from left to right.

BACK

Using smaller needles and D, cast on 86 sts.
Work 19 rows in K1, P1 rib in stripes as foll:
4 rows A, 1 row D, 4 rows B, 1 row D, 4 rows A, 1 row D, 4 rows B.
Inc row (ws) With D, * rib 3, make 1; rep from * to last 2 sts, rib to end. 114 sts.
Change to larger needle and cont in patt as foll: Beg with a K row and working backwards and for-wards in rows of st st throughout, cont in patt from Chart starting and ending rows as indicated, rep rows 1-10 to form patt.
Cont until 44 rows in all have been worked in patt, so ending with a ws row.

Sleeve Shaping

Keeping patt correct, cast on 3 sts at beg of next 36 rows, then 5 sts at beg of foll 2 rows. 232 sts.
Cont without shaping until 114 rows in all have been worked in patt.

Neck Shaping

Next row (rs) Patt 104, cast(bind) off 24 sts, patt to end.
Cont on last set of sts only for left side as foll:
Next row Patt to end.

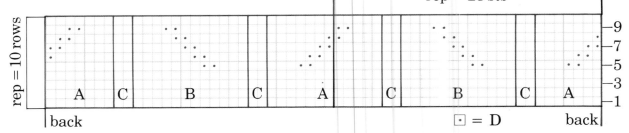

rep = 28 sts

rep = 10 rows

9
7
5
3
1

A   C   B   C   A   C   B   C   A

back   ⊡ = D   back

Next row Cast(bind) off 9 sts, patt to end.
95 sts. (This is now the shoulder line)
Keeping patt correct, work 7 rows without shap-ing. (From now on work yarn D in the same colour sequence as on Back, ie. rows 125-129 the same as on rows 105-109, 135-139 the same as on rows 95-99 and so on).
Work 2 rows without shaping.
** Cast on one st at beg of next and foll 2 alt rows, 2 sts at beg of foll 3 alt rows, then 3 sts at beg of foll 2 alt rows. 110 sts. **
Work 1 row without shaping.
Leave these sts on a spare needle.
Return to sts which were left for right side; with ws facing rejoin yarn to neck edge, cast(bind) off 9 sts and patt to end. 95 sts.
Work 1 row without shaping. (This is now the shoulder line)
Cont in patt in reverse as for left side as foll:
Work 10 rows without shaping.
Rep from ** to ** once.

Join Fronts
Next row (rs) Patt across sts of right front, with A,

cast on 12 sts, cont in patt across rem 110 sts.
232 sts.
Cont without shaping, work 8 rows, so ending with a rs row. 151 rows in all have been worked in patt.

Sleeve Shaping
Keeping patt correct, cast(bind) off 5 sts at beg of next 2 rows, then 3 sts at beg of next 36 rows.
114 sts.
Cont without shaping, work 44 rows, so ending with a rs row. 233 rows in all have been worked in patt.
Change to smaller needles.
Dec row (ws) With D, * P2, P2 tog; rep from * to last 2 sts, P2.
86 sts.
*** Work 20 rows in K1, P1 rib in stripes as foll:
4 rows B, 1 row D, 4 rows A, 1 row D, 4 rows B, 1 row D, 4 rows A, 1 row D.
Using D, cast(bind) off *loosely* in rib. ***

FINISHING
Press work lightly on ws according to instructions on bands, omitting ribbing.

PREVIOUS PAGE AND BELOW
Photographed amidst the flowers of London's Kew Gardens are the Adult's Brushstrokes Crewneck Sweater, page 71, pink and orange Baby's Brushstrokes Shorts, which are the same shape as the Baby's Yellow Plaid Shorts on page 25, and the Child's Brushstrokes Scoopneck Sweater.

CUFFS

With smaller needles, D and with rs facing, pick up and K 48 sts (approximately 3 sts for every 4 rows) along sleeve edge.

Work as given for Front from *** to ***.

Work a 2nd cuff in the same way.

Using backstitch on main knitting and an edge to edge st on rib, join side and sleeve seams. Press seams.

Using D and with rs facing, work 2 rounds in double crochet around neck edge, beginning and ending at centre back. Fasten off. Press neck edge.

ADULT'S COMB SHAWL COLLAR SWEATER

MATERIALS

General yarn weight used – lightweight double knitting (sport)

Rowan *Lightweight DK* (25g/1oz hanks) in the foll 11 colours:

A (89) light emerald – 3[4,4] hanks
B (52) steel blue – 3[4,4] hanks
C (122) pale blue -3[3,3] hanks
D (90) emerald – 3[4,4] hanks
E (50) china blue – 2[2,3] hanks
F (43) cerise – 3[3,3] hanks
G (25) tangerine – 3[3,3] hanks
H (66) salmon – 4[4,4] hanks
J (41) pink – 3[3,4] hanks
L (23) orange – 2[2,2] hanks
M (125) turquoise – 3[3,4] hanks

Rowan *Light Tweed* (25g/1oz hanks) in the foll 2 colours:

N (221) pacific – 2[3,3] hanks
Q (214) blossom – 1[1,1] hank

One pair each 3mm (US size 3) and 3¾mm (US size 5) knitting needles *or size to obtain correct tension(gauge)*

SIZES

To fit 96[102,107]cm/38[40,42]in chest.

Figures for larger sizes are given in square brackets; where there is only one set of figures, it applies to all sizes.

For finished measurements see diagram (page 84).

TENSION(GAUGE)

25.5 sts and 28 rows to 10cm/4in over patt on 3¾mm (US size 5) needles.

COLOUR SEQUENCE TABLE

Rows	☐	☒
1-12	F	A
13-24	Q	B
25-36	G	C
37-48	H	D
49-60	J	E
61-72	L	N
73-84	H	M
85-96	F	A
97-108	G	C
109-120	J	B
121-132	H	D
133-144	L	M
145-156	J	N
157-168	H	E
169-180	G	A

Check your tension(gauge) before beginning.

NOTES

When working in patt from Chart, read odd rows (K) from right to left and even rows (P) from left to right and carry colour not in use loosely across back of work.

BACK

Using smaller needles and F, cast on 110[122,132] sts.

Work 21 rows in K1, P1 rib in stripes as foll:
4 rows D, 2 rows H, 4 rows B, 2 rows L, 4 rows N, 2 rows J, 3 rows M.

Inc row (ws) With M, rib 5[6,6], make 1, * rib 5, make 1; rep from * to last 5[6,6] sts, rib to end. 131[145,157] sts.

Change to larger needles and cont in patt as foll:
Beg with a K row and working in st st throughout cont in patt from Chart, beginning and ending

OVERLEAF *The Adult's Comb Shawl Collar Sweater, which is also shown as the background detail, and a Child's Comb Sleeveless Sweater.*

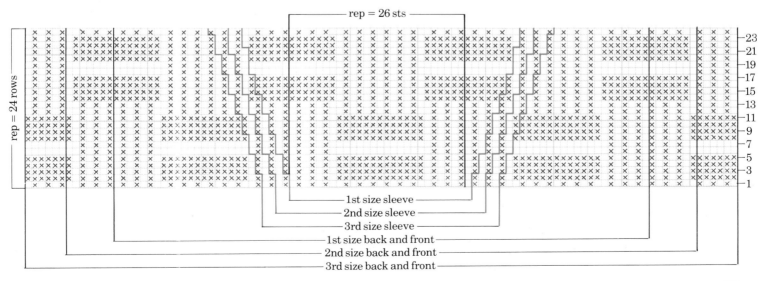

rep = 26 sts

rep = 24 rows

—23
—21
—19
—17
—15
—13
—11
—9
—7
—5
—3
—1

1st size sleeve
2nd size sleeve
3rd size sleeve
1st size back and front
2nd size back and front
3rd size back and front

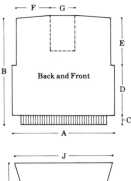

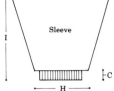

ADULT'S COMB SHAWL
COLLAR SWEATER
A = 51.5[57,61.5]cm/
20½[22¾,24½]in
B = 62[64.5,67.5]cm/
24½[25¾,26¾]in
C = 6cm/2¼in
D = 29.5[30.5,32]cm/
11¾[12¼,12¾]in
E = 26.5[28,29.5]cm/
10½[11¼,11¾]in
F = 15.5[18.5,21]cm/
6¼[7¼,8¼]in
G = 15.5cm/6¼in
H = 31[32.5,34]cm/
12¼[13,13½]in
I = 48[50.5,53]cm/
19¼[20,21¼]in
J =
53[56,59]cm/21[22½,23½]in

rows as indicated and changing colours as given in colour sequence table. Cont until 82[86,90] rows in all have been worked in st st, so ending with a ws row.

Armhole Shaping

Keeping patt correct, cast(bind) off 6 sts at beg of next 2 rows. 119[133,145] sts.
Cont without shaping until 156[164,172] rows in all have been worked in st st, so ending with a ws row.

Shoulder Shaping

Keeping patt correct, cast(bind) off 14[16,18] sts at beg of next 2 rows, 13[16,18] sts at beg of next 2 rows, then 13[15,17] sts at beg of next 2 rows. Leave rem 39 sts on a holder for collar.

FRONT

Work as given for Back until 98[106,114] rows in all have been worked in st st.

Neck Shaping

Next row (rs) Patt 40[47,53], cast(bind) off 39 sts, patt to end.
Cont on last set of sts only for right front:
Keeping patt correct, cont without shaping until 157[165,173] rows in all have been worked in st st, so ending with a rs row.

Shoulder Shaping

Cast(bind) off 14[16,18] sts at beg of next row, then 13[16,18] sts at beg of foll alt row. Work 1 row without shaping, then cast(bind) off rem 13[15,17] sts. Return to sts which were left; with ws facing rejoin yarns to neck edge and patt to end.
Complete to match first side, reversing shaping.

SLEEVES

Using smaller needles and F, cast on 62[64,66] sts and work 21 rows in striped rib as for Back.
Inc row (ws) With M, rib 7[5,3], make 1, * rib 3, make 1; rep from * to last 7[5,3] sts, rib to end. 79[83,87] sts.
Change to larger needles and cont in patt as foll:
Beg with a K row and working in st st throughout cont in patt from Chart, beginning and ending rows as indicated and working in same colour sequence as for Back AND AT THE SAME TIME, inc one st at each end of every 3rd row, working inc sts into patt until there are 91[97,103] sts, then every foll 4th row until there are 135[143,151] sts. Cont without shaping until 118[124,132] rows in all have been worked in patt, so ending with a ws row. Cast(bind) off loosely.
Make a 2nd sleeve in the same way.

FINISHING

Press work lightly on ws according to instructions on bands, omitting ribbing.
Using backstitch, join shoulder seams. Using backstitch, join cast-(bound-)off edge of sleeves to armhole edge, matching centre of top of sleeve to shoulder seam and sewing last few rows of sleeves to cast-(bound-)off sts at underarm. Press all seams. Using backstitch on main knitting and an edge to edge st on rib, join side and sleeve seams. Press seams.

COLLAR

Using smaller needles, M and with rs facing, pick up and K 64 sts (one st for every row) up right front neck, K back neck sts from holder, then pick up and K 64 sts (one st for every row) down left front neck.
167 sts.
Work 56 rows in K1, P1 rib in stripes as foll:
9 rows M, 4 rows B, 6 rows A, 14 rows N, 4 rows M, 2 rows J, 4 rows N, 2 rows L, 4 rows B, 2 rows H, 4 rows D, 1 row F.
Using F, cast(bind) off loosely in rib.
Using an edge to edge st, cross left side of collar over right and sew row ends to cast-(bound-)off sts at centre front.

PREVIOUS PAGE *The Adult's Comb Shawl Collar Sweater, and the Adult's Cable Jacket, page 131, are shown against a New Mexico wall.*

RIGHT *The Adult's Comb Shawl Collar Sweater and a Child's Comb Sleeveless Sweater.*

CHILD'S COMB DRESS

MATERIALS

General yarn weight used – lightweight cotton Rowan *Soft Cotton* (50g/1¾oz balls) in the foll 10 colours:

A (546) strawberry ice – 1[1,1,2,2,3] balls
B (545) sugar pink – 1[1,1,2,2,2] balls
C (531) fiord – 1[1,1,1,1,1] ball
D (534) frolic – 1[1,1,1,1,1] ball
E (528) rain cloud – 1[1,1,1,1,1] ball
F (539) bermuda – 1[1,1,1,1,1] ball
G (533) antique pink – 1[1,1,1,2,2] balls
H (542) bluebell – 1[1,1,1,1,1] ball
J (548) eau de nil – 1[1,1,1,1,1] ball
L (547) mermaid – 1[1,1,1,1,1] ball

One pair each 2¼mm (US size 1) and 3mm (US size 3) knitting needles *or size to obtain correct tension(gauge)*
2¼mm (US size 1) and 3mm (US size 3) circular needles
5[5.6,6,6,6] buttons
Elastic thread (optional)

SIZES

To fit 6months[12months,18months, 2yrs,4yrs, 6yrs] or 45[48,51,53,56,61]cm/18[19,20,21,22,24]in chest.
Figures for larger sizes are given in square brackets; where there is only one set of figures, it applies to all sizes.
For finished measurements see diagram (page 86).

TENSION(GAUGE)

31 sts and 33.5 rows to 10cm/4in over patt on 3mm (US size 3) needles.
Check your tension(gauge) before beginning.

NOTES

The dress is worked in one piece with cuffs neck-band, button and buttonhole bands added afterwards.
There are 2 charts for this dress, Chart 1 for the skirt and Chart 2 for the bodice and sleeves (page 86). The patt and colour sequence finish at the shoulder line and are worked in reverse down the back of the dress so as to make patt match up at side seams. When working patt from charts for front, read odd rows (K) from right to left and even rows (P) from left to right, when working charts for back, read rows K for P and P for K. Carry colour not in use loosely across back of work.

FRONT

Using smaller circular needle and A, cast on 163[173,183,193,203,213] sts. Work backwards and forwards in rows throughout.
Beg with a K row, work 6 rows in st st to form hem.
Picot edge row (rs) (K2 tog, yfwd) to last st, K1.
Next row P to end.
Change to larger needles and cont in patt as foll:
Beg with a K row and working in st st throughout cont in patt from Chart 1, beginning and ending rows as indicated, rep rows 1-24 to form patt, but work in colours as shown in sequence table.
Cont until 72[84,96,108,120,132] rows in all have been worked from Chart.

Waistband

Change to smaller circular needle.
Dec row (rs) With B, K1, K4 tog, K 0[2 tog,0,2 tog,0,2 tog], (K1, K3 tog) to last 6 sts, K4 tog, K 2[2 tog,2,2 tog,2,2 tog].

81[85,91,95,101,105] sts.
Work 8[8,10,10,12,12] rows in K1, P1 rib in stripes as foll:
3[3,4,4,5,5] rows B, 2 rows C, 3[3,4,4,5,5] rows B.
Next row With B, P to end.
Change to larger circular needle.
Beg with a K row and working in st st throughout cont in patt from Chart 2, beginning and ending rows as indicated and working colours as shown in sequence table, work 4 rows.

Sleeve Shaping

Next row Cast on 22[25,28,31,34,37] sts, patt across these and 81[85,91,95,101,105] sts of bodice, with spare piece of yarn cast on 22[25,28,31,34,37] sts on to left hand needle, then patt across these.
125[135,147,157,169,179] sts.
Keeping patt correct, cont without shaping until 34[36,38,38,40,40] rows in all have been worked from Chart 2.

Neck Shaping

Next row (rs) Patt 55[60,65,70,75,80], cast(bind) off 15[15,17,17,19,19] sts, patt to end.
Cont on last set of sts only for right front:
Work 1 row without shaping.
Keeping patt correct, cast(bind) off 2 sts at beg of next and foll 2 alt rows, then one st at beg of foll 3 alt rows.
46[51,56,61,66,71] sts.
Cont without shaping until 51[53,55,57,59,61] rows in all have been worked from Chart 2, so ending with a rs row.
(This is now the shoulder line – row 11[13,15,17,19,1] of patt)
From now on the patt and colour sequence table are reversed by first rep the row just worked then cont down through rows so that back matches front, as foll:
Work 1 row without shaping on these sts for right back.
** Cast on 5 sts at beg of next row, then 9[9,10,10,11,11] sts at beg of foll alt row.
60[65,71,76,82,87] sts.
Cont without shaping until 41[43,45,47,49,51] rows have been worked from shoulder line. **
Leave sts on a spare needle. Return to sts which were left; with ws facing rejoin yarns to neck edge of left front and cont as foll:
Cast(bind) off 2 sts at beg of next and foll 2 alt rows, then one st at beg of foll 3 alt rows.
46[51,56,61,66,71] sts.
Cont without shaping until 51[53,55,57,59,61] rows in all have been worked from Chart 2, so ending with a rs row.
This is now the shoulder line – row 11[13,15,17,19,1] of patt.
Cont with patt and colour sequence table in reverse as for right back.
Rep from ** to ** once.

Join Pieces

Next row Patt 60[65,71,76,82,87] sts of left back, cast on 5 sts to form base of opening, then patt to end across sts of right back. 125[135,147, 157,169,179] sts.
Work 5 rows without shaping.
Next row (rs) Cast(bind) off 22[25,28,31,34,37] sts, patt 81[85,91,95,101,105] including st already on needle, cast(bind) off rem 22[25,28,31,34,37] sts.
With ws facing, rejoin yarns to rem sts and work 3 rows without shaping.
Change to smaller circular needle.
Next row With B, K to end.

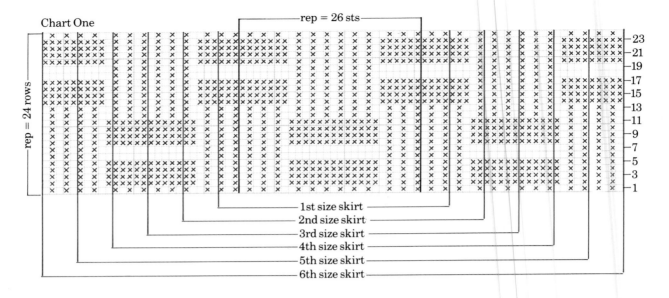

Chart One

rep = 26 sts

rep = 24 rows

1st size skirt
2nd size skirt
3rd size skirt
4th size skirt
5th size skirt
6th size skirt

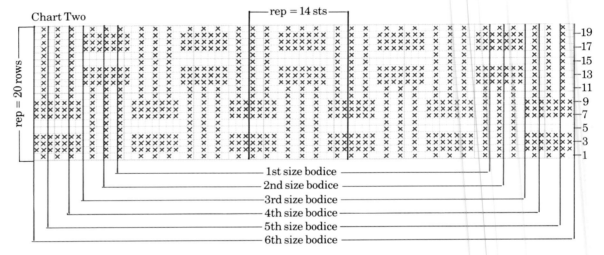

Chart Two

rep = 14 sts

rep = 20 rows

1st size bodice
2nd size bodice
3rd size bodice
4th size bodice
5th size bodice
6th size bodice

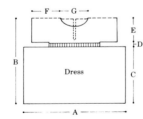

CHILD'S COMB DRESS

A =
52.5[56,59,62,65.5,68.5]cm/
21[22¼,23½,24¾,26,27½]in
B = 38.5[42.5,47,51,56,60]cm/
15[16¾,18¾,20¼,22¼,24]in
C = 21.5[25,28.5,32,36,39.5]cm/
8½[10,11½,12¾,14¼,15¾]in
D = 1.5[1.5,2,2,2.5,2.5]cm/
½[½,¾,¾,1,1]in
E = 15.5[16,16.5,17,17.5,18]cm/
6[6¼,6½,6¾,7,7¼]in
F = 15[16.5,18,19.5,21,23]cm/
6[6½,7¼,7¾,8½,9]in
G =
10.5[10.5,11.5,11.5,12,12]cm/
4¼[4¼,4½,4½,4¾,4¾]in

RIGHT *The Child's Comb Dress, available in kit form, and the Child's Red Tulip Jacket, page 110.*

COLOUR SEQUENCE TABLE

For Chart 1			For Chart 2		
Rows	☒	☐	Rows	☒	☐
1-12	B	C	1-10	D	J
13-24	D	E	11-20	G	H
25-36	A	F	21-30	A	F
37-48	G	H	31-40	B	L
49-60	D	J	41-50	G	C
61-72	B	L	51-60	D	E
73-84	G	C	61	A	F
85-96	A	J			
97-108	B	L			
109-120	G	H			
121-132	A	F			

Waistband

Work 8[8,10,10,12,12] rows in K1, P1 rib in stripes as for Front.

<u>Inc row</u> With B, (P1, K1 tbl, P1) all into first st, (P into front and back of every st) to last 0[2,0,2,0,2] sts, (P1, K1 tbl, P1) all into next st 0[2,0,2,0,2] times.

163[173,183,193,203,213] sts.
Change to larger circular needle.
Beg with a K row, work patt and colours as for front of skirt, but with patt and colour sequence table in reverse order, beg with row 24[12,24,12,24,12] so that patt matches at side seams, work 72[84,96,108,120,132] rows, so ending

RIGHT AND OPPOSITE *The Adult's Comb Shawl Collar Sweater, page 79, and the Child's Comb Dress.*

with row 1.
Change to smaller circular needle and cont in A only.

Next row K to end.

Picot edge row (P2 tog, yrn) to last st, P1.

Beg with a K row, work 6 rows in st st to form hem. Cast(bind) off *loosely.*

CUFFS

With smaller needles, J and with rs facing, pick up and K 49[51,53,55,57,59] sts (approximately one st for every other row) along sleeve edge.

Change to larger needles.

Beg with a P row, work in st st as foll:

1st–7th rows 1B, (1C, 1B) to end.

Change to smaller needles and cont in A only.

Next row K to end.

Picot edge row (P2 tog, yrn) to last st, P1.

Beg with a K row, work 5 rows in st st to form hem. Cast(bind) off *loosely.*

FINISHING

Press work lightly on ws according to instructions on ball bands, omitting ribbing. Using backstitch, join side and sleeve seams. Press all seams. Turn up and press hems at picot edge on cuffs and lower edge of skirt and sl st lightly on ws.

BUTTON BAND

Using smaller needles, J and with rs facing, pick up and K 38[40,42,44,46,48] sts evenly along back opening (one st for every row). **

Work 5 rows in K1, P1 rib in stripes as foll:

4 rows B, 1 row J.

Using J, cast(bind) off in rib.

BUTTONHOLE BAND

Work as given for Button Band to **.

1st row With B, (K1, P1) to end.

2nd row With B, rib 3[4,2,3,4,5], cast(bind) off 2 sts, * rib 7 including st already on needle, cast(bind) off 2 sts; rep from * 2[2,3,3,3,3] times more, rib to end.

3rd row With B, rib to end casting on 2 sts over each 2 cast(bound) off.

Work 1 more row in rib as set using B, then 1 row using J.

Using J, cast(bind) off in rib.

Join ends of bands to cast on sts at centre back, overlapping bands.

NECKBAND

Using smaller circular needle, J and with rs facing, pick up and K 21[21,22,22,23,23] sts evenly across left back neck including Button Band, 54[54,56,60,62,66] sts around front neck and 21[21,22,22,23,23] sts across right back neck and Buttonhole Band.

96[96,100,104,108,112] sts.

Work backwards and forwards in rows throughout.

Change to larger circular needle and cont as foll:

1st row P (1B, 1C) to end.

2nd row K (1C, 1B) to last 4 sts, cast (bind) off 2 sts, 1C, 1B.

3rd row P 1B, 1C, cast on 2 sts, (1B, 1C) to end.

4th row K (1C, 1B) to end.

Change to smaller needles and cont in A only.

5th row P to end.

Picot edge row (K2 tog, yfwd) to last 2 sts, K2.

7th row P to end.

8th row K to end.

9th row P2, cast(bind) off 2 sts, P to end.

10th row K to last 4 sts, cast on 2 sts, K2.

11th row P to end. Cast(bind) off.

Turn in and press neckband at picot edge to inside and sl st lightly on ws. Oversew hem and neckband tog at centre back edges. Sew on buttons. If desired thread elastic through rib at waistband on ws of work, catching in on every other st.

STARS AND MOSAICS

I don't think there is any single geometric shape as lively as a star. For years I have been attracted to the stars in Islamic and oriental decoration; embroideries, carpets, tiles and architectural detail from the Islamic world are sprirkled with stars of every shape and scale. Whorling Star is the latest of my versions from tiles in the Spanish Alhambra in Granada. So far I've not been there but hear it is a treasure trove of patterns. These dancing motifs are endlessly exciting to design for; I'm sure I'll go on and on playing with the pinwheel madness of it. If you try with a background in just two contrasting colours (or tones of colours), you will emphasize the pinwheel effect. The stars can be bright pastels or dark shades of grey with off-white creams and bright white as the backgrounds. I want to try it in black and dark bronzy tones for a man's dress sweater.

In our pattern version of Whorling Star (page 94), the body is worked in intarsia, the sleeves in fairisle. Try to look ahead and knit in the yarn so that it will be in the right place on the next row.

The Spanish architect Gaudi used mosaic to give astounding and exciting beauty to his contorted shapes. His public buildings in Barcelona have a joyful aesthetic that speaks as much to this generation as it did to his. I based a series of paintings on his mosaics in the Parque Güell. Because of this early enthusiasm, I was doubly thrilled when I found Zoë using Gaudi mosaics as the inspiration for such intricately beautiful knitting. I love the range of colour she has discovered from the earthy naturals of the man's sleeveless sweater (page 103), to the deep richness of royal blue and violet in the child's jacket (page 101). The delicate candy pastels of the baby's jacket (page 107) should give knitters further ideas about alternative colourways.

There is a chart for the child's jacket and once you have digested the idea of the mosaic pattern, you should be able to make up your own shapes and colours. Just remember the background colour (or grouting between bits of mosaic) is carried across each row and should be kept to a minimum. Try to avoid long lines of background in any direction as these stand out and 'cut' the design. The Mosaic is worked in a combination of intarsia and fairisle methods. Further notes to explain these techniques are in the pattern.

RIGHT *The bright pastel Whorling Star Button Shoulder Sweater looks sunny on the Key West porch and in close-up as the background. The blond boy is wearing a Turkish Lattice Button Shoulder Sweater.*

ABOVE *Child's Whorling Star Button Shoulder Sweater (left) pictured with a bright pastel Whorling Star Sweater.*

RIGHT *The Child's Whorling Star Button Shoulder Sweater.*

OVERLEAF *On this heavenly Moroccan hillside you can see the Baby's Mosaic Jacket, and the Adult's Mosaic Batwing Sweater. The pale pastel Mosaic is knitted in cotton and Zoë has replaced the rib with a picot-edged hem.*

Neck Shaping

<u>Next row</u> (rs) Patt 46, cast(bind) off 24 sts, patt to end.

Cont on last set of sts only for right front:

<u>Next row</u> Patt to end.

Keeping patt correct, cast(bind) off 3 sts at beg of next and foll alt row, then 2 sts at beg of foll alt row. 38 sts.

<u>Next row</u> Patt 20, turn and leave rem sts on a spare needle.

Work 3 rows without shaping, so ending with a rs row.

Cast(bind) off *loosely*.

Return to sts which were left; with ws facing rejoin yarns to neck edge, cast(bind) off 3 sts and patt to end.

Work 1 row without shaping. Cast(bind) off 3 sts at beg of next row, then 2 sts at beg of foll alt row. 38 sts.

Work 1 row without shaping. Cut yarns.

<u>Next row</u> (ws) Slip first 18 sts on to a spare needle, rejoin yarns to rem sts and patt to end. 20 sts.

Work 3 rows without shaping, so ending with a rs row.

Cast(bind) off *loosely*.

SLEEVES

Using smaller needles and AY, cast on 33 sts and work 13 rows in striped rib as for Back.

<u>Inc row</u> (ws) With CC, rib 3, make 1, * rib 2, make 1; rep from * to last 4 sts, rib to end. 47 sts.

Change to larger needles and cont in patt as foll:

Beg with a K row and working in st st throughout, cont in patt from Chart 2 beginning and ending rows as indicated, rep rows 1-8 to form patt working colours as shown in colour sequence table AND AT THE SAME TIME, inc one st at each end of the 3rd and every foll 4th row, working inc sts into patt until there are 69 sts.

Cont without shaping until 48 rows in all have been worked in patt.

Cast(bind) off *loosely*.

Make a 2nd sleeve in the same way.

FINISHING

Press work lightly on ws according to instructions on bands, omitting ribbing.

BACK NECKBAND

Using smaller needles, CC and with rs facing, K across 18 sts of right shoulder, pick up and K 46 sts evenly around back neck, then K across 18 sts of left shoulder. 82 sts.

Work 4 rows in K1, P1 rib in stripes as foll:

1 row JJ, 1 row HZ, 1 row FF, 1 row AY.

Using AY, cast(bind) off *loosely* in rib.

FRONT NECKBAND

Using smaller needles, CC and with rs facing, K across 18 sts of left shoulder, pick up and K 50 sts evenly around front neck, then K across 18 sts of right shoulder. 86 sts.

<u>1st row</u> With JJ, work in K1, P1 rib to end.

<u>2nd row</u> With HZ, rib 4, cast(bind) off one st, * rib 5 including st already on needle, cast(bind) off one st *; rep from * to * once more, rib 52 including st already on needle, cast(bind) off one st; rep from * to * twice more, rib to end.

<u>3rd row</u> With FF, rib to end, casting on one st over each one cast(bound) off.

<u>4th row</u> With AY, rib to end.

Using AY, cast(bind) off *loosely* in rib.

Press back and front lightly stretching neckbands so that they lie flat. Using backstitch join shoulder seams. Press seams.

Overlap front neckband on to back neckband and oversew at side edges. Using backstitch, join cast-(bound-)off edge of sleeves to back and front, matching centre of top of sleeve to shoulder. Press seams. Using backstitch on main knitting and an edge to edge st on rib, join side and sleeve seams. Press all seams. Sew on buttons.

BABY'S MOSAIC JACKET

MATERIALS

General yarn weight used – 4 ply (fingering)
Rowan *Botany* (25g/1oz hanks) in the foll 7 colours:
 A (616) donkey – 1 hank
 B (633) peacock – 1 hank
 C (125) turquoise – 1 hank
 D (634) midnight – 1 hank
 E (126) purple – 1 hank
 F (501) lavender – 1 hank
 G (51) cornflower – 1 hank
Rowan *Fine Fleck Tweed* (25g/1oz hanks) in the foll 4 colours:
 H (54) marine – 1 hank
 J (410) pink – 2 hanks
 L (611) violet – 1 hank
 M (56) royal – 1 hank
One pair each 2¼mm (US size 1) and 3mm (US size 3) knitting needles *or size to obtain correct tension (gauge)*
3mm (US size 3) circular needle
6 buttons

SIZE

To fit 12 months or 48cm/19in chest.
For finished measurements see diagram (page 105).

TENSION(GAUGE)

31 sts and 38 rows to 10cm/4in over patt on 3mm (US size 3) needles.
Check your tension(gauge) before beginning.

NOTES

The jacket is worked in one piece with cuffs neck-band, button and buttonhole bands added afterwards. When working mosaic patt (rows 9-89) on the Chart (pages 104-105) the background is worked in 2 colours throughout – 2 rows J, 2 rows A – the yarn in use is carried across back of work to the end of each row. The background yarn not in use should be left at side edge of work.
To avoid holes, twist each 'mosaic' colour round the 'mosaic' colour just worked and the background colour tog.

BACK

Using smaller needles and D, cast on 80 sts.
Work 19 rows in K1, P1 rib in stripes as foll:
1 row A, 2 rows J, 1 row A, 2 rows C, 1 row A, 2 rows J, 1 row A, 2 rows F, 1 row A, 2 rows J, 1 row A, 2 rows G, 1 row A.
Inc row (ws) With J, * rib 4, make 1, rib 4; rep from * to end. 90 sts.
Change to larger needles and cont in patt as foll:
Beg with a K row and working in st st throughout cont in patt from Chart, reading odd rows (K) from right to left and even rows (P) from left to right, until 34 rows in all have been worked in patt, so ending with a ws row.

Sleeve Shaping

Keeping patt correct and using the circular needle when necessary (working backwards and forwards in rows), cast on 6 sts at beg of next 20 rows.
210 sts. Cont without shaping until 86 rows in all have been worked in patt.

Neck Shaping

Next row (rs) Patt 95, cast(bind) off 20 sts, patt to end of row.
Cont on last set of sts only for left side:
Work 1 row without shaping.
Next row Cast(bind) off 7 sts, with J, patt to end. (This is now the shoulder line)
From now on the patt is reversed as foll:
TURN CHART UPSIDE DOWN. Working P rows from left to right and K rows from right to left, rep row 89.
Cont in patt as shown on Chart down through the rows to row 1 for left front, working as foll:
Work 6 rows without shaping.
** Cast on one st at beg of next row, 2 sts at beg of foll 2 alt rows, 3 sts at beg of foll alt row, then 4 sts at beg of foll 2 alt rows.
104 sts. **
Cont without shaping until row 52 of Chart is complete.

Sleeve Shaping

Keeping patt correct, cast(bind) off 6 sts at beg of next and every foll alt row until 44 sts rem.
Cont without shaping until row 1 of Chart is complete.
Change to smaller needles.
Dec row (rs) With J, K3, K2 tog, * K7, K2 tog; rep from * to last 3 sts, K to end.
39 sts.
Work 20 rows in K1, P1 rib in stripes as foll:
1 row A, 2 rows G, 1 row A, 2 rows J, 1 row A, 2 rows F, 1 row A, 2 rows J, 1 row A, 2 rows C, 1 row A, 2 rows J, 1 row A, 1 row D.
Using D, cast(bind) off in rib.
Return to sts which were left; with ws facing rejoin yarns to neck edge of right side, cast(bind) off 7 sts and patt to end.
Work 1 row without shaping. (This is now the shoulder line)
Cont with patt in reverse as for left front, TURN CHART UPSIDE DOWN. Working P rows from left to right and K rows from right to left, rep row 89.
Cont in patt as shown on Chart down through the rows to row 1 for right front as foll:
Work 7 rows without shaping.
Rep from ** to ** once.
Cont without shaping until row 53 of Chart is complete.

Sleeve Shaping

Keeping patt correct, cast(bind) off 6 sts at beg of next and every foll alt row until 44 sts rem.
Complete to match first side.

CUFFS

With smaller needles, A and with rs facing, pick up and K 50 sts (approximately 2 sts for for every 3 rows) along sleeve edge.
Work 10 rows in K1, P1 rib in stripes as foll:
2 rows J, 1 row A, 2 rows C, 1 row A, 2 rows J, 1 row A, 1 row D.
Using D, cast(bind) off in rib.
Work a 2nd cuff in the same way.

BUTTON BAND

Work on left for girls and right for boys.
Using smaller needles, A and with rs facing, pick up and K 78 sts (15 sts along edge of rib and approximately 7 sts for every 8 rows on main knitting) along front edge.
Working throughout in J only: **
1st row P to end.
2nd row K to end.
3rd row K to end to form fold line.
Beg with a K row, work 6 rows in st st to form hem.

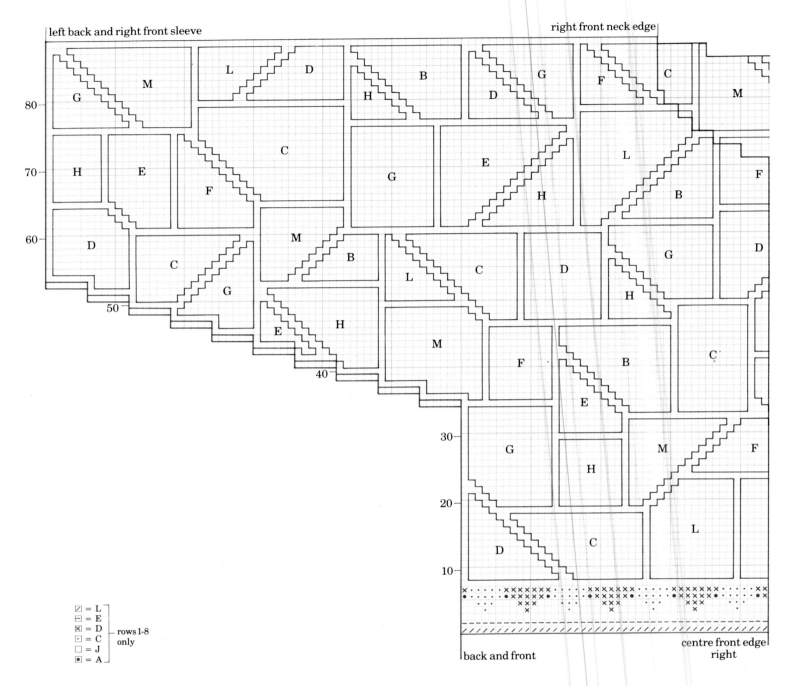

left back and right front sleeve

right front neck edge

G M L D B G F C
H D M

80

H E C E L F

70 F G H B

60 D M G D

C B C D G H

G L H

50 E H C

40 M F B E

30 G M F

H L

20

D C

10

☑ = L
⊟ = E
☒ = D   — rows 1-8
⊡ = C   only
☐ = J
⊙ = A

centre front edge
right

back and front

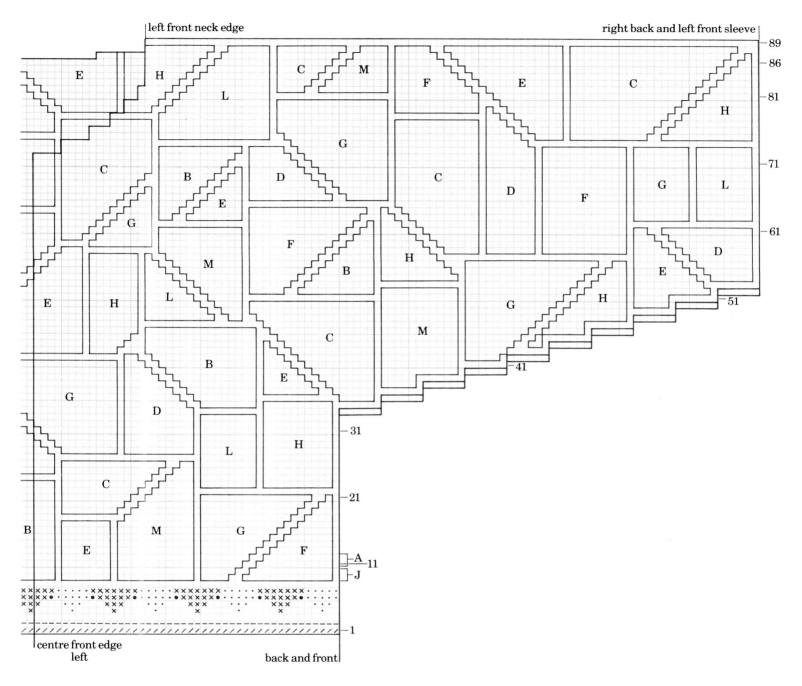

left front neck edge

right back and left front sleeve

— 89
— 86

— 81

— 71

— 61

— 51

— 41

— 31

— 21

—A—11
—J

— 1

centre front edge
left

back and front

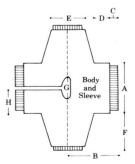

BABY'S MOSAIC JACKET
A = 29cm/11½in
B = 28cm/11in
C = 4.5cm/1¾in
D = 9cm/3½in
E = 19cm/7½in
F = 21.5cm/8½in
G = 11cm/4¼in
H = 14cm/5¾in

ABOVE Zoë's original Mosaic Batwing Sweater and the Adult's Cable Jacket, page 131, glow in the Key West sunshine.

RIGHT The Baby's Mosaic Jacket and a pale pastel version in cotton with picot edge.

Cast(bind) off *loosely*.

BUTTONHOLE BAND
Work on right for girls and left for boys.
Work as given for Button Band to **.
1st row P3, * sl 2 sts on to right hand needle, pass first st over 2nd st, sl another st on to right hand needle, pass 2nd st over this st, thus casting(binding) off 2 sts, return last slipped st back on to left hand needle, cast on 2 sts over those 2 cast(bound) off, P12; rep from * 5 times more, ending last rep with P3 instead of P12.
2nd row K to end.
3rd row K to end to form fold line.
4th row K3, cast(bind) off 2 sts, * K12 including st already on needle, cast(bind) off 2 sts; rep from * to last 3 sts, K3.
5th row P to end, casting on 2 sts over each 2 cast(bound) off.

Beg with a K row, work 4 rows in st st.
Cast(bind) off *loosely*.

FINISHING
Press work lightly on ws according to instructions on bands, omitting ribbing. Turn up and press hems on fold line and sl st *loosely* on ws. Using backstitch on main knitting and an edge to edge st on rib, join side and sleeve seams. Press all seams.

NECKBAND
Using smaller needles, A and with rs facing, pick up and K 32 sts evenly up right front neck including band, 38 sts around back neck and 32 sts down left front neck including band. 102 sts.
Work 4 rows in K1, P1 rib in stripes as foll:
2 rows J, 1 row A, 1 row D.
Using D, cast(bind) off in rib.
Sew round double buttonholes. Sew on buttons.

FLOWERS
AND BOWS

Zoë found this classic Ottoman tulip design on some Turkish embroidery. It is a theme that crops up again and again in Turkish decoration. This compact version is easy to knit in two colours, as our chart for the child's jacket shows (page 110). It can become more intricate in colour tones if knitted by the intarsia method (pages 112 and 117). Either way you should have fun putting your own colours into this pattern and seeing how much it changes with light or dark grounds, for example. Better still, find other examples of the Turkish Tulip and try quite different versions. There are some lovely, long, graceful styles in this motif to be found in museums and books on Ottoman art. Playing with different borders on this pattern could bring a new slant – the borders of the Bright Diagonal Box (page 54) are oriental enough to look good with the Tulips.

The green and pink children's version of Tulips is worked in fairisle throughout. The adult's version is worked in a combination of techniques – fairisle for the leaves and intarsia for the flowers.

Zoë found the Bows pattern on a ceiling in Istanbul. We see it as amusing bow-ties, though I'm sure the Turks never did. Interlocking patterns of this sort are intriguing to knit, particularly when Zoë works them out with such a good knitting rhythm. After a few repeats, you can practically memorize the stitch sequence and move along at a good rate. Seeing how this simple pattern unfolds with its many colour possibilities should alert you to other Islamic geometrics that are waiting to be utilized. It gives a whole new excitement to travelling when you are on the look-out for special patterns.

You will notice that we have worked out the colours in a formula similar to Plaids – keeping the direction of the colours constant and working only with two contrasting groups of colours. I felt it should be fairly contrasty, although close tweedy or shell colours would work as well. The large areas of colour would read well with similar tones too. You could go mad and have each area a different colour, or shade the occasional row of bows to give an old Victorian effect, or make the odd bow in a polka dot or stripe to emphasize it.

Zoë found it easiest to knit this pattern carrying the yarns for the horizontal row of bows across the work, and working the vertical bows by the intarsia method.

RIGHT *Two versions of Zoë's Tulip design: her easy-to-knit two-colour-in-a-row Child's Red Tulip Jacket, page 110, and my more complicated Adult's Tulip Shirt Collar Sweater, page 117, also available in kit form.*

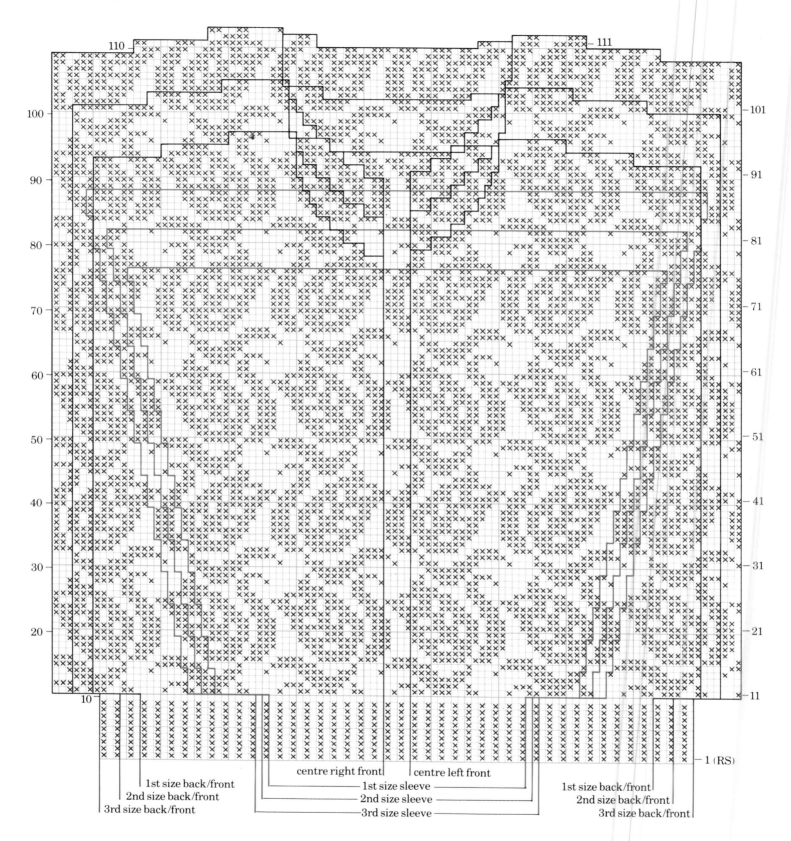

centre right front | centre left front

1st size back/front
2nd size back/front
3rd size back/front

1st size sleeve
2nd size sleeve
3rd size sleeve

1st size back/front
2nd size back/front
3rd size back/front

1 (RS)

RIGHT *The Child's Red Tulip Jacket and the Adult's Tulip Shirt Collar Sweater, page 117.*

COLOUR SEQUENCE TABLE

Rows	☐	☒	Rows	☐	☒	Rows	☐	☒
1-2	A	J	20-21	H	L	35	G	B
3	A	C	22	H	E	36	G	D
4-5	A	B	23	A	L	37-38	H	L
6-7	A	L	24	A	F	39	H	E
8-9	A	F	25	G	F	40	A	L
11	A	L	26	G	E	41	A	F
12	H	B	27	A	F	42	G	F
13-14	H	J	28	A	L	43	G	E
15	A	J	29	H	B	44	A	F
16	A	C	30-31	H	J			
17	A	B	32	A	J			
18	G	B	33	A	C	Rows 11-44		
19	G	D	34	A	B	are repeated as		
						necessary.		

CHILD'S RED TULIP JACKET

MATERIALS

General yarn weight used – lightweight double knitting (sport)

Rowan *Lightweight DK* (25g/1oz hanks) in the foll 6 colours:

A (90) emerald – 3[3,4] hanks
B (41) pink – 1[2,2] hanks
C (115) flame – 1[1,1] hank
D (23) orange – 1[1,1] hank
E (66) salmon – 1[1,1] hank
F (19) lipstick pink – 2[2,2] hanks

Rowan *Fine Cotton Chenille* (50g/1¾oz balls) in the foll colour:

G (383) turquoise – 1[1,1] ball

Rowan *Knobbly Cotton* (50g/1¾oz balls) in the foll 2 colours:

H (569) jade – 1[1,1] ball
J (568) bright pink – 1[1,1] ball

Rowan *Mulberry Silk* (50g/1¾oz hanks) in the foll colour:

L (872) flamingo – 1[1,1] hank

One pair each 3mm (US size 3) and 3¾mm (US size 5) knitting needles *or size to obtain correct tension(gauge)*

7 buttons

SIZES

To fit 2[4,6]yrs or 53[56,61]cm/21[22,24]in chest.
Figures for larger sizes are given in square brackets; where there is only one set of figures, it applies to all sizes.
For finished measurements see diagram (page 114).

TENSION(GAUGE)

27 sts and 30 rows to 10cm/4in over patt on 3¾mm (US size 5) needles.
Check your tension(gauge) before beginning.

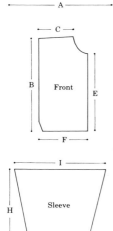

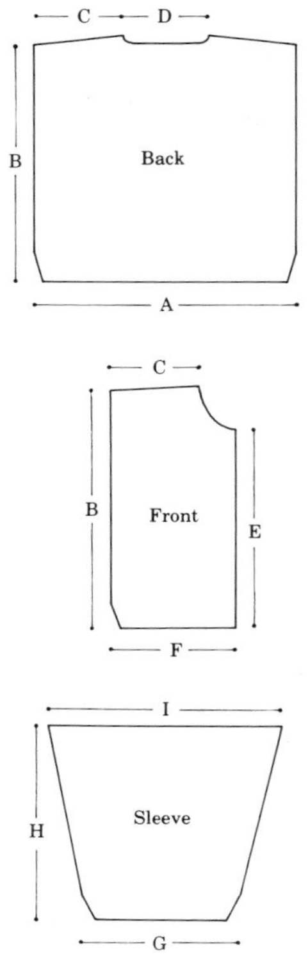

CHILD'S RED TULIP JACKET
A = 33[36,37.5]cm/
13½[14¼,15]in
B = 30.5[33.5,36]cm/
12¼[13¼,14½]in
C = 11[12,12.5]cm/4½[4¾,5]in
D = 11[12,12.5]cm/4½[4¾,5]in
E = 26[28,30]cm/10½[11¼,12]in
F = 16[17,18]cm/6¼[6¾,7¼]in
G = 20[21.5,23]cm/8[8½,9]in
H = 25.5[27.5,29.5]cm/
10[11,11¾]in
I = 30[32,34]cm/
11¾[12¾,13½]in

PREVIOUS PAGE AND RIGHT
*Adult's and Child's
Tulip Sweaters. The two
pastel intarsia versions
are pictured in a
Tangier garden. The
pattern for the adult's
version is on page 117
and is available in kit
form. Think of all the
different colours you can
try on this classic
Turkish pattern!*

NOTES
When working in patt from Chart, read odd rows (K) from right to left and even rows (P) from left to right.

BACK
Using smaller needles and J, cast on 76[82,88] sts.
** Beg with a K row, work 5 rows in st st to form hem. Break off J and join in F.
Next row P to end.
Picot edge row (rs) K1, (K2 tog, yfwd) to last st, K1.
Next row P to end.
Change to larger needles and work border patt as foll:
Beg with a K row and working in st st throughout cont in patt from Chart, beginning and ending rows as indicated, rows 1-9 form patt but work in different colours as shown in sequence table. **
Inc row (ws) With A, first size: P3, * P2, (work into front and back of next st, P3) twice; rep from * to last 3 sts, P3, 2nd and 3rd sizes: P [2,5], work into front and back of next st, * P5, work into front and back of next st; rep from * to last [1,4] sts, P to end. 90[96,102] sts.
Cont in tulip patt as foll:
Cont in st st as set from Chart, beginning and ending rows as indicated start at row 11, working in different colours as shown in sequence table. Cont until 92[100,108] rows in all have been worked from Chart.

Shoulder and Neck Shaping
Keeping patt correct, cast(bind) off 10[11,12] sts at beg of next 2 rows. 70[74,78] sts.
Next row Cast(bind) off 10[11,11] sts, patt 15[15,16] including st already on needle, cast(bind) off 20[22,24] sts, patt to end.
Cont on last set of sts only for left back as foll:
Cast(bind) off 10[11,11] sts at beg of next row, then 5 sts at beg of foll row.
Cast(bind) off rem 10[10,11] sts.
Return to sts which were left; with ws facing rejoin yarns to neck edge, cast(bind) off 5 sts and patt to end. Cast(bind) off rem 10[10,11] sts.

LEFT FRONT
Using smaller needles and J, cast on 36[39,42] sts.
Beg with a K row, work 5 rows in st st to form hem. Break off J and join in F.
6th row P to end.
Picot edge row (rs) K1, (K2 tog, yfwd) to last 1[2,1] sts, K to end.
8th row P to end. ***
Change to larger needles and work border patt to match Back, beginning and ending rows as indicated.
Inc row (ws) With A, P 3[1,3], work into front and back of next st, * first size: P5, work into front and back of next st, P3, work into front and back of next st, 2nd and 3rd sizes: P5, work into front and back of next st, all sizes: rep from * to last 2[1,2] sts, P to end. 43[46,49] sts.
Cont in tulip patt to match Back, beginning and ending rows as indicated until 79[85,91] rows in all have been worked from Chart, so ending with a rs row.

Neck Shaping
Keeping patt correct, cast(bind) off 3 sts at beg of next and foll alt row, 2 sts at beg of foll 2[3,3] alt rows, then one st at beg of foll 3[2,3] alt rows. 30[32,34] sts.
Work 0[2,2] rows without shaping, so ending with a ws row.

Shoulder Shaping
Keeping patt correct, cast(bind) off 10[11,12] sts at beg of next row, then 10[11,11] sts at beg of foll alt row. Work 1 row without shaping, then cast(bind) off rem 10[10,11] sts.

RIGHT FRONT
Work as given for Left Front to ***.
Change to larger needles and work border patt to match Back, beginning and ending rows as indicated.
Inc row (ws) With A, P 3[2,3], work into front and back of next st, * first size: P3, work into front and back of next st, P5, work into front and back of next st, 2nd and 3rd sizes: P5, work into front and back of next st, all sizes: rep from * to last 2[0,2]sts, P 2[0,2]. 43[46,49] sts.
Cont in tulip patt to match Back, beginning and ending rows as indicated until 78[84,90] rows in all have been worked from Chart, so ending with a ws row.

Neck Shaping
Keeping patt correct, cast(bind) off 3 sts at beg of next and foll alt row, 2 sts at beg of foll 2[3,3] alt rows, then one st at beg of foll 3[2,3] alt rows. 30[32,34] sts. Cont without shaping until 93[101,109] rows in all have been worked from Chart, so ending with a rs row.

Shoulder Shaping
Work as given for Left Front.

SLEEVES
Using smaller needles and J, cast on 38[40,42] sts and work as given for Back from ** to **.
Inc row (ws) With A, P 4[3,2], work into front and back of next st, * P1, work into front and back of next st; rep from * to last 3[2,1] sts, P to end. 54[58,62] sts. Cont in tulip patt as foll:
Cont in st st as set from Chart, beginning and ending rows as indicated start at row 11, working in different colours as shown in sequence table AND AT THE SAME TIME, inc one st at each end of every 5th row, working inc sts into patt until there are 80[86,92] sts. Cont without shaping until 76[82,88] rows in all have been worked from Chart. Cast(bind) off *loosely*.
Make a 2nd sleeve in the same way.

BUTTON BAND
Work on left for girls and right for boys.
Using smaller needles, A and with rs facing, pick up and K 80[86,92] sts along front edge (2 sts from picot edge and one st for every row on main knitting).
Change to larger needles and cont as foll: *
1st row (ws) P (1C, 1A) to end.
2nd row K (1A, 1J) to end.
3rd row P (1J, 1A) to end.
Change to smaller needles and cont in F as foll:
4th row K to end.
Picot edge row P1, (P2 tog, yrn) to last st, P1.
6th row K to end.
With J, beg with a P row, work 5 rows in st st. Cast(bind) off *loosely*.

BUTTONHOLE BAND
Work on right for girls and left for boys.
Work as given for Button Band to *.
1st row (ws) P (1A, 1C) to end.
2nd row Work in colour sequence as set to match Button Band AND AT THE SAME TIME, patt 3, cast(bind) off 2 sts, * patt 10[11,12] including st

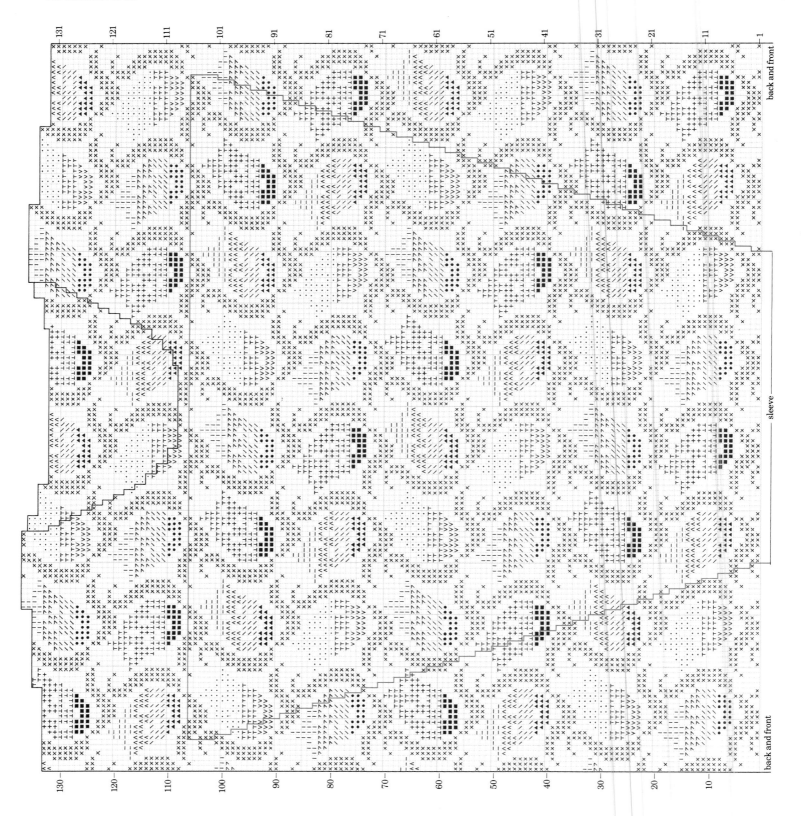

already on needle, cast(bind) off 2 sts; rep from * 5 times more, patt to end.

3rd row Work in colour sequence as set to match Button Band AND AT THE SAME TIME, cast on 2 sts over each 2 cast(bound) off.

Change to smaller needles and cont in F as foll:

4th row K to end.

Picot edge row P1, (P2 tog, yrn) to last st, P1.

6th row K to end.

Cont in J only:

7th row P3, cast(bind) off 2 sts, * P 10[11,12] including st already on needle, cast(bind) off 2 sts; rep from * 5 times more, P to end.

8th row K to end, casting on 2 sts over each 2 cast(bound) off.

Beg with a P row work 3 rows in st st.

Cast(bind) off *loosely*.

FINISHING

Press work lightly on ws according to instructions on bands. Turn up and press hems, cuffs and bands at picot edge to inside. Using backstitch, join shoulder seams. Mark back and fronts at side edges 15[16,17]cm/6[6¼,6¾]in from shoulders. Using backstitch, join cast-(bound-)off edge of sleeves to back and fronts between markers, matching centre of top of sleeve to shoulder seam. Using backstitch, join side and sleeve seams. Press all seams. Fold hems, cuffs and bands to inside on picot row and sl st lightly on ws. Sew round double buttonholes.

COLLAR

Using smaller needles, A and with ws facing, pick up and K 31[33,35] sts evenly up left front neck including band, 35[37,39] sts around back neck and 31[33,35] sts down right front neck including band. 97[103,109] sts. Change to larger needles.

Beg with a P row, work 3 rows in st st.

4th row K 1F, (1A, 1F) to end.

5th row P 1F, (1A, 1F) to end.

6th row K 1L, (1A, 1L) to end.

7th row P 1L, (1A, 1L) to end.

8th row K 1B, (1A, 1B) to end.

9th row P 1B, (1A, 1B) to end.

10th row K 1C, (1A, 1C) to end.

11th row P 1J, (1A, 1J) to end.

12th row K 1J, (1A, 1J) to end.

Cont in F as foll:

13th row P to end.

Picot edge row K1, (K2 tog, yfwd) to last 2 sts, K2.

15th row P to end.

Change to smaller needles and J. Beg with a K row, work 8 rows in st st. Cast(bind) off *loosely*. Press collar, turn up and press hem at picot edge to inside and sl st lightly on ws. Oversew hem and collar tog at centre front edges. Sew on buttons.

ADULT'S TULIP SHIRT COLLAR SWEATER

MATERIALS

General yarn weight used – lightweight double knitting (sport)

Rowan *Lightweight DK* (25g/1oz hanks) in the foll 16 colours:

A (76) pistachio – 12 hanks
B (89) light emerald – 12 hanks
C (41) pink – 1 hank
D (19) lipstick pink – 2 hanks
E (68) sugar pink – 2 hanks
F (103) flesh – 1 hank
G (12) sunshine – 2 hanks
H (7) gold – 1 hank
J (4) cream – 1 hank
L (30) champagne – 1 hank
M (63) eau de nil – 1 hank
N (47) baby blue – 2 hanks
Q (110) white – 2 hanks
R (127) amethyst – 2 hanks
S (121) mauve – 3 hanks
T (48) cloud blue – 1 hank

One circular needle in each of 3¼mm (US size 3) 40cm or 16in long for collar and 4mm (US size 6) *or size to obtain correct tension(gauge)*

SIZE

To fit up to 96cm/38in bust.
For finished measurements see diagram (page 118).

TENSION(GAUGE)

26 sts and 24 rows to 10cm/4in over patt on 4mm (US size 6) needles.
Check your tension(gauge) before beginning.

NOTES

The Back, Front and Sleeves may be worked on straight needles if preferred.
When working in patt from Chart, read odd rows (K) from right to left and even rows (P) from left to right.

BELOW *The Adult's Tulip Shirt Collar Sweater and a pastel version of a Child's Tulip Jacket.*

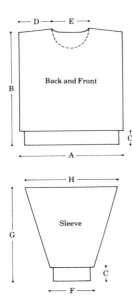

ADULT'S TULIP SHIRT COLLAR SWEATER
A = 54cm/21½in
B = 62.5cm/25in
C = 7.5cm/3in
D = 17.5cm/7in
E = 19cm/7½in
F = 23cm/9¼in
G = 51.5cm/20½in
H = 49cm/19½in

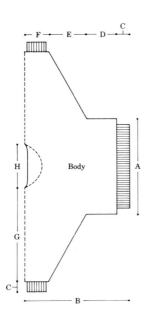

CHILD'S BOW SCOOPNECK SWEATER
A = 41.5[45,48]cm/
16½[18,19¼]in
B = 41.5[45.5,50]cm/
16½[18½,20¼]in
C = 5.5cm/2¼in
D = 9.5[12,14.5]cm/
3¾[5,6]in
E = 15.5[16.5,18]cm/
6¼[6¾,7¼]in
F = 11[11.5,12]cm/
4¼[4½,4¾]in
G = 39.5[43,46.5]cm/
15½[17¼,18½]in
H = 20.5[21.5,22.5]cm/
8¼[8½,9]in

BACK

Using smaller needle and B, cast on 125 sts.
** Beg with a K row and working backwards and forwards in rows, work 6 rows in st st to form hem.
Picot edge row (rs) (K2 tog, yfwd) to last st, K1.
8th row P to end.
Change to larger needle and work border patt in st st, beg with a K row as foll:
1st and 2nd rows 1B, (1A, 1B) to end.
3rd and 4th rows 1B, (1S, 1B) to end.
5th to 7th rows 1B, (1E, 1B) to end.
8th row 1B, (1D, 1B) to end.
9th and 10th rows As 1st and 2nd rows.
11th to 13th rows 1R, (1A, 1R) to end.
14th to 16th rows 1S, (1A, 1S) to end.
17th row 1S, (1G, 1S) to end.
18th and 19th rows 1S, (1B, 1S) to end. **
Inc row (ws) With A, P7, make 1, * P8, make 1; rep from * to last 6 sts, P to end. 140 sts.
Cont in tulip patt as foll:
Beg with a K row and working in st st throughout cont in patt from Chart, starting and ending rows as indicated.
Cont until 132 rows in all have been worked from Chart.

Shoulder and Neck Shaping

Next row (rs) Cast(bind) off 16 sts, patt 39 including st already on needle, cast(bind) off 30 sts, patt to end.
Cont on last set of sts only for left back as foll:
Keeping patt correct, cast(bind) off 16 sts at beg of next row, 6 sts at beg of foll row, 15 sts at beg of next row, then 3 sts at beg of foll row.
Cast(bind) off rem 15 sts.
Return to sts which were left; with ws facing rejoin yarns to neck edge, cast(bind) off 6 sts and patt to end.
Cast(bind) off 15 sts at beg of next row, then 3 sts at beg of foll row.
Cast(bind) off rem 15 sts.

FRONT

Work as given for Back until 108 rows in all have been worked from Chart.

Neck Shaping

Next row (rs) Patt 62, cast(bind) off 16 sts, patt to end.
Cont on last set of sts only for right front as foll:
Next row Patt to end.
Keeping patt correct, cast(bind) off 3 sts at beg of next row, * cast(bind) off 2 sts at beg of foll 2 alt rows, then one st at beg of foll 9 alt rows. 46 sts.

Shoulder Shaping

Cast(bind) off 16 sts at beg of next row, then 15 sts at beg of foll alt row. Work 1 row without shaping.
Cast(bind) off rem 15 sts. *
Return to sts which were left; with ws facing rejoin yarns to neck edge, cast(bind) off 3 sts and patt to end.
Work as given for first side from * to *.

SLEEVES

Using smaller needle and B, cast on 49 sts and work as given for Back from ** to **.
Inc row (ws) With A, P5, * make 1, P4; rep from * to end. 60 sts.
Cont in tulip patt as foll:
Beg with a K row and working in st st throughout cont in patt from Chart, beginning and ending rows as indicated AND AT THE SAME TIME, inc one st at each end of 3rd and every foll 3rd row, work-

ing inc sts into patt until there are 128 sts.
Cont without shaping until 106 rows in all have been worked from Chart.
Cast(bind) off loosely.
Make a 2nd sleeve in the same way.

FINISHING

Press work lightly on ws according to instructions on bands. Turn up and press hems at picot edge to inside. Using backstitch, join shoulder seams. Press seams.

COLLAR

Using smaller needle, A and with rs facing, beg at centre front, pick up and K 38 sts evenly up right front neck, 51 sts around back neck and 38 sts down left front neck.
127 sts.
Work 2 ROUNDS knitwise.
Change to larger needle.
Beg with a P row and working backwards and forwards in ROWS, cont in st st as for Back Border but in reverse order, beg with 17th row and working back to row 1.
Cont in B only as foll:
Next row K to end.
Picot edge row (ws) (P2 tog, yrn) to last st, P1.
Next row K to end.
Change to smaller needle.
Beg with a P row, work 8 rows in st st to form hem.
Cast(bind) off loosely.
Turn up and press hem at picot edge to inside. Mark back and front at side edges 24.5cm/9¾in from shoulders. Using backstitch, join cast-(bound-)off edge of sleeves to back and front between markers, matching centre of top of sleeve to shoulder seam. Using backstitch, join side and sleeve seams. Press all seams. Fold hems to inside on picot row and sl st lightly on ws. Oversew hem and collar tog at centre front edges.

CHILD'S BOW SCOOPNECK SWEATER

MATERIALS

General yarn weight used – lightweight double knitting (sport)
Approximately 200[250,300]g/8[10,12]oz of mixed yarns in each of two groups of colours, A and B
One pair 3mm (US size 3) knitting needles
3¾mm (US size 5) circular needle 100cm or 40in long or size to obtain correct tension(gauge)
One 2.50mm (US size B1) crochet hook

SIZES

To fit 8[10,12]yrs or 66[71,76]cm/26[28,30]in chest.
Figures for larger sizes are given in square brackets; where there is only one set of figures, it applies to all sizes.
For finished measurements see diagram.

TENSION(GAUGE)

25 sts and 31 rows to 10cm/4in over patt on 3¾mm (US size 5) needles.
Check your tension(gauge) before beginning.

NOTES

The sweater is worked in one piece with cuffs added afterwards. Chart on page 124.
The vertical 'bows' are worked in group A colours and the horizontal 'bows' are worked in group B

colours which are carried to the end of each row.

BACK

Using smaller needles cast on 88[94,100] sts. Work 21 rows in K1, P1 rib in random stripes.
Inc row (ws) Rib 6[5,3], make 1, * rib 5, make 1; rep from * to last 7[4,2] sts, rib to end. 104[112,120] sts.
Change to larger needles and cont in patt as foll:
Beg with a K row and working backwards and forwards in rows of st st throughout, cont in patt from Chart reading odd rows (K) from right to left and even rows (P) from left to right, rep rows 1-26 to form patt introducing a new yarn B on the 14th and every foll 13th row.
Cont until 30[38,46] rows in all have been worked in patt, so ending with a ws row.

Sleeve Shaping

Keeping patt correct cast on 3 sts at beg of next 48[52,56] rows. 248[268,288] sts.
Cont without shaping until 108[121,134] rows in all have been worked in patt.

Neck Shaping

Next row Patt 105[114,123], cast(bind) off 38[40,42] sts, patt to end.
Cont on last set of sts only for left[right,left] back.
Next row Patt to end.
Next row Cast(bind) off 7 sts, patt to end.
(This is now the shoulder line)
From now on the patt and colours are reversed by repeating the row just worked then working DOWN through patt rows. (NOTE the horizontal 'bow' at the shoulder line has one more row than all the other horizontal 'bows' and that these 'bows' now end with points of a single st and begin with points

of two sts. The rhythm of the design changes and it is easy to make a mistake.)
Work 7 rows without shaping.
** Cast on one st at beg of next and foll alt row, 2 sts at beg of foll 2 alt rows, 3 sts at beg of foll 2 alt rows, then 4 sts at beg of foll 2 alt rows. 118[127,136] sts. ** Work 1 row without shaping.
Return to sts which were left; with ws[rs,ws] facing rejoin yarn to neck edge, cast(bind) off 7 sts and patt to end.
Work 1 row without shaping. (This is now the shoulder line)
Cont with patt in reverse as for left[right,left] front as foll:
Work 8 rows without shaping.
Rep from ** to ** once.

Join Fronts

Next row With rs[ws,rs] facing, patt across sts of right[left,right] front, cast on 12 [14,16] sts, then patt across rem 118[127,136] sts. 248[268,288] sts.
Cont without shaping until 144[158,172] rows in all have been worked in patt, so ending with a ws row.

Sleeve Shaping

Keeping patt correct cast(bind) off 3 sts at beg of next 48[52,56] rows. 104[112,120] sts.
Cont without shaping, work 30[38,46] rows so ending with a ws row.
(222[248,274] rows in all have been worked in patt)
Change to smaller needles.
Dec row (rs) K 6[4,2], K2 tog, * K4, K2 tog; rep from * to last 6[4,2] sts, K to end.
88[94,100] sts.

BELOW AND OVERLEAF
Child's Bow Scoopneck Sweater with batwing sleeves. The ragdoll is wearing a Child's Flags Crewneck Sweater.

Work 21 rows in K1, P1 rib in stripes to match Back. Cast(bind) off *loosely* in rib.

FINISHING

Press work lightly on ws according to instructions on bands, omitting ribbing.

CUFFS

With smaller needles and with rs facing, pick up and K 44[46,48] sts (approximately 2 sts for for every 3 rows) along sleeve edge.

Work 21 rows in K1, P1 rib in stripes to match Front.

Cast(bind) off in rib.

Work a 2nd cuff in the same way.

Using backstitch on main knitting and an edge to edge st on rib, join side and sleeve seams. Press seams.

Work 3 rows in double crochet in random stripes around neck edge. Fasten off.

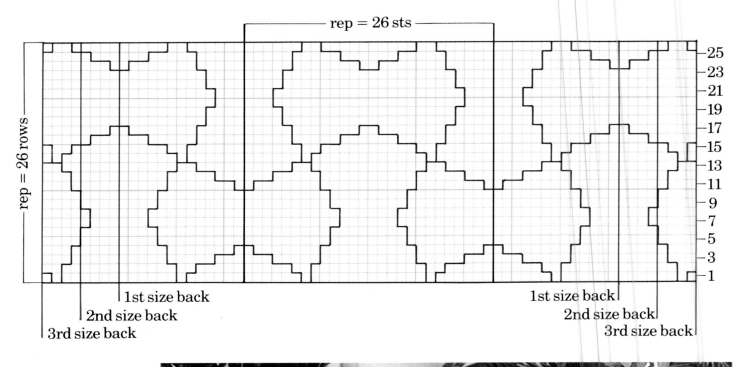

rep = 26 sts

rep = 26 rows

25
23
21
19
17
15
13
11
9
7
5
3
1

1st size back
2nd size back
3rd size back

1st size back
2nd size back
3rd size back

PREVIOUS PAGE *An adult's and child's version of a Pink Brocade Sweater. I took the idea from an eighteenth-century brocade fragment combining the flowers and bowl motifs to make a damask-like two-colour-a-row pattern. The adult's version is available in kit form.*

RIGHT *Children's versions of a Bright Whorling Star Sweater, the Bow Scoopneck Sweater and Flags Crewneck Sweater.*

FAR RIGHT *The Child's Bow Scoopneck Sweater is shown with a Child's Flags Crewneck Sweater.*

CABLES AND FLAGS

I never felt the slightest need for fancy stitches when I started my adventure into knitting, I had my palette and my canvas and it was simply a matter of making as much magic as possible with pure colour. Adding textured stitches seemed like trickery – like a painter adding textures to paints. I noticed that the people doing fancy stitches seemed to limit the colour to one or two tones so that the stitches would show. The reasons for my stand were my own inability to knit textured stitches without making obvious mistakes, and my claim that anyone can do what I do because I only ever use stocking stitch. Then along comes Zoë and produces the most colourful and mouthwatering cable knits. The luxurious intertwining of the fabric captivated me at once and I find myself drooling over the garments! I still can't knit them myself, but many knitters will tackle these designs with skill and relish.

All the Cables designs are difficult to work with balls attached. You will get into a frightful tangle. I think it is easier to pull off long lengths of yarn, then at least, in the event of a tangle, you can pull each one out. It is worth spending time untangling the yarns periodically as this makes the actual knitting less stressful.

There is only so much you can do with a two-colour-in-a-row repeating design, so when a designer stumbles across a two-colour pattern that carries the eye up and down the garment, instead of the usual horizontal structure, it's like pure gold. Flags is one of Zoë's most brilliant inventions. You can see how many colour schemes can be fed through this pattern. This particular design often occurs to me when thinking up new colour ideas. It's a gift to machine knitters who can cope best with only two colours in a row.

Zoë found this pattern in a book on oriental carpets. These books are superb sources for studying the layout of a design but are often limited in the colourways used. If you add lots of your own shades of colour to what exists in your design source, you will begin to build up that rich beauty of vegetable-dyed yarns. They are so wonderfully irregular and multi-toned – no dye-lot angst amongst the carpet weavers!

Flags can be done in quite close tones, but really dances to life with colourful contrasts; picking tones of one colour is a good start and then add complementary darks and lights, such as my yellow version (page 144). Zoë's tweedy, wearable colourway (page 136) was her first attempt at the design. We often stumble on the best combination the first time we try a new idea. Though we created this somewhat vertical look using the intarsia technique, using fairisle and two contrasting groups of colours also helps to create a powerful diagonal sweater.

RIGHT *The background is the Adult's Cable Jacket, page 131, and the inset shows an Adult's Cable Sweater and the Child's Cable Shawl Collar Jacket, page 130.*

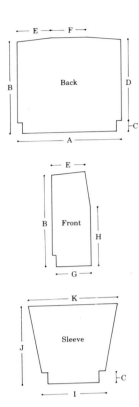

CHILD'S CABLE SHAWL
COLLAR JACKET
A = 39cm/15½in
B = 36.5cm/14½in
C = 4.5cm/1¾in
D = 32cm/12¾in
E = 12.5cm/5in
F = 14cm/5½in
G = 14.5cm/5¾in
H = 22.5cm/9in
I = 24cm/9½in
J = 31cm/12¼in
K = 34cm/13½in

PREVIOUS PAGE *Adult's
Cable Jacket, and the
Child's Cable Shawl
Collar Jacket, which is
also shown as the
background.*

CHILD'S CABLE SHAWL
COLLAR JACKET

MATERIALS

General yarn weight used – lightweight double
knitting(sport)
Rowan *Lightweight DK* (25g/1oz hanks) in the foll
12 colours:
A (53) sea blue – 4 hanks
B (501) lavender – 2 hanks
C (91) pine forest – 2 hanks
D (90) emerald – 2 hanks
E (43) cerise – 3 hanks
F (41) pink – 2 hanks
G (42) cherry red – 2 hanks
H (46) maroon – 2 hanks
J (96) magenta – 2 hanks
L (67) lacquer red – 2 hanks
M (70) grape – 2 hanks
N (44) scarlet – 2 hanks
One pair each 2¾mm (US size 2) and 3¼mm
(US size 3) knitting needles *or size to obtain correct
tension(gauge)*
One cable needle (cn)
2¾mm (US size 2) circular needle
6 buttons

SIZE

To fit 4yrs or 56cm/22in chest.
For finished measurements see diagram.

TENSION(GAUGE)

40 sts and 34 rows to 10cm/4in over patt on 3¼mm
(US size 3) needles.
Check your tension(gauge) before beginning.

NOTES

*The jacket has an unusual rib; 2 colours are used in
every row making it less stretchy than normal rib.
It is an ordinary K2, P2 rib but the K sts are worked
in one colour and the P sts in another. Take care not
to pull yarns too tightly across ws of work and
always take both colours right to end of row.
T8k – sl next 4 sts on to cn and hold at back of work,
K4 in their own colour taking yarn loosely across
back of work and twisting it around colour just
worked, then K4 from cn in their own colour – the
colours are now in reverse order in the row.
make one K – pick up loop lying between sts
and K into back of it.
make one P – pick up loop lying between sts and P
into back of it.*

BACK

Using smaller needles and D, cast on 104 sts.
Break off D.
1st row (rs) K1C, (take F to rs, P2F, take F to ws,
K2C) to last 3 sts, take F to rs, P2F, take F to ws,
K1C.
2nd row P1A, (take E to rs, K2E, take E to ws, P2A)
to last 3 sts, take E to rs, K2E, take E to ws, P1A.
3rd row As first row, *but* using A and E instead of C
and F.
4th row As 2nd row, *but* using B instead of A.
5th row As first row, *but* using B and E instead of C
and F.
6th row As 2nd row.
7th row As first row, *but* using G instead of F.
8th row As 2nd row, *but* using C and G instead of A
and E.
9th row As first row, *but* using A and G instead of C
and F.

10th row As 2nd row, *but* using H instead of E.
11th row As first row, *but* using A and H instead of
C and F.
12th row As 10th row.
13th row As first row, *but* using A and J instead of
C and F.
14th row As 2nd row, *but* using L instead of E.
15th row As first row, *but* using A and L instead of
C and F.
Inc row (ws) With A, P into front and back of first
st, (take L to rs, with L, K1, make one K, K1, take L
to ws, with A, P1, make one P, P1) to last 3 sts, take
L to rs, with L, K1, make one K, K1, take L to ws,
P1A. 156 sts.
Change to larger needles and cont in cable patt as
foll:
1st row (rs) (K1, P1)A, K4E, K4H, (P1, K2, P1)C,
K4J, K4M, (P1, K2, P1)D, K4F, * K4L, (P1, K2,
P1)A, K4N, K4H, (P1, K2, P1)B, K4E, K4L, (P1,
K2, P1)C, K4F, K4G, (P1, K2, P1)A, K4J, K4L, (P1,
K2, P1)D, K4N, K4M, (P1, K2, P1)C, K4E, K4H,
(P1, K2, P1)B, K4J, K4G, (P1, K2, P1)A, K4F, **
K4L, (P1, K2, P1)D, K4N, K4M, (P1, K2, P1)B,
K4E, K4J, (P1, K1)A.
2nd row Working in colours as set and twisting
yarns tog as you go; P1, K1, (P8, K1, P2, K1) to last
10 sts, P8, K1, P1.
3rd-6th rows Rep first and 2nd rows twice.
7th row Keeping colours correct; K1, P1, (T8k, P1,
K2, P1) to last 10 sts, T8k, P1, K1.
8th row As 2nd row, *but* with colours in new
positions.
9th-12th rows Working in colours as set, rep first
and 2nd rows twice.
13th row As 7th row, colours now return to
original positions.
Rows 2-13 form the rep of patt. Cont until 110 rows
in all have been worked in cable patt.

Shoulder Shaping

Keeping patt correct, cast(bind) off 17 sts at beg of
next 4 rows, then 16 sts at beg of next 2 rows.
Leave rem 56 sts on a holder for collar.

LEFT FRONT

Using smaller needles and D, cast on 39 sts. Break
off D.
1st row (rs) K1C, (take F to rs, P2F, take F to ws,
K2C) to last 2 sts, take F to rs, P2F.
Keeping rib as now set, work 14 more rows using
same colour sequence as on Back.
Inc row (ws) (With L, K1, make one K, K1, take L to
ws, with A, P1, make one P, P1, take L to rs) to last
3 sts, with L, K1, make one K, K1, take L to ws,
P1A. 58 sts.
Change to larger needles and cont in cable patt as
foll:
1st row (rs) (K1, P1)A, K4E, K4H, (P1, K2, P1)C,
K4J, K4M, (P1, K2, P1)D, K4F, K4L, (P1, K2,
P1)A, K4N, K4H, (P1, K2, P1)B, K4E, K4L.
This sets position of patt. Cont to match Back until
62 rows in all have been worked in cable patt.

Front Edge Shaping

Keeping colours correct as set by previous row and
twisting cable at front edge with rem sts work dec
as foll:
Next row Patt to last 8 sts, K4, K2 tog, K2.
Work 5 rows.
Next row Patt to last 7 sts, K3, K2 tog, K2.
Work 5 rows.
Next row Patt to last 6 sts, K3, K2 tog, K1.
Work 5 rows.
Next row Patt to last 5 sts, K2, K2 tog, K1.

Work 5 rows.
Next row Patt to last 4 sts, K2, K2 tog.
Work 5 rows.
Next row Patt to last 3 sts, K1, K2 tog. Work 5 rows.
Next row Patt to last 2 sts, K2 tog. Work 5 rows.
Next row Patt to last 2 sts, P2 tog B. 50 sts.
Keeping patt correct, cont without shaping until work measures same as Back to shoulders, ending with a ws row.

Shoulder Shaping
Keeping patt correct, cast(bind) off 17 sts at beg of next and foll alt row. Work 1 row without shaping, then cast(bind) off rem 16 sts.

RIGHT FRONT
Using smaller needles and D, cast on 39 sts.
Break off D.
1st row (rs) (P2F, take F to ws, K2C, take F to rs) to last 3 sts, P2F, take F to ws, K1C.
Keeping rib as now set, work 14 more rows using same colour sequence as on Back.
Inc row (ws) P1A, (take L to rs, with L, K1, make one K, K1, take L to ws, with A, P1, make one P, P1) to last 2 sts, take L to rs, with L, K1, make one K, K1. 58 sts.
Change to larger needles and cont in cable patt as foll:
1st row K4E, K4H, (P1, K2, P1)B, K4J, K4G, (P1, K2, P1)A, K4F, K4L, (P1, K2, P1)D, K4N, K4M, (P1, K2, P1)B, K4E, K4J, (P1, K1)A.
This sets position of patt. Cont to match Back until 62 rows in all have been worked in cable patt.

Front Edge Shaping
Keeping colours correct as set by previous row and twisting cable at front edge with rem sts work dec as foll:
Next row K2, K2 tog, K4, patt to end.
Work 5 rows.
Next row K2, K2 tog, K3, patt to end.
Work 5 rows.
Next row K1, K2 tog, K3, patt to end.
Work 5 rows.
Next row K1, K2 tog, K2, patt to end.
Work 5 rows.
Next row K2 tog, K2, patt to end. Work 5 rows.
Next row K2 tog, K1, patt to end. Work 5 rows.
Next row K2 tog, patt to end. Work 5 rows.
Next row P2 tog B, patt to end. 50 sts.
Cont to match Left Front, reversing shaping.

SLEEVES
Using smaller needles and D, cast on 56 sts.
Break off D. Work 15 rows in rib as for Back.
Inc row (ws) P1A, * take L to rs, with L, K1, make one K, K1, take L to ws, (with A, P into front and back of next st) twice; rep from * to last 3 sts, take L to rs, with L, K1, make one K, K1, take L to ws, P1A. 96 sts. Change to larger needles and cont in cable patt as foll:
Work from * to ** as on first patt row of Back.
This sets position of patt. Cont to match Back AND AT THE SAME TIME, inc one st at each end of the 5th and every foll 4th row, working inc sts into patt until there are 136 sts. Cont without shaping until 90 rows in all have been worked in cable patt.
Cast(bind) off loosely in patt.
Make a 2nd sleeve in the same way.

FINISHING
Using backstitch, join shoulder seams. Mark back and fronts at side edges 17cm/6¾in from shoulder seam. Using backstitch, join cast-(bound-)off edge of sleeves to back and fronts between markers, matching centre of top of sleeve to shoulder seam. Press all seams taking care not to flatten cables. Join side seams, using an edge to edge seam. Using backstitch, join sleeve seams. Press seams.

FRONT BANDS AND COLLAR
Using circular needle and C and with rs facing, pick up and K 15 sts evenly up right front edge to top of rib and 96 sts to shoulder seam (picking up 5 sts along each cable, plus one extra st at neck), K back neck sts from holder, then pick up and K 96 sts evenly down left front edge to top of rib and 15 sts to lower edge. 278 sts.
Working backwards and forwards in rows, work 7 rows in K1, P1 rib, in stripe sequence of 3 rows C, 2 rows M, 1 row J and 1 row A.
Next row (for Boy) With A, rib 220, * cast(bind) off 2 sts, rib 24 including st already on needle; rep from * once more, cast(bind) off 2 sts, rib 4.
Next row (for Girl) With A, rib 4, * cast(bind) off 2 sts, rib 24 including st already on needle; rep from * once more, cast(bind) off 2 sts, rib to end.
Next row (either version) With A, rib to end, casting on 2 sts over each 2 cast(bound) off.
Work 20 rows in rib as set, working in stripes of 3 rows A, 2 rows L, 3 rows B, 1 row E, 2 rows D, 4 rows A, 1 row J, 3 rows G and 1 row M.
Rep 2 buttonhole rows once more.
Work 8 rows in rib as set, working in stripes of 1 row A, 1 row H, 2 rows A, 1 row B, 1 row N, 1 row F, 1 row D. Cast(bind) off loosely in rib using D. Stretch rib gently to same length as main knitting, pin out and steam press lightly. Sew on buttons.

ADULT'S CABLE JACKET

MATERIALS
General yarn weight used – Aran (heavy worsted)
All yarns are used double throughout.
Rowan *Botany* (25g/1oz hanks) in the foll 8 colours:
  A (501) periwinkle – 8[8,9] hanks
  B (125) turquoise – 8[9,10] hanks
  C (55) china – 7[8,9] hanks
  D (56) royal – 8[9,10] hanks
  E (96) magenta – 4[5,6] hanks
  F (115) scarlet – 5[5,6] hanks

ABOVE *An Adult's Cable Sweater and the Child's Cable Shawl Collar Jacket.*

131

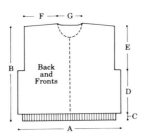

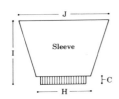

ADULT'S CABLE JACKET
A = 56.5[64.5,72.5]cm/
22½[25¾,29]in
B = 61.5[66,71]cm/
24¾[26½,28½]in
C = 5cm/2in
D = 28.5[31,34]cm/
11½[12½,13¾]in
E = 28[30,32]cm/11¼[12,12¾]in
F = 16.5[20,23.5]cm/
6½[8,9½]in
G = 16[16.5,17.5]cm/
6¼[6½,6¾]in
H = 36[37.5,38.5]cm/
14½[15,15½]in
I = 42[44,46.5]cm/
16¾[17½,18½]in
J =
56[60,64]cm/22½[24,25½]in

BELOW *The Adult's Cable Jacket and Child's Cable Shawl Collar Jacket, page 130.*

G (44) ruby – 4[5,6] hanks
H (41) pink – 4[5,6] hanks
One pair each 4mm (US size 6) and 5mm (US size 8) knitting needles *or size to obtain correct tension (gauge)*
One cable needle (cn)
Open-ended zip fastener 56[61,66]cm/22[24,26]in long

SIZES
To fit 86-91[96-102,107-112]cm/34-36[38-40,42-44]in bust/chest.
Figures for larger sizes are given in square brackets; where there is only one set of figures, it applies to all sizes.
For finished measurements see diagram.

TENSION(GAUGE)
30 sts and 28 rows to 10cm/4in over patt slightly stretched on 5mm (US size 8) needles.
Check your tension(gauge) before beginning.

NOTES
T8k – see Notes on page 130.

BACK
Using smaller needles and F, cast on 92[104,116] sts.
Work 17 rows in K1, P1 rib in stripes as foll:
3 rows D, 2 rows H, 3 rows C, 2 rows E, 3 rows B, 2 rows G, 2 rows A.
Inc row (ws) With A, rib 3, (work into front and back of next st, rib 1) 4 times, (work into front and back of next st) to last 11 sts, (rib 1, work into front and back of next st) 4 times, rib 3. 170[194,218] sts.
Change to larger needles and cont in cable patt as foll:
1st row (rs) First size: (K2, P1)H[2nd size: (K2, P1)G, K4D, K4C, (P1, K2, P1)H, 3rd size: (K2, P1)E, K4C, K4B, (P1, K2, P1)G, K4D, K4C, (P1, K2, P1)H], all sizes: * K4B, K4A, (P1, K2, P1)F, K4A, K4D, (P1, K2, P1)E, K4C, K4B, (P1, K2, P1)G, K4D, K4C, (P1, K2, P1)H **; rep from * to ** twice more, then work from * until 3 sts rem, (P1, K2)E[(P1, K2)G, (P1, K2)H].
2nd row Working in colours as set and twisting yarns tog as you go; P2, K1, (P8, K1, P2, K1) to last 11 sts, P8, K1, P2.
3rd and 4th rows Rep 1st and 2nd rows once.
5th row Keeping colours correct; K2, P1, (T8k, P1, K2, P1) to last 11 sts, T8k, P1, K2.

6th row As 2nd row, *but* with colours in new positions.
7th-10th rows Working in colours as set, rep 1st and 2nd rows twice.
11th row As 5th row, colours now return to original positions.
12th row As 2nd row.
Rows 1-12 form the rep of patt. Cont until 80[88,96] rows in all have been worked in cable patt.

Armhole Shaping
Keeping patt correct, cast(bind) off 12 sts at beg of next 2 rows. 146[170,194] sts.
Cont without shaping until 158[172,186] rows in all have been worked in cable patt, so ending with a ws row.

Shoulder and Neck Shaping
Keeping patt correct, cast(bind) off 17[20,23] sts at beg of next 2 rows.
Next row Cast(bind) off 16[20,24] sts, patt 23[27,31] including st already on needle, cast(bind) off 34[36,38] sts, patt to end.
Cont on last set of sts only for left back:
Keeping patt correct, cast(bind) off 16[20,24] sts at beg of next row, then 7 sts at beg of foll row.
Cast(bind) off rem 16[20,24] sts.
Return to sts which were left; with ws facing rejoin yarns to neck edge, cast(bind) off 7 sts and patt to end. Cast(bind) off rem 16[20,24] sts.

LEFT FRONT
Using smaller needles and F, cast on 46[52,58] sts.
Work 17 rows in K1, P1 rib in stripes as for Back. **
Inc row (ws) Rib 3, (work into front and back of next st, rib 1) 4 times, (work into front and back of next st) to end. 85[97,109] sts.
Change to larger needles and cont in cable patt as foll:
1st row (rs) First size: (K2, P1)H[2nd size: (K2, P1)G, K4D, K4C, (P1, K2, P1)H, 3rd size: (K2, P1)E, K4C, K4B, (P1, K2, P1)G, K4D, K4C, (P1, K2, P1)H], all sizes: K4B, K4A, (P1, K2, P1)F, K4A, K4D, (P1, K2, P1)E, K4C, K4B, (P1, K2, P1)G, K4D, K4C, (P1, K2, P1)H, K4B, K4A, (P1, K2, P1)F, K4A, K4D, (P1, K2, P1)E, K4C, K4B, (P1, K1)G.
This sets position of patt. Cont to match Back until 80[88,96] rows in all have been worked in cable patt, so ending with a ws row.

Armhole Shaping
Keeping patt correct, cast(bind) off 12 sts at beg of next row. 73[85,97] sts. Cont without shaping until 135[149,163] rows in all have been worked in cable patt, so ending with a rs row.

Neck Shaping
Keeping patt correct, cast(bind) off 6[7,8] sts at beg of next row, 4 sts at beg of foll 2 alt rows, 3 sts at beg of foll 2 alt rows, 2 sts at beg of foll alt row, then one st at beg of foll 2 alt rows. 49[60,71] sts.
Work 8 rows without shaping.

Shoulder Shaping
Cast(bind) off 17[20,23] sts at beg of next row, then 16[20,24] sts at beg of foll alt row. Work 1 row without shaping, then cast (bind) off rem 16[20,24] sts.

RIGHT FRONT
Work as given for Left Front to **.
Inc row (ws) (Work into front and back of next st) to last 11 sts, (rib 1, work into front and back of next st) 4 times, rib 3. 85[97,109] sts.

Change to larger needles and cont in cable patt as foll:

1st row (rs) * (K1, P1)G, K4D, K4C, (P1, K2, P1)H, K4B, K4A, (P1, K2, P1)F, K4A, K4D, ** (P1, K2, P1)E, K4C, K4B, (P1, K1)G; rep from * to ** once more, first size: (P1, K2)E [2nd size: (P1, K2, P1)E, K4C, K4B, (P1, K2)G, 3rd size: (P1, K2, P1)E, K4C, K4B, (P1, K2, P1)G, K4D, K4C, (P1, K2)H].
This sets position of patt. Cont to match Back until 81[89,97] rows in all have been worked in cable patt, so ending with a rs row.

Armhole Shaping
Keeping patt correct, cast(bind) off 12 sts at beg of next row. 73[85,97] sts.
Cont without shaping until 136[150,164] rows in all have been worked in cable patt, so ending with a ws row.

Neck Shaping
Keeping patt correct, cast(bind) off 6[7,8] sts at beg of next row.
Complete to match Left Front reversing all shaping.

SLEEVES
Using smaller needles and F, cast on 54[56,58] sts.
Work 17 rows in K1, P1 rib in stripes as for Back.
Inc row (ws) Work into front and back of every st to end. 108[112,116] sts.
Change to larger needles and cont in cable patt as foll:

1st row (rs) K 0[2,4]C, K4B, (P1, K2, P1)G, K4D, K4C, (P1, K2, P1)H, work from * to ** as first patt row of Back, K4B, K4A, (P1, K2, P1)F, K4A, K4D, (P1, K2, P1)E, K4C, K4B, (P1, K2, P1)G, K4D, K 0[2,4]C.
This sets position of patt. Cont to match Back AND AT THE SAME TIME, inc one st at each end of the 3rd and every foll alt row, working inc sts into patt until there are 116 [128,140] sts, then every foll 3rd row until there are 168[180,192] sts.
Cont without shaping until 104[110,116] rows in all have been worked in cable patt, so ending with a ws row. Cast(bind) off *loosely* in patt.
Make a 2nd sleeve in the same way.

FINISHING
DO NOT PRESS. Using backstitch, join shoulder seams. Using backstitch, join cast-(bound-) off edge of sleeves to back and front armholes, matching centre of top of sleeve to shoulder seam and sewing last few rows of sleeve to cast-(bound-)off sts at underarm. Press all seams taking care not to flatten cables. Using backstitch, join side and sleeve seams. Press seams.

COLLAR
Using smaller needles, B and with rs facing, pick up and K 32[33,34] sts evenly up right front neck, 31[33,35] sts around back neck, then 32[33,34] sts down left front neck. 95[99,103] sts.
Work in K1, P1 rib shaping collar as foll:
1st row Rib 63[66,69], turn.
2nd row Sl 1, rib 30[32,34], turn.
3rd row Sl 1, rib 37[38,39], turn.
4th row Sl 1, rib 44[44,44], turn.
5th row Sl 1, rib 49[50,49], turn.
6th row Sl 1, rib 54[56,54], turn.
7th row Sl 1, rib 59[62,60], turn.
8th row Sl 1, rib 64[68,66], turn.
9th row With G, sl 1, rib 69[73,72], turn.
10th row Sl 1, rib 74[78,78], turn.
11th row Sl 1, rib 79[83,84], turn.

12th row Sl 1, rib 84[88,90], turn.
13th row With B, sl 1, rib 89[93,96].
14th row Rib to end. 95[99,103] sts.
Work 4 rows in rib as set without shaping.
Cast(bind) off 5[5,6] sts at beg of next 2 rows.
With G, cast(bind) off 5[5,6] sts at beg of next 4 rows. With B, cast(bind) off 5[6,6] sts at beg of next 2 rows, 5[6,5] sts at beg of foll 2 rows then 7[6,5] sts at beg of next 2 rows. Cast(bind) off rem 31[33,35] sts. Tack zip in place at centre front being careful not to stretch or gather knitting. When you have tried jacket on and are sure zip is correct, using backstitch sew zip into place. Fold collar in half to inside and sl st on to ws.

BABY'S CABLE JUMPSUIT

MATERIALS
General yarn weight used – lightweight cotton
Rowan *Soft Cotton* (50g/1¾oz balls) in the foll 7 colours:
  A (542) bluebell – 2[2] balls
  B (533) antique pink – 1[2] balls
  C (547) mermaid – 1[1] ball
  D (534) frolic – 1[2] balls
  E (531) fiord – 1[1] ball
  F (546) strawberry ice – 1[2] balls
  G (545) sugar pink – 1[2] balls
One pair each 2¼mm (US size 1) and 3mm (US size 3) knitting needles *or size to obtain correct tension(gauge)*
One cable needle (cn)
9 buttons
Elastic thread (optional)

SIZES
To fit 6[12]months or 45[48]cm/18[19]in chest.
Figures for larger size are given in square brackets; where there is only one set of figures, it applies to both sizes.
For finished measurements see diagram.

TENSION(GAUGE)
48 sts and 37 rows to 10cm/4in over patt on 3mm (US size 3) needles.
Check your tension(gauge) before beginning.

NOTES
T8k-sl next 4 sts on to cn and hold at back of work, K4 twisting yarn around colour just worked, then K4 from cn.

LEGS
Using smaller needles and F, cast on 72[84] sts. (NOTE: If working ends into back of work, remember that cuff will be folded so that 19th row becomes ws.)
Beg with a rs row work 18 rows in K1, P1 rib, working in stripes of * 3 rows E, 3 rows D, 3 rows C, 3 rows B *, 3 rows A, 3 rows F.
Work 14 more rows in rib (next row is ws), working in stripes as from * to *, ending with 2 rows A.
Inc row (ws) With A, rib working into front and back of every st to end. 144[168] sts. Change to larger needles and cont in cable patt as foll:
1st row (rs) (K1, P1)A, * K8B, (P1, K2, P1)E, K8D, (P1, K2, P1)A, K8G, (P1, K2, P1)C, K8F, (P1, K2, P1)A **; rep from * to ** 1[2] times more, then work from * until 2 sts rem, (P1, K1)A.
2nd row Working in colours as set and twisting yarns tog as you go; P1, K1, (P8, K1, P2, K1) to last

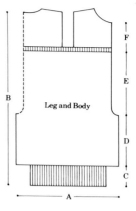

Leg and Body

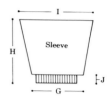

Sleeve

BABY'S CABLE JUMPSUIT
A = 30[35]cm/12[14]in
B = 54.5[62]cm/21½[24½]in
C = 7cm/2¾in
D = 15.5[18]cm/6[7¼]in
E = 18.5[22]cm/7½[8¾]in
F = 10[11.5]cm/4[4½]in
G = 16.5[18]cm/6½[7¼]in
H = 19[22.5]cm/7¾[9]in
I = 22.5[25]cm/9[10]in
J = 3cm/1¼in

10 sts, P8, K1, P1.
<u>3rd and 4th rows</u> As first and 2nd rows.
<u>5th row</u> Working in colours as set K1, P1, (T8k, P1, K2, P1) to last 10 sts, T8k, P1, K1.
<u>6th row</u> As 2nd row.
These 6 rows form the rep of patt. Cont until 56[68] rows in all have been worked in cable patt.

Crotch Shaping
Keeping patt correct, cast(bind) off 4 sts at beg of next 2 rows, 3 sts at beg of next 2 rows, 2 sts at beg of next 2 rows, then one st at beg of next 2 rows. Leave rem 124[148] sts on a spare needle.
Make a 2nd leg in the same way.

BELOW AND RIGHT Baby's Cable Jumpsuit in cottons and the Adult's Cable Jacket. Instructions are given for these colours but do try other combinations of colours.

Body
Join legs to beg Body as foll:
Using larger needles and with rs facing, beg with right leg and keeping colours correct, cast(bind) off 2 sts, patt as set to last 3 sts, sl 1, K2 tog, psso, with left leg, K3 tog, patt to end. 242[290] sts.
<u>Next row</u> Cast(bind) off 2 sts, patt to end. 240[288] sts.
Cont until 125[149] rows in all have been worked

in cable patt, so ending with a rs row.

Waistband
Working in colours as set:
<u>Dec row</u> (ws) P1, K1, (P2 tog) to last 2 sts, K1, P1. 122[146] sts. Change to smaller needles.
<u>Next row</u> (K1, P1) 60[72] times, K2, (P1, K1) to end.
Work 8 more rows in rib as set, working 2 sts at centre back in st st on every row.
<u>Inc row</u> Rib 2, (P into front and back of next 4 sts, K into front and P into back of next st, P into front and K into back of next st) to last 6 sts, P into front and back of next 4 sts, rib 2. 240[288] sts.
Change to larger needles.

Armhole Shaping
Keeping colours correct, beg first patt row, cont in cable patt as before:
<u>Next row</u> (rs) Patt 50[62], cast(bind) off 20 sts, patt 100[124] including st already on needle, cast(bind) off 20 sts, patt to end. 50[62] sts.

Left Front
Cont on last set of sts only for Left Front until 29[35] rows in all have been worked in cable patt from top of waistband, so ending with a rs row.

Neck Shaping
Keeping patt correct, cast(bind) off 6 sts at beg of next row, 5 sts at beg of foll 0[1] alt row, 4 sts at beg of foll 2[3] alt rows, 3 sts at beg of foll 1[2] alt rows, then 2 sts at beg of foll 3[0] alt rows. 27[33] sts.

Shoulder and Neck Shaping
Cast(bind) off 9[11] sts at beg of next row, one st at beg of next row, then 9[11] sts at beg of next row. Work 1 row without shaping, then cast(bind) off rem 8[10] sts.

Back
Return to sts which were left for Back; with larger needles and ws facing, cont in patt until 42[48]

rows in all have been worked in cable patt from top of waistband, so ending with a ws row.

Shoulder and Neck Shaping
Keeping patt correct, cast(bind) off 9[11] sts at beg of next 2 rows.

Next row (rs) Cast(bind) off 9[11] sts, patt 14[18] including st already on needle, cast(bind) off 36[44] sts, then patt to end.

Next row Cast(bind) off 9[11] sts, patt to neck edge, turn slipping rem sts on to holder. Cast(bind) off 6[8] sts at beg of next row (neck edge).

Cast(bind) off rem 8[10] sts.

Return to sts which were left for right shoulder; with ws facing rejoin yarn, cast (bind) off 6[8] sts, patt to end. Work 1 row without shaping, then cast(bind) off rem 8[10] sts.

Right Front
Return to sts which were left for Right Front; with larger needles and ws facing, cont in patt until 30[36] rows in all have been worked in cable patt from top of waistband.

Neck Shaping
Keeping patt correct and twisting cable before shaping, cast(bind) off 6 sts at beg of next row. Cont to match Left Front, reversing all shaping.

SLEEVES
Using smaller needles and F, cast on 40[44] sts. Work 13 rows in K1, P1 rib, working in stripes of 3 rows E, 3 rows D, 3 rows C, 3 rows B and 1 row A.

Next row With A, work into front and back of every st to end. 80[88] sts.

Change to larger needles and cont in cable patt as foll:

1st row (rs) (P1, K2, P1)A 0[1] time, * K8B, (P1, K2, P1)E, K8D, (P1, K2, P1)A, K8G, ** (P1, K2, P1)C, K8F, (P1, K2, P1)A; rep from * to ** once more, (P1, K2, P1)C 0[1] time.

This sets position of patt. Cont to match Legs AND AT THE SAME TIME, inc one st at each end of the 2nd row and then every foll 4th row, working inc sts into patt in same sequence as on Legs until there are 108[120] sts. Cont without shaping until 60[72] rows in all have been worked in cable patt.

Cast(bind) off *loosely* in patt.

Make a 2nd sleeve in the same way.

FINISHING
If desired run elastic thread along ws of work through every rib row at waistband, catching in on every other st. Using backstitch, join shoulder seams then join cast-(bound-)off edge of sleeves to back and front armholes, matching centre of top of sleeve to shoulder seam and sewing last few rows of sleeves to cast-(bound-)off sts at underarm. Press all seams taking care not to flatten cables. Using backstitch, join sleeve seams to top of cuff, using an edge to edge seam, join cuffs.

NECKBAND
Using smaller needles, E and with rs facing, pick up and K 22[28] sts evenly up right front neck, 40[48] sts around back neck, then 22[28] sts down left front neck. 84[104] sts.

Work 4 rows in K1, P1 rib, working in stripes of 3 rows E and 1 row F. Cast(bind) off in rib using F. Using an edge to edge seam, join inside leg seams below crotch shaping, reversing seam on rib to allow for turning. Join centre back seam along shaping and corresponding seam on front up to base of opening. Press seams.

BUTTON BAND
Button Band is on left for girls and right for boys. Using smaller needles, E and with rs facing, pick up and K 102[120] sts (approximately one st for every row end) evenly along front edge including neckband. * With E, work 3 rows in K1, P1 rib. Cast(bind) off in rib using E.

BUTTONHOLE BAND
Buttonhole Band is on right for girls and left for boys. Work as given for Button Band to *.

Next row With E, rib 2[3], * cast(bind) off 2 sts, rib 10[12] including st already on needle; rep from * 7 more times, cast(bind) off 2 sts, rib to end.

Next row With E, rib to end, casting on 2 sts over each 2 cast(bound) off.

Next row With E, rib to end.

Cast(bind) off in rib using E.

Overlap ends of front bands at lower edge and sew to cast-(bound-)off sts at base of opening. Sew on buttons. Turn up rib at ankles, if necessary catch down at inside edge to hold in place.

BABY'S FLAGS JUMPSUIT

MATERIALS
General yarn weight used – 4 ply (fingering) Rowan *Botany* (25g/1oz hanks) in the foll 16 colours:

A (1) white – 1[1,1] hank
B (4) cream – 1[1,1] hank
C (6) custard – 1[1,1] hank
D (12) sunshine – 1[1,1] hank
E (89) light emerald – 1[2,2] hanks
F (416) almond – 1[2,2] hanks
G (76) pistachio – 1[1,1] hank
H (49) sky blue – 1[1,1] hank
J (123) duck egg – 1[1,1] hank
L (48) cloud blue – 1[1,1] hank
M (103) flesh – 1[1,1] hank
N (121) mauve – 1[1,1] hank
Q (120) platinum – 1[1,1] hank
R (68) sugar pink – 1[1,1] hank
S (621) shocking pink – 2[2,2] hanks
T (83) powder – 1[1,1] hank

One pair each 2¼mm (US size 1) and 3mm (US size 3) knitting needles *or size to obtain correct tension(gauge)*

8 buttons

Elastic thread (optional)

SIZES
To fit 6[12,18]months or 45[48,51]cm/18[19,20]in chest.

Figures for larger sizes are given in square brackets; where there is only one set of figures, it applies to all sizes.

For finished measurements see diagram (page 142).

TENSION(GAUGE)
33 sts and 35 rows to 10cm/4in over patt on 3mm (US size 3) needles.

Check your tension(gauge) before beginning.

NOTES
When working in patt from Chart, read odd rows (K) from right to left and even rows (P) from left to right.

LEGS
Using smaller needles and R, cast on 76[80,84] sts.

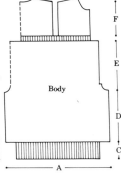

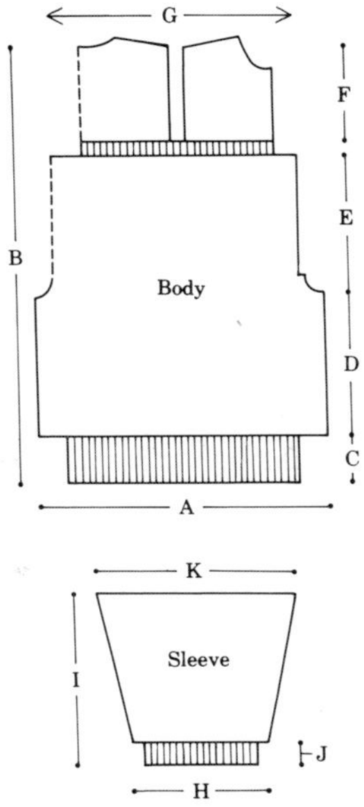

BABY'S FLAGS JUMPSUIT
A = 39.5[42.5,45.5]cm/
15¾[17,18]in
B = 60.5[64.5,69]cm/
24[26,27¼]in
C = 7.5cm/3in
D = 19[20.5,22]cm/
7½[8¼,8¾]in
E = 19[20.5,22]cm/
7½[8¼,8¾]in
F = 13[14,15.5]cm/
5¼[5¾,6]in
G = 50[55,60]cm/
20[22,24]in all round
H = 19[20,21]cm/
7½[8,8½]in
I = 24[25.5,27.5]cm/
9½[10¼,11]in
J = 3.5cm/1¼in
K = 26[28.5,31]cm/
10½[11½,12¼]in

OVERLEAF *In the brilliant New Hampshire sunshine, we can see Zoë's original colourway of the Flags pattern as sleeveless sweaters. The background fabric shows that she has used the intarsia method with about 40 shades and textures of blues, greys and greeny-browns.*

135

NOTE: If working ends into back of work, remember that cuff will be folded so that 24th row becomes rs.)

Beg with a rs row, work 23 rows in K1, P1 rib in stripes as foll:

3 rows E, 2 rows A, 3 rows S, 2 rows G, 3 rows H, 2 rows C, 3 rows F, 2 rows T, 3 rows F.

Work 15 more rows in rib (next row is rs), working in stripes as foll:

2 rows C, 3 rows H, 2 rows G, 3 rows S, 2 rows A, 3 rows E.

Inc row (ws) With R, first size: rib 2, * (rib 1, make 1) 3 times, rib 1; rep from * to last 2 sts, rib 2[2nd size: * (rib 1, make 1) 3 times, rib 1; rep from * to end, 3rd size: * (rib 1, make 1) 8 times, * (rib 1, make 1) 3 times, rib 1; rep from * to last 8 sts, (rib 1, make 1) 7 times, rib 1. 130[140,150] sts.

Change to larger needles and cont in patt as foll:

Beg with a K row and working in st st throughout cont in patt from Chart, beginning and ending rows as indicated, rep rows 1-30 to form patt, but changing colours as given in colour sequence table. Cont until 66[72,78] rows in all have been worked in patt, so ending with a ws row.

Crotch Shaping

Keeping patt correct, cast(bind) off 3 sts at beg of next 2 rows, 2 sts at beg of foll 4 rows, then one st at beg of next 6 rows.

Leave rem 110[120,130] sts on a spare needle.

Make a 2nd leg in the same way.

Body

Join legs to beg body as foll:

Using larger needles and with rs facing, beg with right leg and keeping patt correct, cast (bind) off 3 sts, patt to end, then cont in patt across sts of left leg. 217[237,257] sts.

Next row (ws) Cast(bind) off 3 sts, patt to end. 214[234,254] sts.

Cont without shaping until 132[144,156] rows in all have been worked in patt.

Waistband

Change to smaller needles.

Dec row (rs) With R, K1, (K2 tog, K3) to last 3 sts, K2 tog, K1. 171[187,203] sts.

Next row With E and working in K1, P1 rib, rib 12[16,20], * work 2 tog, rib 34[36,38]; rep from * to last 15[19,23] sts, work 2 tog, rib to end. 166[182,198] sts. Work 8 more rows in K1, P1 rib in stripes as foll: 2 rows E, 2 rows A, 3 rows S, 1 row G. Change to larger needles.

Armhole Shaping

Cont in st st and patt from row 1 of Chart, rep colours from row 49 of colour sequence table and cont as foll:

Next row (rs) (3N, 7A) 3[4,4] times, 3[0,3] N, 3[0,1]A, cast(bind) off 8 sts, (3N, 7A) 7 [8,9] times including st already on needle, 3N, 5[3,1]A, cast(bind) off 8 sts, (3N, 7A) 3[4,4] times including st already on needle, 3[0,3]N, 3[0,1]A.

Left Front

Cont on last set of 36[40,44] sts only for left front until 33[37,41] rows in all have been worked in patt from top of waistband, ending with a rs row.

Neck Shaping

** Keeping patt correct, cast(bind) off 4 sts at beg of next row, 3 sts at beg of foll 1[2,3] alt rows, 2 sts at beg of foll 4[3,2] alt rows, then one st at beg of foll alt row. 20[23,26] sts.

Shoulder Shaping

Cast(bind) off 7[8,9] sts at beg of next and foll alt row. Work 1 row without shaping.

Cast(bind) off rem 6[7,8] sts. **

Back

Return to 78[86,94] sts which were left for back; with larger needles and ws facing rejoin yarns and cont in patt as set until 46[50,54] rows in all have been worked in patt from top of waistband.

Shoulder and Neck Shaping

Next row (rs) Cast(bind) off 7[8,9] sts, patt 22[24,26] including st already on needle, cast(bind) off 20[22,24] sts, patt to end.

Cont on last set of sts only for left shoulder as foll: Keeping patt correct, cast(bind) off 7[8,9] sts at beg of next row, 6 sts at beg of foll row, 7[8,9] sts at beg of next row, then 3 sts at beg of foll row.

Cast(bind) off rem 6[7,8] sts.

Return to sts which were left for right shoulder; with ws facing rejoin yarns to neck edge, cast(bind) off 6 sts and patt to end. Cast(bind) off 7[8,9] sts at beg of next row, then 3 sts at beg of foll row.

Cast(bind) off rem 6[7,8] sts.

Right Front

Return to 36[40,44] sts which were left for right front; with larger needles and ws facing, rejoin yarns to armhole edge and cont in patt until 34[38,42] rows in all have been worked in patt from top of waistband.

Neck Shaping

Work as given for Left Front from ** to **.

SLEEVES

Using smaller needles and R, cast on 42[44,46] sts and work 17 rows in striped rib as for Legs (working ends in on ws throughout).

Inc row (ws) With F, first size: rib 1, * rib 1, make 1, rib 1; rep from * to last st, rib 1[2nd size: * rib 1, make 1, rib 1; rep from * to end, 3rd size: (rib 1, make 1) twice, * rib 1, make 1, rib 1; rep from * to end. 62[66,70] sts.

Change to larger needles and cont in patt as foll:

1st row (rs) K (3H, 7B) to last 2[6,0] sts, 2[3,0]H, 0[3,0]B.

Cont in patt from Chart as set, working in colours as for Legs AND AT THE SAME TIME, inc one st at each end of every foll 5th[5th,4th] row, working inc sts into patt until there are 86[94,102] sts.

Cont without shaping until 72[78,84] rows in all have been worked in patt. Cast(bind) off *loosely*.

Make a 2nd sleeve in the same way.

FINISHING

Press work lightly on ws according to instructions on bands, omitting ribbing. If desired run elastic thread along ws of work through every rib row at waistband, catching in on every other st. Using backstitch, join shoulder seams, then join cast-(bound-)off edge of sleeves to back and front armholes, matching centre of top of sleeve to shoulder seam and sewing last fews rows of sleeves to cast-(bound-)off sts at underarm. Press all seams. Using backstitch, join back crotch seam below where legs were joined, then join front crotch seam below cast-(bound-)off sts for front opening. Using backstitch on main knitting and an edge to edge st on rib, join sleeve seams, then leg seams, reversing seam to allow for turn ups. Press all seams.

PAGES 138-139 *All in a Moroccan garden: an Adult's pastel Flags Crewneck and a Child's Button Shoulder Sweater in Flags.*

LEFT *The Baby's Flags Jumpsuit, and the Adult's Squares Jacket, page 22. Both patterns are available in kit form. Zoë had fun making up the hat using the colours from the Squares jacket. The shape is like a traditional bonnet with its Chinese-style tassel (page 143).*

rep = 10 sts

rep = 30 rows

—29
—27
—25
—23
—21
—19
—17
—15
—13
—11
—9
—7
—5
—3
—1

beg and end of rows for both legs all sizes

COLOUR SEQUENCE TABLE

Rows	☒	☐	Rows	☒	☐
1-6	H	B	79-84	F	D
7-12	F	S	85-90	E	R
13-18	J	R	91-96	G	S
19-24	Q	D	97-102	N	M
25-30	N	T	103-108	L	D
31-36	G	S	109-114	E	A
37-42	E	M	115-120	Q	C
43-48	L	D	121-126	J	R
49-54	N	A	127-132	F	S
55-60	F	C	133-138	H	B
61-66	H	T	139-144	L	D
67-72	Q	S	145-150	E	M
73-78	J	B	151-156	G	S

RIGHT *The Baby's Flags Jumpsuit and the Adult's Squares Jacket, page 22.*

OVERLEAF *Yellow Flags Crewneck Sweaters and the Child's Bow Scoopneck Sweater, page 118.* These colourways depend on finding as many yellows and golds as possible and adding some bright pastels to make them sing.

NECKBAND

Using smaller needles, A and with rs facing, pick up and K 27[28,29] sts evenly up right front neck, 40[42,44] sts around back neck, then 27[28,29] sts down left front neck.
94[98,102] sts.
** Work 5 rows in K1, P1 rib, working in stripes as foll:
1 row A, 3 rows E, 1 row R.
Using R, cast(bind) off in rib.

BUTTON BAND

Button Band is on left for girls and right for boys.
Using smaller needles, A and with rs facing, pick up and K 102[112,122] sts (approximately one st for every row) along front edge including neckband. *
Work as given for Neckband from ** to end.

BUTTONHOLE BAND

Buttonhole Band is on right for girls and left for boys.
Work as given for Button Band to *.
<u>1st row</u> With A, rib to end.
<u>2nd row</u> With E, rib to end.
<u>3rd row</u> With E, rib 4[2,4], * cast (bind) off 2 sts, rib 11[13,14] including st already on needle; rep from * 6 times more, cast (bind) off 2 sts, rib to end.
<u>4th row</u> With E, rib to end, casting on 2 sts over each 2 cast(bound) off.
<u>5th row</u> With R, rib to end.
Using R, cast(bind) off in rib.
Overlap ends of front bands at lower edge and sew to cast-(bound-)off sts at base of opening. Sew on buttons. Turn up rib at ankles, if necessary catch down at inside edge to hold in place.

TURKS AND
HARLEQUINS

Zoë originally discovered the Harlequin design by acci-
dent some years ago while trying to make a waistcoat for
her brother. She began by working the small diamonds
all over the bottom of the back (she always starts with
the back of a garment – by the time she gets to the front
she has ironed out the problems). This became far too
laborious and, realizing that she would never get it done
in time, she began to enlarge some of the areas of colour
by treating four small diamonds as if they were a large
one, and keeping diagonal bands of the small diamonds
in between. In both versions, Zoë has imposed restrictions – the large diamonds are
in one group of colours and the small diamonds in another. She feels much more at
home with this kind of formula. I, on the other hand, have imposed no restrictions
and have used a mixture of strong dark colours in a less predictable way so that the
eye has to examine the design more closely to discover its anatomy. The garments
are worked by the intarsia method.

When you begin to design things for yourself, you may find it helpful to make
these kinds of rules so that you limit your range of possibilities. Once you feel more
confident, you can try the same design with no restrictions. Contrary to what you
might think, it is actually harder to design with so much freedom.

When it comes to designs to break up or organize the surface of a sweater, the lattice takes a lot of beating. All through history, from primitive times, this tilted
grid has served as a basis for many patterns. Classics like garden lattice fencing
keep being produced and never seem to lose their appeal and elegance. Argyll, an
offshoot of the lattice, is stronger than ever as a fashion perennial. Lattice patterns
still delight the eye of even the most severe decorator.

This Lattice, with its little square decorations, is a variation that Zoë found in a
castle in Switzerland. It was an old piece of printed silk from that treasure house of
patterns, Turkey. She was able to do a thumbnail sketch on the spot and commit it
to graph paper for knitting later. There are many looks to be brought out of this
geometry. If you knit the large areas as background, all in shades of a given colour,
the little squares will float in the foreground (page 162). If you knit the large areas
in a more varied colouring, they become pointed crosses and the squares recede
into the background (page 162). You can knit the lattice line itself in one colour as
it is here or change it at every square. Turkish Lattice is worked in a combination
of fairisle for the lattice and intarsia for the small squares and the large cross
shapes. On the last row of each small square, carry the yarn of the appropriate
large cross along and knit it in so it will be in the right place on the next row.

RIGHT *An Adult's Harlequin Sweater and the Baby's*
Harlequin Button Shoulder Sweater, page 150. The
background is a Child's Harlequin Turtleneck Sweater.
Both the children's sweaters are available in kit form.

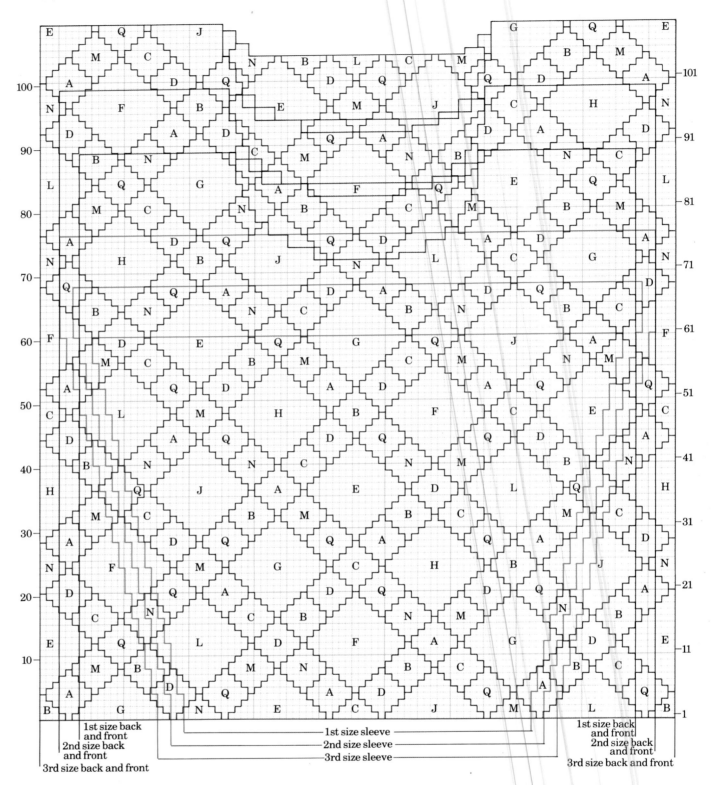

1st size back and front
2nd size back and front
3rd size back and front

1st size sleeve
2nd size sleeve
3rd size sleeve

1st size back and front
2nd size back and front
3rd size back and front

BABY'S HARLEQUIN BUTTON SHOULDER SWEATER

MATERIALS

General yarn weight used – 4 ply (fingering)
Rowan *Botany* (25g/1oz hanks) in the foll 10 colours:

A (34) bright green – 1[1,1] hank
B (38) grass green – 1[1,1] hank
C (124) kelly green – 1[1,1] hank
D (89) light emerald – 1[1,1] hank
E (41) pink – 1[1,1] hank
F (25) tangerine – 1[1,1] hank
G (631) raspberry – 1[1,1] hank
H (115) flame – 1[1,1] hank
J (44) scarlet – 1[1,1] hank
L (45) pillar box – 1[1,1] hank
Rowan *Fine Fleck Tweed* (25g/1oz hanks) in the foll 2 colours:
M (90) emerald – 1[1,1] hank
N (100) sage – 1[1,1] hank
Rowan *Light Tweed* (25g/1oz hanks) in the foll colour:
Q (220) jade – 1[1,2] hanks
One pair each 2¼mm (US size 1) and 3mm (US size

3) knitting needles *or size to obtain correct tension(gauge)*
6 buttons

SIZES

To fit 6[12,18] months or 45[48,51]cm/18[19,20]in chest.
Figures for larger sizes are given in square brackets; where there is only one set of figures, it applies to all sizes.
For finished measurements see diagram.

TENSION(GAUGE)

29 sts and 38 rows to 10cm/4in over patt on 3mm (US size 3) needles.
Check your tension(gauge) before beginning.

NOTES

When working in patt from Chart, read odd rows (K) from right to left and even rows (P) from left to right.

BACK

Using smaller needles and H, cast on 74[78,82] sts.
Work 23 rows in K1, P1 rib in stripes as foll:
4 rows C, 1 row E, 4 rows A, 1 row F, 4 rows M, 1 row G, 4 rows Q, 1 row H, 3 rows B.
Inc row (ws) With B, rib 7[3,6], make 1, * rib 6[6,5], make 1; rep from * to last 7[3,6] sts, rib to end. 85[91,97] sts.
Change to larger needles and cont in patt as foll:
Beg with a K row and working in st st throughout, cont in patt from Chart beginning and ending rows as indicated.
Cont until 84[94,104] rows in all have been worked in patt.

Neck and Shoulder Shaping

Next row (rs) Patt 28[30,32], cast(bind) off 29[31,33] sts, patt to end.
Cont on last set of sts only for left shoulder:
Next row Patt to end.
Keeping patt correct, cast(bind) off 2 sts at beg of next and foll alt row. 24[26,28] sts. Leave these sts

on a spare needle.
Return to sts which were left; with ws facing rejoin yarns to neck edge, cast(bind) off 2 sts, patt to end.
Next row Patt to end.
Next row Cast(bind) off 2 sts, patt to end.
Next row Patt to end.
Leave rem 24[26,28] sts on a spare needle.

FRONT

Work as given for Back until 72[82,92] rows in all have been worked in patt.

Neck Shaping

Next row (rs) Patt 36[38,40], cast(bind) off 13[15,17] sts, patt to end.
Cont on last set of sts only for right front:
Next row Patt to end.
Keeping patt correct, cast(bind) off 4 sts at beg of next row, 3 sts at beg of foll alt row, 2 sts at beg of foll alt row, then one st at beg of foll 3 alt rows. 24[26,28] sts.
Work 4 rows without shaping. 89[99,109] rows in all have been worked in patt.
Leave rem sts on a spare needle.
Return to sts which were left; with ws facing rejoin yarns to neck edge, cast(bind) off 4 sts and patt to end.
Next row Patt to end.
Keeping patt correct, cast(bind) off 3 sts at beg of next row, 2 sts at beg of foll alt row, then one st at beg of foll 3 alt rows.
24[26,28] sts.
Work 5 rows without shaping, so ending with a rs row.
Leave rem sts on a spare needle.

SLEEVES

Using smaller needles and H, cast on 38[40,42] sts and work 23 rows in striped rib as for Back.
Inc row (ws) With B, rib 5[4,3], make 1, * rib 2, make 1; rep from * to last 5[4,3] sts, rib to end. 53[57,61] sts.
Change to larger needles and cont in patt as foll:
Beg with a K row and working in st st throughout,

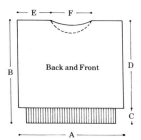

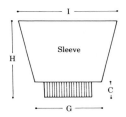

BABY'S HARLEQUIN BUTTON SHOULDER SWEATER
A = 30[31.5,33]cm/ 11¾[12½,13¼]in
B = 28[30.5,33]cm/ 11[12¼,13¼]in
C = 4.5cm/1¾in
D = 23.5[26,28.5]cm/ 9¼[10½,11½]in
E = 8.5[9,9.5]cm/ 3¼[3½,3¾]in
F = 13[13.5,14]cm/ 5¼[5½,5¾]in
G = 18[19.5,21]cm/ 7¼[7¾,8½]in
H = 20.5[22.5,24.5]cm/ 8[9,9¾]in
I = 28[30,31.5]cm/ 11¼[12,12½]in

LEFT *The Adult's Harlequin Sweater, the Child's Harlequin Turtleneck Sweater and the Baby's Harlequin Button Shoulder Sweater.*

151

cont in patt from Chart beginning and ending rows as indicated AND AT THE SAME TIME, inc one st at each end of the 5th and every foll 4th row, working inc sts into patt until there are 81[87,91] sts. Cont without shaping until 60[68,76] rows in all have been worked in patt. Cast(bind) off *loosely*. Make a 2nd sleeve in the same way.

FINISHING
Press work lightly on ws according to instructions on bands, omitting ribbing.

BACK NECKBAND
Using smaller needles, C and with ws facing, P across 24[26,28] sts of left shoulder, pick up and P 42[44,46] sts evenly around back neck, then P across 24[26,28] sts of right shoulder. 90[96,102] sts.
Work 5 rows in K1, P1 rib in stripes as foll:
4 rows C, 1 row H.
Using H, cast(bind) off *loosely* in rib.

FRONT NECKBAND
Using smaller needles, C and with ws facing, P across 24[26,28] sts of right shoulder, pick up and

P 58[60,62] sts evenly around front neck, then P across 24[26,28] sts of left shoulder. 106[112,118] sts.
<u>1st row</u> With C, work in K1, P1 rib to end.
<u>2nd row</u> With C, rib 7, cast(bind) off 2 sts, * rib 5[6,7] including st already on needle, cast(bind) off 2 sts *; rep from * to * once more, rib 60[62,64] including st already on needle, cast(bind) off 2 sts; rep from * to * twice more, rib to end.
<u>3rd row</u> With C, rib to end, casting on 2 sts over each 2 cast(bound) off.
<u>4th row</u> With C, rib to end.
<u>5th row</u> With H, rib to end.
Using H, cast(bind) off *loosely* in rib.
Press back and front lightly stretching neckbands so that they lie flat. Overlap front neckband on to back neckband and oversew at side edges. Mark back and front at side edges 14[15,16]cm/5½[6,6¼]in down from centre of shoulders. Using backstitch, join cast-(bound-)off edge of sleeves to back and front between markers, matching centre of top of sleeve to shoulder. Press seams. Using backstitch on main knitting and an edge to edge st on rib, join side and sleeve seams. Press all seams. Sew on buttons.

PREVIOUS PAGE AND BELOW
Boy and girl in Harlequin sweaters in a field of New Hampshire sorghum. The pattern for the Child's Harlequin Shawl Collar Sweater is on this page.

CHILD'S HARLEQUIN SHAWL COLLAR SWEATER

MATERIALS
General yarn weight used – double knitting (knitting worsted)
Rowan *Designer DK* (50g/1¾oz doughnuts) in the foll 17 colours:
  A (628) navy – 1[1,2] hanks
  B (99) clerical purple – 1[1,1] hank
  C (56F) royal – 1[1,1] hank
  D (77F) sienna fleck – 1[1,1] hank
  E (90) emerald – 1[1,1] hank
  F (647) peacock – 1[1,1] hank
  G (639) sludge – 1[1,1] hank
  H (127) amethyst – 1[1,1] hank
  J (655) forest – 1[1,1] hank
  L (65) dark airforce – 1[1,1] ball
  N (71) chestnut – 1[1,1] hank
  Q (62) black – 1[1,1] hank
  R (654) blue grey – 1[1,1] hank
  S (501) lavender – 1[1,1] hank
  T (652) grape – 1[1,1] hank
  U (650) gold – 1[1,1] hank
  V (660) citrine – 1[1,1] hank
Rowan *Lightweight DK* (25g/1oz hanks) in the foll colour:
  W (57) lapis – 1[1,1] hank
Rowan *Silkstones* (50g/1¾oz hanks) in the foll 2 colours:
  X (830) mulled wine – 1[1,1] hank
  Y (831) orchid – 1[1,1] hank
One pair each 3¼mm (US size 3) and 4mm (US size 6) knitting needles *or size to obtain correct tension(gauge)*
3¼mm (US size 3) circular needle

SIZES
To fit 2[4,6]yrs or 53[56,61]cm/21[22,24]in chest.
Figures for larger sizes are given in square brackets; where there is only one set of figures, it applies to all sizes.
For finished measurements see diagram (page 156).

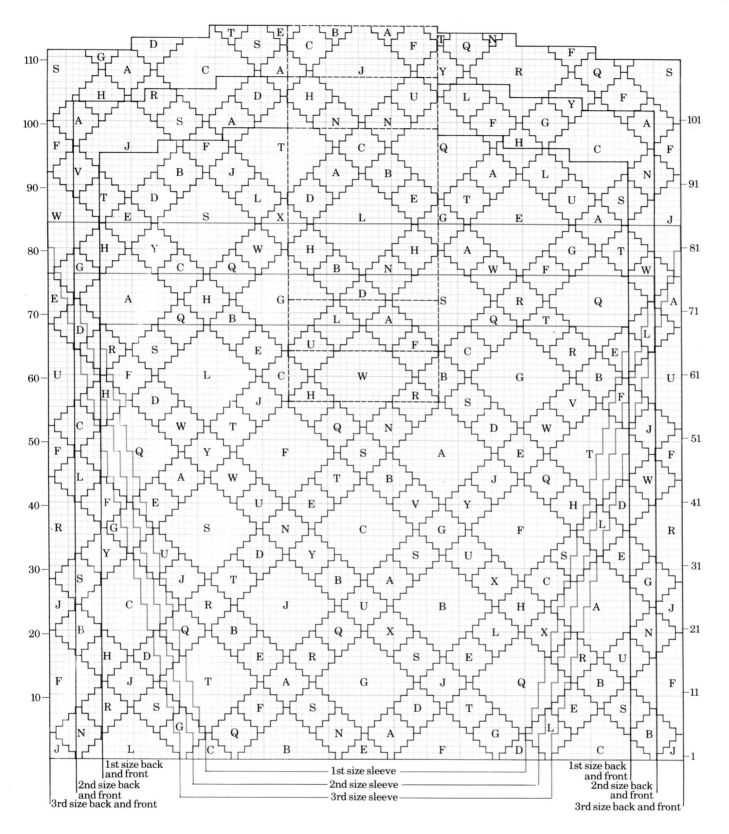

RIGHT *Grandmother's Sunday best looks good against the wonderful purple colourway of the Child's Harlequin Shawl Collar Sweater.*

TENSION(GAUGE)

23 sts and 29 rows to 10cm/4in over patt on 4mm (US size 6) needles.
Check your tension(gauge) before beginning.

NOTES

Yarns X and Y are used double throughout. When working in patt from Chart, read odd rows (K) from right to left and even rows (P) from left to right.

BACK

Using smaller needles and A, cast on 69[75,81] sts.
Work 17 rows in K1, P1 rib in stripes as foll:
2 rows A, 3 rows B, 1 row C, 3 rows D, 1 row E, 1 row F, 3 rows G, 1 row H, 1 row C, 1 row A.
Inc row (ws) With A, rib 7[5,3], make 1, * rib 5, make 1; rep from * to last 7[5,3] sts, rib to end. 81[89,97] sts.
Change to larger needles and cont in patt as foll:
Beg with a K row and working in st st throughout cont in patt from Chart, beginning and ending rows as indicated until 94[102,110] rows in all have been worked in patt, so ending with a ws row.

Shoulder Shaping

Keeping patt correct, cast(bind) off 9[11,13] sts at beg of next 2 rows, then 10[11,12] sts at beg of foll 4 rows. Leave rem 23 sts on a holder for collar.

FRONT

Work as given for Back until 56[64,72] rows in all have been worked in patt.

Neck Shaping

Next row (rs) Patt 29[33,37], cast(bind) off 23 sts, patt to end.
Cont on last set of sts only for right front:
Work without shaping until 95[103,111] rows in all have been worked in patt, so ending with a rs row.

Shoulder Shaping

Keeping patt correct, cast(bind) off 9[11,13] sts at

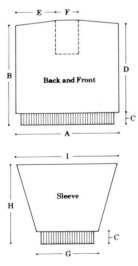

CHILD'S HARLEQUIN
SHAWL COLLAR SWEATER
A = 35[39,42]cm/14[15½,17]in
B = 37.5[40,43]cm/15[16,17]in
C = 5cm/2in
D = 32.5[35,38]cm/13[14,15]in
E = 12.5[14.5,16]cm/
5[5¾,6½]in
F = 10cm/4in
G = 21.5[23,24.5]cm/
8½[9¼,9¾]in
H = 28.5[31,34]cm/
11¼[12½,13½]in
I = 35[39,42]cm/14[15½,16¾]in

156

beg of next row, then 10[11,12] sts at beg of foll alt row.
Work 1 row without shaping, then cast(bind) off rem 10[11,12] sts.
Return to sts which were left; with ws facing rejoin yarns to neck edge and patt to end. Complete to match first side, reversing shaping.

SLEEVES

Using smaller needles and A, cast on 41[43,45] sts and work 17 rows in striped rib as for Back.
Inc row (ws) With A, rib 3[4,6], make 1, * rib 5[4,3], make 1; rep from * to last 3[3,6] sts, rib to end. 49[53,57] sts.
Change to larger needles and cont in patt as foll:
Beg with a K row and working in st st throughout cont in patt from Chart, beginning and ending rows as indicated AND AT THE SAME TIME, inc one st at each end of the 5th and every foll 4th row, working inc sts into patt until there are 81[89,97] sts.
Cont without shaping until 68[76,84] rows in all have been worked in patt, so ending with a ws row.
Cast(bind) off *loosely*.
Make a 2nd sleeve in the same way.

FINISHING

Press work lightly on ws according to instructions on bands, omitting ribbing.
Using backstitch, join shoulder seams.

COLLAR

Using circular needle, A and with rs facing, pick up and K 43 sts evenly up right front neck, K back neck sts from holder, then pick up and K 43 sts evenly down left front neck.
109 sts.
Work backwards and forwards in rows.
Work 33 rows in P1, K1 rib in stripes as foll:
2 rows A, 3 rows B, 1 row C, 3 rows D, 1 row E, 1 row F, 3 rows G, 1 row H, 1 row C, 2 rows A, 2 rows Q, 1 row J, 3 rows S, 1 row Y, 2 rows B, 1 row C, 1 row E, 4 rows J.
Using J, cast(bind) off *very loosely* in rib.
Overlap right side of collar over left and using an edge to edge st sew row ends to cast-(bound-)off sts at centre front. Mark back and front at side edge 17.5[19.5,21]cm/7[7¾,8½]in down from shoulder. Using backstitch, join cast-(bound-)off edge of sleeves to back and front between markers, matching centre of top of sleeve to shoulder. Press seams. Using backstitch on main knitting and an edge to edge st on rib, join side and sleeve seams. Press all seams.

CHILD'S TURKISH LATTICE BUTTON SHOULDER SWEATER

MATERIALS

General yarn weight used – double lightweight knitting (sport)
Rowan *Lightweight DK* (25g/1oz hanks) in the foll 9 colours:
  A (52) steel blue – 1[2,2,2,3,3] hanks
  B (108) indigo – 1[1,1,1,1,1] hank
  C (53) sea blue – 1[1,1,2,2,2] hanks
  D (122) pale blue – 1[1,1,2,2,2] hanks
  E (50) china blue – 1[1,1,2,2,2] hanks
  F (55) lobelia – 1[1,2,2,2,3] hanks
  G (60) silver – 1[1,1,1,1,1] hank

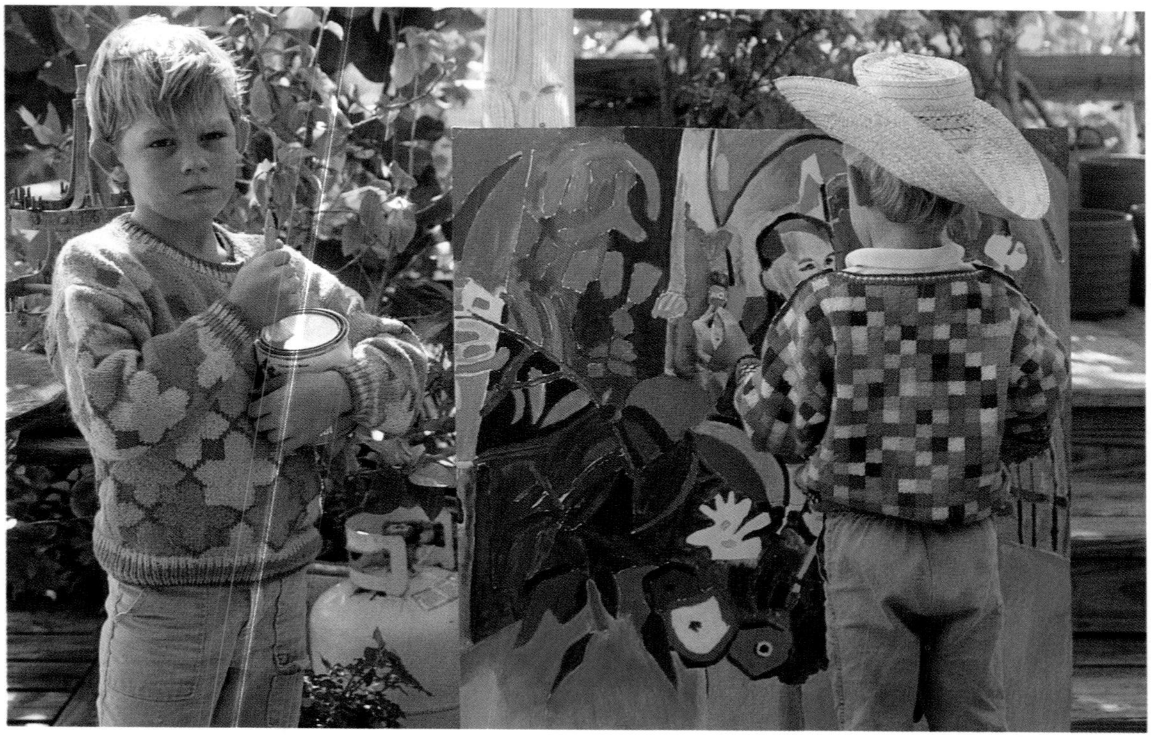

LEFT *A Child's Turkish Lattice Crewneck Sweater and a Child's Squares Button Shoulder Sweater, page 12.*

OVERLEAF *An Adult's Turkish Lattice Scoopneck Sweater and a Child's Turkish Lattice Crewneck Sweater photographed in Morocco and in Key West. The adult's sweater is also seen as the background and is available in kit form.*

H (616) donkey – 1[1,1,1,1,1] hank
J (82) camel – 1[1,1,1,1,1] hank
Rowan *Light Tweed* (25g/1oz hanks) in the foll 6 colours:
L (223) atlantic – 1[1,1,1,2,2] hanks
M (221) pacific – 1[1,1,1,1,1] hanks
N (210) charcoal – 1[1,1,2,2,2] hanks
Q (205) autumn – 1[1,1,1,1,1] hank
R (203) pebble – 1[1,1,1,1,1] hank
S (222) lakeland – 1[1,1,1,2,2] hanks
Rowan *Grainy Silks* (50g/1¾oz hanks) in the foll 3 colours:
T (802) crow – 1[1,1,1,1,1] hank
U (812) blackcurrant – 1[1,1,1,1,1] hank
V (804) slate – 1[1,1,1,1,1] hank
Rowan *Silkstones* (50g/1¾oz hanks) in the foll 2 colours:
W (825) dried rose – 1[1,1,1,1,1] hank
Z (832) blue mist – 1[1,1,1,1,1] hank
One pair each 2¾mm (US size 2) and 3¼mm (US size 3) knitting needles *or size to obtain correct tension(gauge)*
6 buttons

SIZES

To fit 2[4,6,8,10,12]yrs or 53[56,61,66,71,76]cm/ 21[22,24,26,28,30]in chest.
Figures for larger sizes are given in square brackets; where there is only one set of figures, it applies to all sizes.
For finished measurements see diagram.

TENSION(GAUGE)

26 sts and 34 rows to 10cm/4in over patt on 3¼mm (US size 3) needles.
Check your tension(gauge) before beginning.

NOTES

Always carry 'lattice' colour (N,T and U) to the end of row when in use. Twist each 'cross' colour (L,A,E,S etc.) round the 'lattice' colour and the 'cross' colour just worked.
When working in patt from Chart (pages 160-161), read odd rows (K) from right to left and even rows (P) from left to right.

BACK

Using smaller needles and F, cast on 76[82,88,94,100,106] sts.
Work 19 rows in K1, P1 rib in stripes as foll:
2 rows N, 1 row R, 2 rows A, 2 rows M, 1 row B, 3 rows S, 2 rows W, 1 row D, 1 row F, 1 row N, 2 rows L, 1 row J.
<u>Inc row</u> (ws) With J, rib 5[2,7,5,3,11], make 1, * rib 6[6,5,5,5,4], make 1; rep from * to last 5[2,6,4,2,11] sts, rib to end.
88[96,104,112,120,128] sts.
Change to larger needles and cont in patt as foll:
Beg with a K row and working in st st throughout cont in patt from Chart, beginning and ending rows as indicated until 99[109,119,129,139,149] rows in all have been worked in patt.

Neck Shaping

<u>Next row</u> (ws) Patt 27[30,33,36,39,42], cast (bind) off 34[36,38,40,42,44] sts, patt to end.
Cont on last set of sts only for right back:
<u>Next row</u> Patt to end.
Keeping patt correct, cast(bind) off 2 sts at beg of next and foll alt row.
Leave rem 23[26,29,32,35,38] sts on a spare needle.
Return to sts which were left; with rs facing rejoin yarns to neck edge, cast(bind) off 2 sts and patt to end. Work 1 row without shaping.
Keeping patt correct, cast(bind) off 2 sts at beg of next row. Work 1 row without shaping.
Leave rem 23[26,29,32,35,38] sts on a spare needle.

FRONT

Work as given for Back until 88[98,108,116, 126,136] rows in all have been worked in patt.

Neck Shaping

<u>Next row</u> (rs) Patt 36[39,42,45,48,51], cast (bind) off 16[18,20,22,24,26] sts, patt to end.
Cont on last set of sts only for right front:
<u>Next row</u> Patt to end.
Keeping patt correct, cast(bind) off 4 sts at beg of next row, 3 sts at beg of foll alt row, 2 sts at beg of

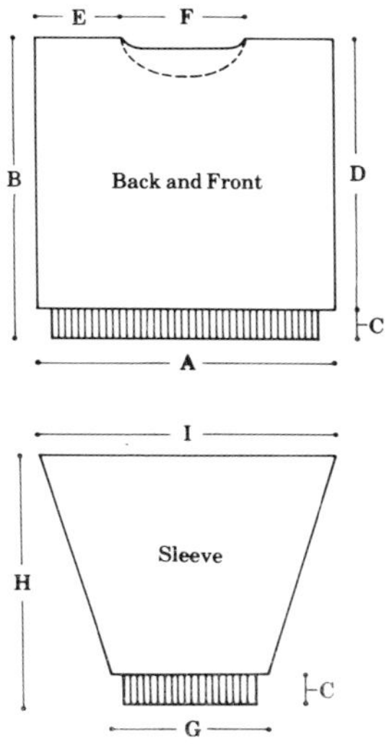

CHILD'S TURKISH LATTICE BUTTON SHOULDER SWEATER
A = 34[37,40,43,46,49]cm/ 13½[14¾,16,17¼,18½,19½]in
B = 35.5[38.5,41.5,44.5,47.5, 50.5]cm/ 14¼[15½,16½,17¾,19,20]in
C = 5cm/2in
D = 30.5[33.5,36.5,39.5,42.5, 45.5]cm/ 12¼[13½,14½,15¾,17,18]in
E = 9[10,11,12.5,13.5,14.5]cm/ 3½[4,4½,5,5½,5¾]in
F = 16[17,18,18,19,20]cm/ 6½[6¾,7,7¼,7½,8]in
G = 18.5[20,21.5,23,24.5,26]cm/ 7½[8,8½,9¼,9¾,10½]in
H = 28[31,34,37,40,43]cm/ 11[12¼,13½,14½,16,17]in
I = 32[35,38,41,44,47]cm/ 13[14,15,16½,18,19]in

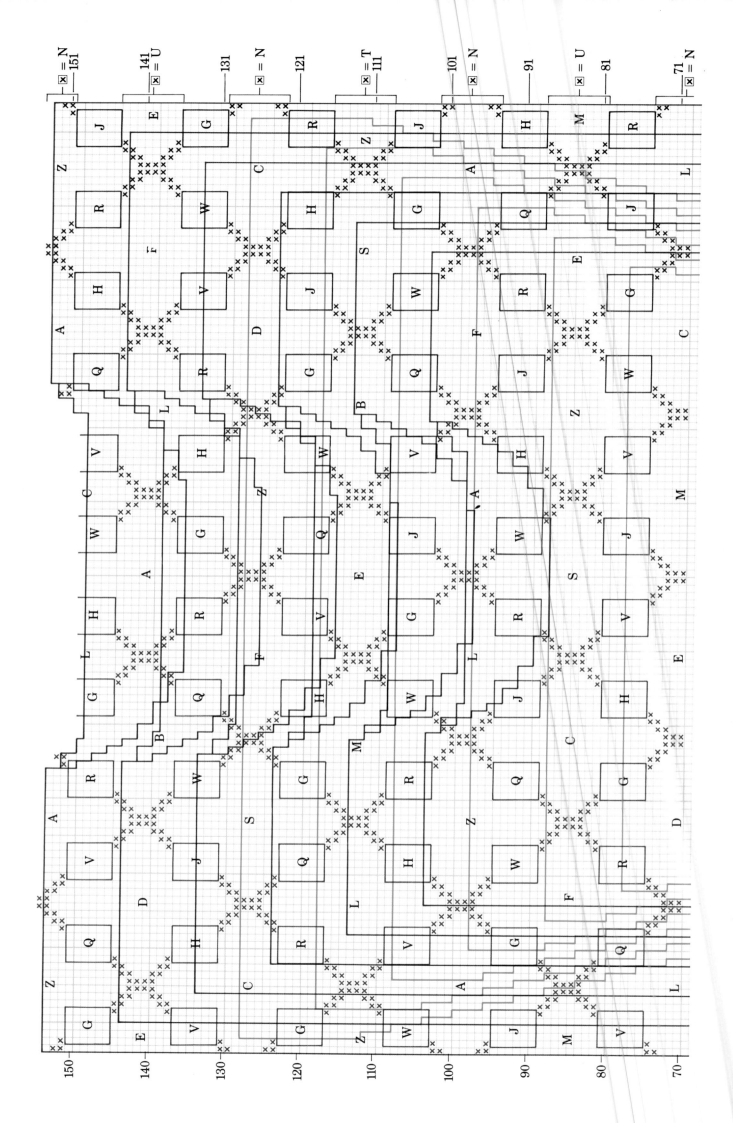

160

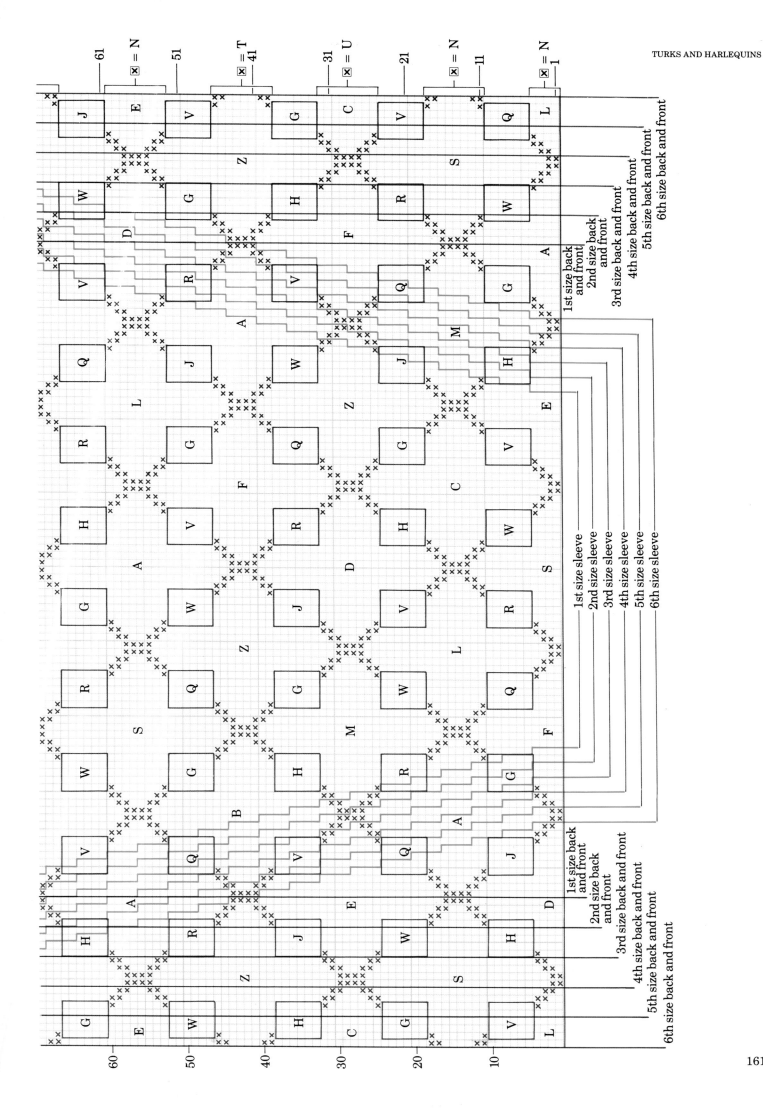

foll alt row, then one st at beg of foll 4 alt rows.
23[26,29,32,35,38] sts.
Work 1[1,1,3,3,3] rows without shaping, so ending
with a ws row. Leave these sts on a spare needle.
Return to sts which were left; with ws facing rejoin
yarns to neck edge, cast(bind) off 4 sts and patt to
end.
Complete to match first side, reversing all shaping.

SLEEVES
Using smaller needles and F, cast on
42[44,46,48,50,52] sts and work 19 rows in striped
rib as for Back.
Inc row (ws) With J, rib 4[5,5,2,6,4], make 1, * rib
7[5,4,4,3,3], make 1; rep from * to last 3[4,5,2,5,3]
sts, rib to end. 48[52,56,60,64,68] sts.
Change to larger needles and cont in patt as foll:
Beg with a K row and working in st st throughout
cont in patt from Chart, beginning and ending
rows as indicated AND AT THE SAME TIME, inc one
st at each end of the 5th and every foll 4th row,
working inc sts into patt until there are
84[92,100,108,116,124] sts.
Cont without shaping until 78[88,98,108,118,128]
rows in all have been worked in st st, so ending
with a ws row.
Cast(bind) off *loosely*.
Make a 2nd sleeve in the same way.

FINISHING
Press work lightly on ws according to instructions
on bands, omitting ribbing.

BACK NECKBAND
Using smaller needles, A and with rs facing, K
across 23[26,29,32,35,38] sts of right shoulder,
pick up and K 46[48,50,52,54,56] sts evenly
around back neck, then K across 23[26,29,
32,35,38] sts of left shoulder.
92[100,108,116,124,132] sts.
Work 6 rows in K1, P1 rib in stripes as foll:
2 rows A, 1 row R, 2 rows N, 1 row F.
Using F, cast(bind) off *loosely* in rib.

Front Neckband
Using smaller needles, A and with rs facing, K
across 23[26,29,32,35,38] sts of left shoulder, pick
up and K 60[62,64,70,72,74] sts evenly around
front neck, then K across 23[26,29,32,35,38] sts of
right shoulder.
106[114,122,134,142,150] sts.
1st row With A, rib to end.
2nd row With A, rib 5[6,7,8,9,10], cast (bind) off 2
sts, * rib 5[6,7,8,9,10] including st already on
needle, cast(bind) off 2 sts *; rep from * to * once
more, rib 64[66,68,74,76,78] including st already
on needle, cast(bind) off 2 sts; rep from * to * twice
more, rib to end.
3rd row With R, rib to end, casting on 2 sts over
each 2 cast(bound) off.
4th and 5th rows With N, rib to end.
6th row With F, rib to end.
Using F, cast(bind) off *loosely* in rib.
Overlap front neckband on to back neckband and
over sew at armhole edges. Mark back and front at
side edge 16[17.5,19,20.5,22,23.5]cm/6½[7,7½,
8¼,9,9½]in down from shoulder. Using backstitch, join cast-(bound-)off edge of sleeves to back
and front between markers, matching centre of
top of sleeve to shoulder. Press seams. Using backstitch on main knitting and an edge to edge st on
rib, join side and sleeve seams. Press all seams.
Sew on buttons.

ADULT'S TURKISH LATTICE SLEEVELESS SWEATER

MATERIALS
General yarn weight used – lightweight double
knitting (sport)
Rowan *Lightweight DK* (25g/1oz hanks) in the foll
10 colours:
  A (88) pale airforce – 1[2,2] hanks
  B (52) steel blue – 1[1,1] hank
  C (108) indigo – 1[1,1] hank
  D (53) sea blue – 1[1,1] hank
  E (122) pale blue – 1[1,1] hank
  F (61) dark grey – 1[1,1] hank
  G (129) elephant – 1[1,1] hank
  H (60) silver – 1[1,1] hank
  J (616) donkey – 1[1,1] hank
  L (82) camel – 1[1,1] hank
Rowan *Light Tweed* (25g/1oz hanks) in the foll 6
colours:
  M (203) pebble – 1[1,1] hank
  N (221) pacific – 1[1,1] hank
  Q (223) atlantic – 1[1,1] hank
  R (222) lakeland – 1[1,1] hank
  S (205) autumn – 1[1,1] hank
  T (210) charcoal – 1[2,2] hanks
Rowan *Fine Cotton Chenille* (50g/1¾oz balls) in
the foll 2 colours:
  U (380) mole – 1[1,1] ball
  V (378) shark – 1[1,1] ball
Rowan *Grainy Silks* (50g/1¾oz hanks) in the foll 6
colours:
  W (804) slate – 1[1,1] hank
  X (801) flint – 1[1,1] hank
  Y (802) crow – 1[1,1] hank
  Z (812) blackcurrant – 1[1,1] hank
  a (809) twine – 1[1,1] hank
  b (810) petrol – 1[1,1] hank
Rowan *Silkstones* (50g/1¾oz hanks) in the foll 2
colours:
  d (832) blue mist – 1[1,1] hank
  e (825) dried rose – 1[1,1] hank
One pair each 2¾mm (US size 2) and 3¼mm (US
size 3) knitting needles *or size to obtain correct ten-
sion(gauge)*
2¾mm (US size 2) circular needle

SIZES
To fit 96[102,107]cm/38[40,42]in chest.
*Figures for larger sizes are given in square
brackets; where there is only one set of figures, it
applies to all sizes.*
For finished measurements see diagram.

TENSION(GAUGE)
26 sts and 34 rows to 10cm/4in over patt on 3¼mm
(US size 3) needles.
Check your tension(gauge) before beginning.

NOTES
*Carry 'lattice' colour (yarn T, Y or Z) to end of the
row when in use. Always twist each 'cross' colour
(W, J, G, etc.) round the 'lattice' colour and the
'cross' colour just worked.*
*When working in patt from Chart (pages 166-167),
read odd rows (K) from right to left and even rows
(P) from left to right.*

BACK
Using smaller needles and A, cast on 116[126,136]
sts. Work 21 rows in K1, P1 rib in stripes as foll:

1 row E, 2 rows a, 1 row T, 1 row D, 2 rows G, 1 row N, 1 row B, 1 row J, 2 rows H, 1 row b, 1 row A, 2 rows d, 1 row E, 2 rows W, 1 row R, 1 row L.

Inc row (ws) With L, rib 7[4,9], make 1, * rib 6[7,7], make 1; rep from * to last 7[3,8] sts, rib to end. 134[144,154] sts.

Change to larger needles and cont in patt as foll: Beg with a K row and working in st st throughout cont to work in patt from Chart, beginning and ending rows as indicated until 102[106,110] rows in all have been worked in patt, so ending with a ws row. **

Armhole Shaping
Keeping patt correct, cast(bind) off 8[9,10] sts at beg of next 2 rows, 3 sts at beg of foll 2 rows, 2 sts at beg of next 4[6,8] rows, then one st at beg of foll 16[14,12] rows. 88[94,100] sts.

Cont without shaping until 180[188,196] rows in all have been worked in patt, so ending with a ws row.

Shoulder Shaping
Keeping patt correct, cast(bind) off 8[9,9] sts at beg of next 2 rows, 8[8,9] sts at beg of foll 2 rows, then 7[8,9] sts at beg of next 2 rows.
Leave rem 42[44,46] sts on a holder for neckband.

FRONT
Work as given for Back to **.

Armhole and Neck Shaping
Next row (rs) Cast(bind) off 10[11,12] sts, patt 55[59,63] including st already on needle, K2 tog, K2 tog tbl, patt to end.
Cont on last set of sts only for right front:
Next row Cast(bind) off 10[11,12] sts, patt to end.
Next row Patt to end.
Next row Cast(bind) off 3 sts, patt to end.
Keeping patt correct, dec one st at beg of next and every foll 4th row AND AT THE SAME TIME, cast(bind) off 2 sts at beg of foll 1[2,3] alt rows, then one st at beg of foll 8[7,6] alt rows.
Keeping armhole edge straight, cont to dec at neck edge only on every 4th row as set until 181[189,197] rows in all have been worked in patt, so ending with a rs row. 24[26,28] sts.

Shoulder and Neck Shaping
Keeping patt correct, cast(bind) off 8[9,9] sts at beg of next row, one st at beg of foll row, then 8[8,9] sts at beg of next row. Work 1 row without shaping, then cast(bind) off rem 7[8,9] sts.
Return to sts which were left; with ws facing rejoin yarns to neck edge and patt to end.
Next row Cast(bind) off 3 sts, patt to end.
Next row Patt to end.
Keeping patt correct, dec one st at end of next and every foll 4th row AND AT THE SAME TIME, cast(bind) off 2 sts at beg of next and foll 0[1,2] alt rows, then one st at beg of foll 8[7,6] alt rows.
Keeping armhole edge straight, cont to dec at neck edge only on every 4th row as set until 180[188,196] rows in all have been worked in patt, so ending with a ws row. 24[26,28] sts.

Shoulder and Neck Shaping
Keeping patt correct, cast(bind) off 8[9,9] sts at beg of next row. Work 1 row without shaping.
Next row Cast(bind) off 8[8,9] sts, patt to last 2 sts, K2 tog.
Work 1 row without shaping, then cast(bind) off rem 7[8,9] sts.

FINISHING
Press work lightly on ws according to instructions on bands, omitting ribbing.
Using backstitch, join left shoulder seam.

NECKBAND
Using circular needle, F and with rs facing, K back neck sts from holder, pick up and K 83[87,91] sts evenly down left front neck and 83[87,91] sts evenly up right front neck.
208[218,228] sts.
Work backwards and forwards in rows.
Beg with K1, cont in K1, P1 rib as foll:
1st row (ws) With e, rib 81[85,89], P2 tog, P2 tog tbl, rib to end.
2nd row With G, rib 122[128,134], K2 tog tbl, K2 tog, rib to end.
Work 6 more rows in rib as set, dec at centre front on every row and working in stripes of 1 row D, 1 row T, 2 rows a, 1 row E, 1 row A. With A, cast(bind) off in rib, still dec at centre front.
Using backstitch on main knitting and an edge to edge st on rib, join right shoulder and neckband seam. Press seams.

Armhole Borders
Using circular needle and a, with rs facing, pick up and K 156[166,176] sts around armhole edge (29[31,33] sts from shaped sections and approximately 7 sts for every 8 straight rows).
Work backwards and forwards in rows.
1st row With E, P to end.
2nd row With A, K to end.
Hem edge row With A, K to end.
Cont in A only as foll:
Beg with a K row work 4 rows in st st to form hem. Cast(bind) off loosely.
Press armhole borders to inside on hemline.
Using backstitch, on main knitting and an edge to edge st on rib, join side and armhole border seams. Press all seams. Turn in hems on armhole borders and sl st lightly on ws.

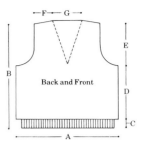

ADULT'S TURKISH LATTICE SLEEVELESS SWEATER
A = 51.5[55.5,59]cm/20½[22,23½]in
B = 58[60,63]cm/23[24,25]in
C = 5cm/2in
D = 30[31,32.5]cm/12[12½,13]in
E = 23[24,25.5]cm/9[9½,10]in
F = 9[9.5,10]cm/3½[4,4¼]in
G = 16[17,18]cm/6½[6¾,7]in

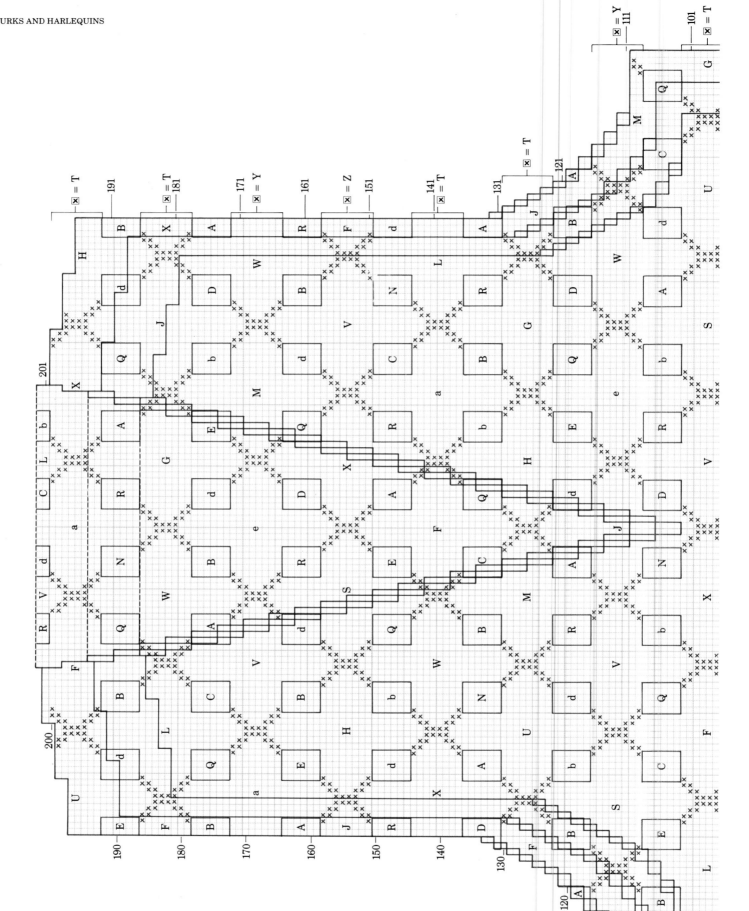

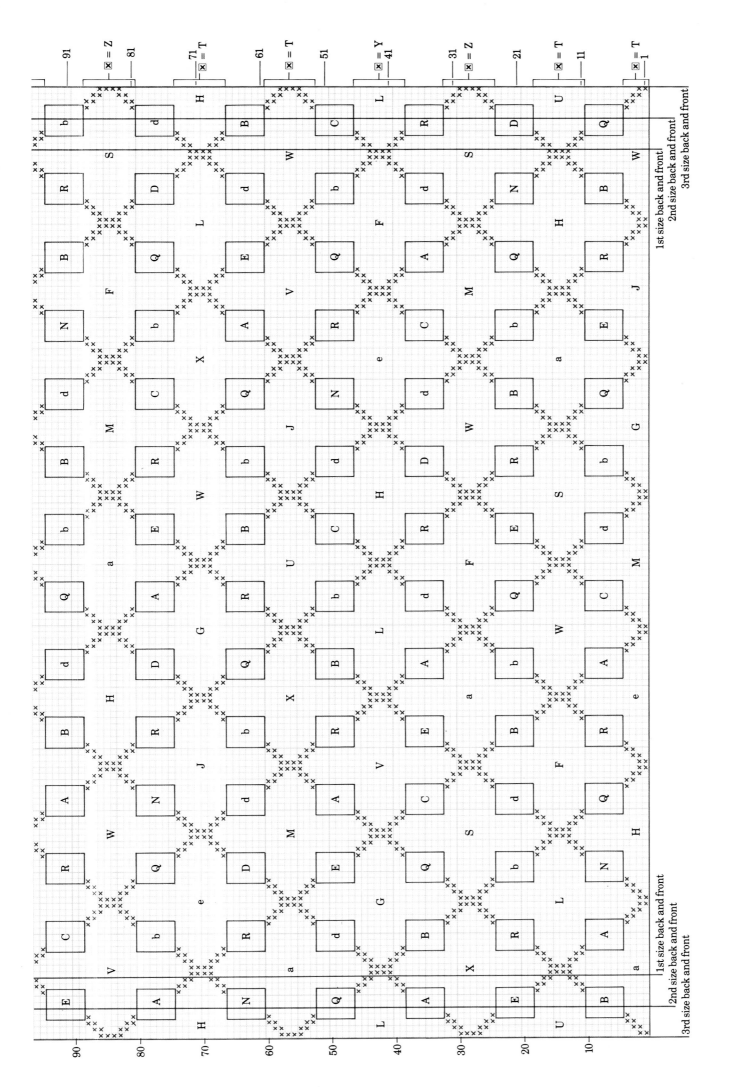

167

DIAMONDS AND PATCHES

I first saw the diamond design on a patterned furnishing fabric and realized then the possibilities for a good fair-isle knitting pattern. When the diamonds are split in half by colour, the crisp, pointed shapes seem to break up the two-colour-in-a-row stripiness, helping to make the eye move over the design. It works well with contrasting colours or many shades of one colour with quite different coloured centres to the diamonds.

I have knitted up a Split Diamond jacket in tweedy muted tones – dark maroon, ochres and forest green. This works well for an antique oriental brocade look, but the design really springs to life in strong pastels. How about shades of yellow from pale primrose to deep golden yellow with sky blue, lavender and mint green centres? Sounds delicious.

Patchwork quilts supply knitters with exciting vehicles for colour. I have often been thrilled by their use of geometric structure and the Circle Square is a case in point. This satisfying design came from an old bed quilt. The segmented circle in its quartered box is a good layout for bright contrasting colours or even for a more monotone effect. The quilt had a smaller circle floating in the centre of the square. We felt that a full circle touching the sides of the square was more stylish, but you could try either version. Perhaps a variety of proportions would be more interesting in the same garment. My own favourite in this book is Zoë's brilliant green and magenta skirt (page 176). It has the richness of stained glass and the tantric art of India. The grey, blue and beige colourway (page 188) is infinitely wearable and looks handsome worn with faded jeans or grey flannel.

We have knitted a solid colour within each segment of the design. You could shade each colour to bring a subtle richness to this motif. It could become as textured as marble mosaic or wood inlay.

The Circle Square design is worked in intarsia throughout. I found the best way was to break off short lengths for the corners of the circle and try to keep the balls attached for the quarters of the circles. If you find you can estimate how long a piece of yarn is needed for each quarter, you will have fewer tangles.

RIGHT *The Child's Split Diamond Button Shoulder Sweater, page 174, amidst a riot of sweet peas in Morocco. This pattern is available in kit form.*

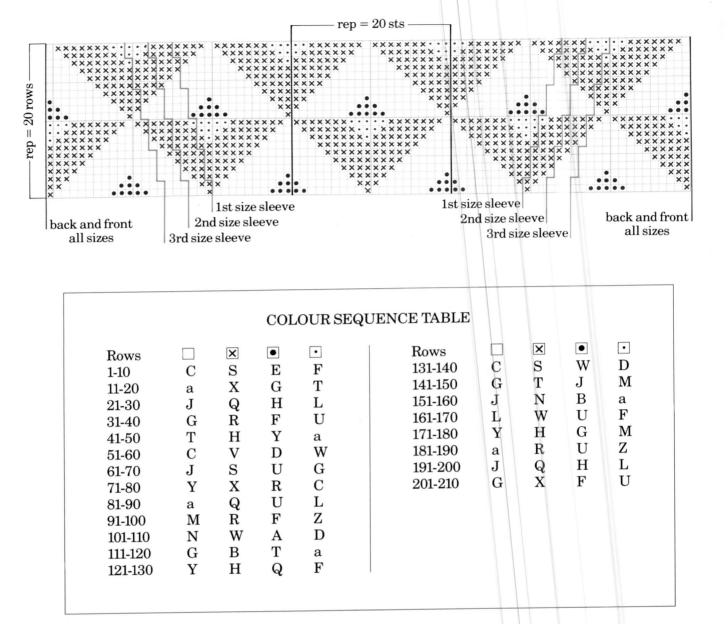

rep = 20 sts

rep = 20 rows

back and front all sizes | 1st size sleeve / 2nd size sleeve / 3rd size sleeve

1st size sleeve / 2nd size sleeve / 3rd size sleeve | back and front all sizes

COLOUR SEQUENCE TABLE

Rows	□	☒	●	·		Rows	□	☒	●	·
1-10	C	S	E	F		131-140	C	S	W	D
11-20	a	X	G	T		141-150	G	T	J	M
21-30	J	Q	H	L		151-160	J	N	B	a
31-40	G	R	F	U		161-170	L	W	U	F
41-50	T	H	Y	a		171-180	Y	H	G	M
51-60	C	V	D	W		181-190	a	R	U	Z
61-70	J	S	U	G		191-200	J	Q	H	L
71-80	Y	X	R	C		201-210	G	X	F	U
81-90	a	Q	U	L						
91-100	M	R	F	Z						
101-110	N	W	A	D						
111-120	G	B	T	a						
121-130	Y	H	Q	F						

ADULT'S SPLIT DIAMOND CREWNECK SWEATER

MATERIALS

General yarn weight used – lightweight cotton
Rowan *Soft Cotton* (50g/1¾oz balls) in the foll 12 colours:

A (546) strawberry ice – 1[1,1] ball
B (543) purple – 1[1,1] ball
C (527) smoke – 1[2,2] balls
D (545) sugar pink – 1[1,1] ball
E (542) bluebell – 1[1,1] ball
F (534) frolic – 1[1,1] ball
G (539) bermuda – 1[2,2] balls
H (531) fiord – 1[1,2] balls
J (533) antique pink – 1[1,2] balls
L (528) rain cloud – 1[1,1] ball
M (549) dove grey – 1[1,1] ball
N (530) polka – 1[1,1] ball

Rowan *Knobbly Cotton* (50g/1¾oz balls) in the foll 7 colours:

Q (569) jade – 1[2,2] balls
R (575) marine – 2[2,2] balls
S (570) electric blue – 1[1,2] balls
T (566) hyacinth – 1[1,1] ball
U (568) bright pink – 1[1,1] ball
V (573) cornflower – 1[1,1] ball
W (571) fresh green – 1[1,1] ball

Rowan *Cabled Mercerised Cotton* (50g/1¾oz balls) in the foll 4 colours:

X (310) rich purple – 1[1,2] balls
Y (311) pale mauve – 1[1,2] balls
Z (323) hydro – 1[1,1] ball
a (314) furnace – 1[2,2] balls

One pair each 2¼mm (US size 1) and 3mm (US size 3) knitting needles *or size to obtain correct tension(gauge)*

SIZES

To fit 86-91[96-102,107-112]cm/34-36[38-40,42-44]in bust/chest.

Figures for larger sizes are given in square brackets; where there is only one set of figures, it applies to all sizes.
For finished measurements see diagram.

PREVIOUS PAGE *The Adult's Split Diamond Crewneck Sweater is shown with the Child's Split Diamond Button Shoulder Sweater, page 174. Both are available in kit form.*

TENSION(GAUGE)
30 sts and 33 rows to 10cm/4in over patt on 3mm (US size 3) needles.
Check your tension(gauge) before beginning.

NOTES
When working in patt from Chart, read odd rows (K) from right to left and even rows (P) from left to right.

BACK
Using smaller needles and R, cast on 136[152,168] sts.
Work 21 rows in K1, P1 rib in stripes as foll:
1 row R, (2 rows Q, 2 rows R) 5 times.
Inc row (ws) With R, rib 8[6,4], make 1, * rib 5, make 1; rep from * to last 8[6,4] sts, rib to end. 161[181,201] sts.
Change to larger needles and cont in patt as foll:
Beg with a K row and working in st st throughout cont in patt from Chart beginning and ending rows as indicated, rep rows 1-20 to form patt *but* work in different colours as shown in colour sequence table.
Cont until 176[186,196] rows in all have been worked in patt.

Shoulder and Neck Shaping
Next row (rs) Cast(bind) off 16[19,22] sts, patt 46[52,58] including st already on needle, cast(bind) off 37[39,41] sts, patt to end.
Cont on last set of sts only for left back:
Keeping patt correct, cast(bind) off 16[19,22] sts at beg of next row, 9 sts at beg of foll row, 15[18,21] sts at beg of next row, then 7 sts at beg of foll row.
Cast(bind) off rem 15[18,21] sts. Return to sts which were left; with ws facing rejoin yarns to neck edge, cast(bind) off 9 sts and patt to end.
Keeping patt correct, cast(bind) off 15[18,21] sts at beg of next row, then 7 sts at beg of foll row.
Cast(bind) off rem 15[18,21] sts.

FRONT
Work as given for Back until 150[160,170] rows in all have been worked in patt.

Neck Shaping
Next row (rs) Patt 69[78,87], cast(bind) off 23[25,27] sts, patt to end.
Cont on last set of sts only for right front:
Next row Patt to end.
Keeping patt correct, cast(bind) off 4 sts at beg of next row, 3 sts at beg of foll 3 alt rows, 2 sts at beg of foll 3 alt rows, then one st at beg of foll 4 alt rows. 46[55,64] sts.
Work 4 rows without shaping.

Shoulder Shaping
Cast(bind) off 16[19,22] sts at beg of next row, then 15[18,21] sts at beg of foll alt row.
Work 1 row without shaping, then cast (bind) off rem 15[18,21] sts.
Return to sts which were left; with ws facing rejoin yarns to neck edge, cast(bind) off 4 sts and patt to end.
Complete to match first side, reversing all shaping.

SLEEVES
Using smaller needles and R, cast on 66[72,76] sts and work 21 rows in striped rib as for Back.
Inc row (ws) With R, rib 3[6,3], make 1, * rib 5, make 1; rep from * to last 3[6,3] sts, rib to end. 79[85,91] sts.
Change to larger needles and cont in patt as foll:
Beg with a K row and working in st st throughout cont in patt from Chart, beginning and ending rows as indicated, working same colour sequence as for Back AND AT THE SAME TIME, inc one st at each end of the 3rd and every foll 4th row, working inc sts into patt until there are 137[149,159] sts.
Cont without shaping until 120[130,140] rows in all have been worked in patt, so ending with a ws row.
Cast(bind) off *loosely*.
Make a 2nd sleeve in the same way.

FINISHING
Press work lightly on ws according to instructions on ball bands, omitting ribbing. Using backstitch, join left shoulder seam.

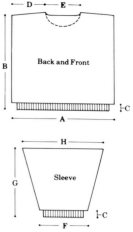

ADULT'S SPLIT DIAMOND CREWNECK SWEATER
A = 53.5[60.5,67]cm/ 21¼[24,26¾]in
B = 58.5[61.5,64.5]cm/ 23½[24½,25¾]in
C = 5cm/2in
D = 15.5[18.5,21.5]cm/ 6[7¼,8½]in
E = 22.5[23.5,24]cm/ 9¼[9½,9¾]in
F = 26.5[28.5,30.5]cm/ 10½[11½,12]in
G = 41.5[44.5,47.5]cm/ 16½[17¾,19]in
H = 45.5[49.5,53]cm/ 18¼[20,21¼]in

LEFT *The Adult's Split Diamond Crewneck Sweater and the Child's Split Diamond Button Shoulder Sweater.*

RIGHT *The Adult's Split Diamond Crewneck Sweater and the Child's Split Diamond Button Shoulder Sweater. The donkey rider is wearing a Child's Diagonal Stripe Sleeveless Sweater.*

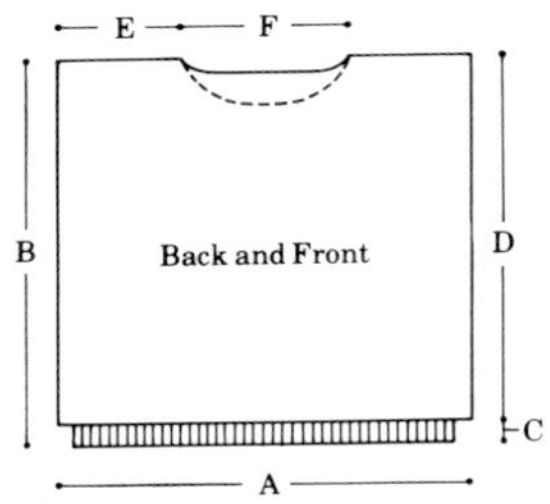

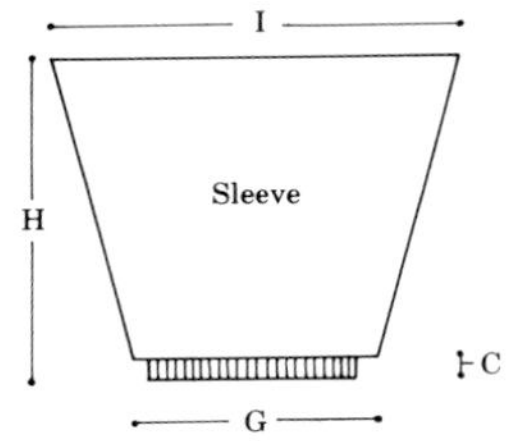

CHILD'S SPLIT DIAMOND BUTTON SHOULDER SWEATER
A = 34[37,40.5,43.5,47, 50.5]cm/ 13½[14¾,16,17½,18½,20]in
B = 33.5[36.5,39.5,42.5, 45.5,48.5]cm/ 13¼[14½,15¾,17,18¼, 19½]in
C = 2.5cm/1in
D = 31[34,37,40,43,46]cm/ 12¼[13½,14¾,16,17¼, 18½]in
E = 9.5[10.5,12,13,14,15]cm/ 3¾[4¼,4¾,5¼,5½,6]in
F = 15[16,16.5,17.5,19, 20.5]cm/ 6[6¼,6½,7,7½,8]in
G = 19[21,23,25,27,29]cm/ 7½[8½,9¼,10,10¾,11½]in
H = 25.5[28.5,31.5,34.5, 37.5,40.5]cm/ 10¼[11½,12½,13¾,15, 16¼]in
I = 31.5[35,38.5,41.5, 45,48.5]cm/ 12½[14,15¼,16½,18,19¼]in

NECKBAND

Using smaller needles, R and with rs facing, pick up and K 73[75,77] sts around back neck and 97[99,101] sts around front neck.
170[174,178] sts.
Work 9 rows in K1, P1 rib in stripes as foll:
1 row R, (2 rows Q, 2 rows R) twice.
Using R, cast(bind) off *loosely* in rib.
Using backstitch on main knitting and an edge to edge st on rib, join right shoulder and neckband seam. Press seams.
Mark back and front at side edge 23[25,26.5]cm/9[10,10½]in down from shoulder seam.
Using backstitch, join cast-(bound-)off edge of sleeves to back and front between markers, matching centre of top of sleeve to shoulder seam. Press seams.
Using backstitch on main knitting and an edge to edge st on rib, join side and sleeve seams.
Press all seams.

CHILD'S SPLIT DIAMOND BUTTON SHOULDER SWEATER

MATERIALS

General yarn weight used – lightweight cotton
Rowan *Knobbly Cotton* (50g/1¾oz balls) in the foll 3 colours:
A (572) rouge – 1[1,2,2,3,3] balls
B (568) bright pink – 1[1,1,2,2,2] balls
C (571) fresh green – 1[1,1,1,1,1] ball
Rowan *Soft Cotton* (50g/1¾oz balls) in the foll 10 colours:
D (534) frolic – 1[1,1,2,2,2] balls
E (545) sugar pink – 1[2,2,2,3,3] balls
F (539) bermuda – 1[1,1,1,1,1] ball
G (542) bluebell – 1[1,1,1,1,1] ball
H (538) pine forest – 1[1,1,1,1,1] ball
J (533) antique pink – 1[1,1,1,1,1] ball
L (546) strawberry ice – 1[1,1,1,2,2] balls
N (527) smoke – 1[1,1,1,1,1] ball
Q (537) apple – 1[1,1,1,1,1] ball
R (528) rain cloud – 1[1,1,1,1,1] ball
Rowan *Cabled Mercerised Cotton* (50g/1¾oz balls) in the foll 7 colours:
S (304) jasmine – 1[1,1,1,1,1] ball
T (313) pastel peach – 1[1,2,2,3,3] balls
U (311) pale mauve – 1[1,1,1,1,1] ball
V (314) furnace – 1[1,1,2,2,2] balls
W (308) french blue – 1[1,1,1,1,1] ball
X (312) old rose – 1[1,1,1,2,2] balls
Y (322) blush – 1[1,1,1,1,1] ball
One pair each 2¼mm (US size 1) and 3mm (US size 3) knitting needles *or size to obtain correct tension(gauge)*
6 buttons

SIZES

To fit 2[4,6,8,10,12]yrs or 53[56,61,66,71,76]cm/ 21[22,24,26,28,30]in chest.
Figures for larger sizes are given in square brackets; where there is only one set of figures, it applies to all sizes.
For finished measurements see diagram.

TENSION(GAUGE)

30 sts and 33 rows to 10cm/4in over patt on 3mm (US size 3) needles.
Check your tension(gauge) before beginning.

NOTES

When working in patt from Chart (page 176), read odd rows (K) from right to left and even rows (P) from left to right.

BACK

Using smaller needles and A, cast on 86[94,102,110,118,126] sts.
Work 11 rows in K1, P1 rib in stripes as foll:
2 rows A, 1 row D, 2 rows E, 2 rows F, 1 row G, 2 rows B, 1 row D.
Inc row (ws) With D, rib 8[7,6,5,4,3], make 1, * rib 5, make 1; rep from * to last 8[7,6,5,4,3] sts, rib to end.
101[111,121,131,141,151] sts.
Change to larger needles and cont in patt as foll:
Beg with a K row and working in st st throughout, *starting with row 5* cont in patt from Chart, beginning and ending rows as indicated work rows 5-20 once, then rep rows 1-20 to form patt, but work in different colours as shown in colour sequence table.
Cont until 96[106,116,126,136,146] rows in all have been worked in patt.

Neck and Shoulder Shaping

Next row (rs) Patt 32[36,40,43,46,49], cast (bind) off 37[39,41,45,49,53] sts, patt to end.
Cont on last set of sts only for left shoulder:
Next row Patt to end.
Keeping patt correct, cast(bind) off 2 sts at beg of next and foll alt row. Work 1 row without shaping.
28[32,36,39,42,45] sts.
Leave these sts on a spare needle.
Return to sts which were left; with ws facing rejoin yarns to neck edge, cast(bind) off 2 sts and patt to end.
Work 1 row without shaping. Cast(bind) off 2 sts at beg of next row. Work 2 rows without shaping.
28[32,36,39,42,45] sts.
Leave these sts on a spare needle.

FRONT

Work as given for Back until 86[96,106,114, 124,134] rows in all have been worked in patt.

Neck Shaping

Next row (rs) Patt 40[44,48,51,54,57], cast (bind) off 21[23,25,29,33,37] sts, patt to end.
Cont on last set of sts only for right front:
Next row Patt to end.
** Keeping patt correct, cast(bind) off 4 sts at beg of next row, 3 sts at beg of foll alt row, 2 sts at beg of foll alt row, then one st at beg of foll 3 alt rows.
28[32,36,39,42,45] sts. **
Work 3[3,3,5,5,5] rows without shaping, so ending with a ws row.
Leave these sts on a spare needle.
Return to sts which were left; with ws facing rejoin yarns to neck edge, work from ** to ** once.
Work 4[4,4,6,6,6] rows without shaping, so ending with a ws row.
Leave these sts on a spare needle.

SLEEVES

Using smaller needles and A, cast on 46[50, 54,58,62,66] sts and work 11 rows in striped rib as for Back.
Inc row (ws) With D, rib 8[7,6,5,4,3], make 1, * rib 3, make 1; rep from * to last 8[7,6,5,4,3] sts, rib to end. 57[63,69,75,81,87] sts.
Change to larger needles and cont in patt as foll:
Beg with a K row and working in st st throughout, *starting with row 5* cont in patt from Chart, begin-

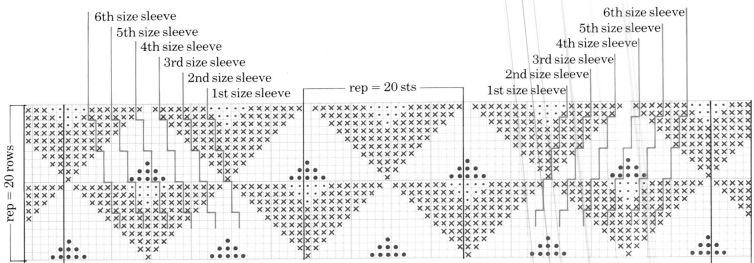

6th size sleeve
5th size sleeve
4th size sleeve
3rd size sleeve
2nd size sleeve
1st size sleeve

rep = 20 sts

6th size sleeve
5th size sleeve
4th size sleeve
3rd size sleeve
2nd size sleeve
1st size sleeve

rep = 20 rows

1st, 3rd and 5th sizes back and front
2nd, 4th and 6th sizes back and front

1st, 3rd and 5th sizes back and front
2nd, 4th and 6th sizes back and front

COLOUR SEQUENCE TABLE

Rows	□	☒	●	·
1-6	D	E		H
7-16	B	T	S	G
17-26	J	U	F	L
27-36	A	E	N	F
37-46	V	T	Q	W
47-56	L	T	U	F
57-66	D	X	N	R
67-76	A	V	S	C
77-86	B	E	Q	F
87-96	Y	T	R	W
97-106	L	X	N	C
107-116	D	E	R	H

Repeat colour sequence,
beginning with row 7
as necessary.

ning and ending rows as indicated work in same colour sequence as for Back AND AT THE SAME TIME, inc one st at each end of the 3rd and every foll 4th row, working inc sts into patt until there are 95 [105,115,125,135,145] sts.
Cont without shaping until 76[86,96,106,116,126] rows in all have been worked in patt. Cast(bind) off *loosely*.
Make a 2nd sleeve in the same way.

FINISHING
Press work lightly on ws according to instructions on ball bands, omitting ribbing.

BACK NECKBAND
Using smaller needles, F and with rs facing, K across 28[32,36,39,42,45] sts of right shoulder, pick up and K 48[50,52,56,60,64] sts evenly around back neck, then K across 28[32,36,39,42,45] sts of left shoulder.
104[114,124,134,144,154] sts.
Work 5 rows in K1, P1 rib in stripes as foll:
1 row F, 2 rows E, 1 row D, 1 row A.
Using A, cast(bind) off *loosely* in rib.

FRONT NECKBAND
Using smaller needles, F and with rs facing, K across 28[32,36,39,42,45] sts of left shoulder, pick up and K 63[65,67,75,79,83] sts evenly around front neck, then K across 28[32,36,39,42,45] sts of right shoulder.
119[129,139,153,163,173] sts.
<u>1st row</u> With F, work in K1, P1 rib to end.
<u>2nd row</u> With E, rib 6[8,10,11,12,13], cast (bind) off 2 sts, * rib 7[8,9,10,11,12] including st already on needle, cast(bind) off 2 sts *; rep from * to * once more, rib 67[69,71,79,83,87] including st already on needle, cast(bind) off 2 sts; rep from * to * twice more, rib to end.
<u>3rd row</u> With E, rib to end, casting on 2 sts over each 2 cast(bound) off.
<u>4th row</u> With D, rib to end.
<u>5th row</u> With A, rib to end.
Using A, cast(bind) off *loosely* in rib.
Overlap front neckband on to back neckband and oversew at armhole edges. Mark back and front at side edge 16[17.5,19.5,21,22.5,24.5]cm/6¼[7,7¾, 8¼,9,9¾]in down from shoulder. Using backstitch, join cast-(bound-)off edge of sleeves to back and front between markers, matching centre of top of sleeve to shoulder. Press seams. Using backstitch on main knitting and an edge to edge st on rib, join side and sleeve seams. Press all seams. Sew on buttons.

CHILD'S CIRCLE SQUARE SKIRT

MATERIALS
General yarn weight used – lightweight double knitting (sport)
Rowan *Lightweight DK* (25g/1oz hanks) in the foll 11 colours:
  A (43) cerise – 3[3,4] hanks

LEFT *The Adult's Split Diamond Crewneck Sweater and the Child's Split Diamond Button Shoulder Sweater.*

OVERLEAF *These generous Red Diamond crewneck sweaters, inspired by the Fez leather dyeing pits, look at home in the old Tangier garden. The Adult's Crewneck is available in kit form.*

PAGES *180-181 The Child's Circle Square Skirt with two views of an Adult's Circle Square Sleeveless Sweater. The adult's sweater is available in kit form.*

B (90) emerald – 2[2,2] hanks
C (91) pine forest – 1[2,2] hanks
D (42) cherry red – 1[1,1] hank
E (25) tangerine – 1[1,1] hank
F (501) lavender – 1[1,1] hank
G (100) sage – 1[1,2] hanks
H (124) kelly green – 1[1,2] hanks
J (38) grass green – 2[2,2] hanks
L (115) flame – 1[1,1] hank
M (67) lacquer red – 1[1,1] hank
Rowan *Fine Cotton Chenille* (50g/1¾oz balls) in the foll 5 colours:
  N (382) steel – 1[1,1] ball

Q (383) turquoise – 1[1,1] ball
R (385) cyclamen – 1[1,1] ball
S (387) saville – 1[1,1] ball
T (379) cardinal – 1[1,1] ball
Rowan *Mulberry Silk* (50g/1¾oz hanks) in the foll 2 colours:
  U (877) peony – 1[1,1] hank
  V (872) flamingo – 1[1,1] hank
One circular needle in each of 2¾mm (US size 2) and 3¼mm (US size 3) *or size to obtain correct tension (gauge)*
4 buttons
Waist length of 18mm/¾in wide elastic

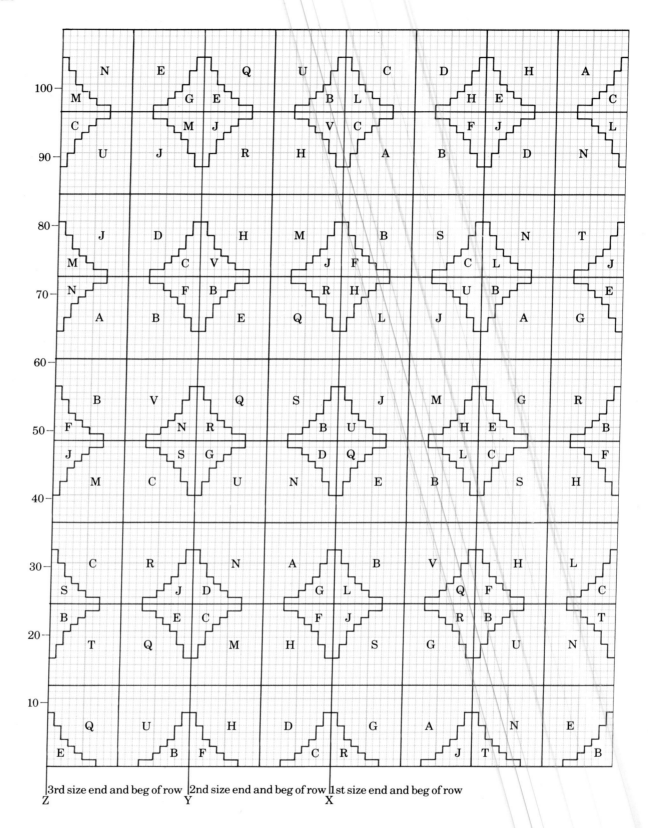

3rd size end and beg of row 2nd size end and beg of row 1st size end and beg of row

Z   Y   X

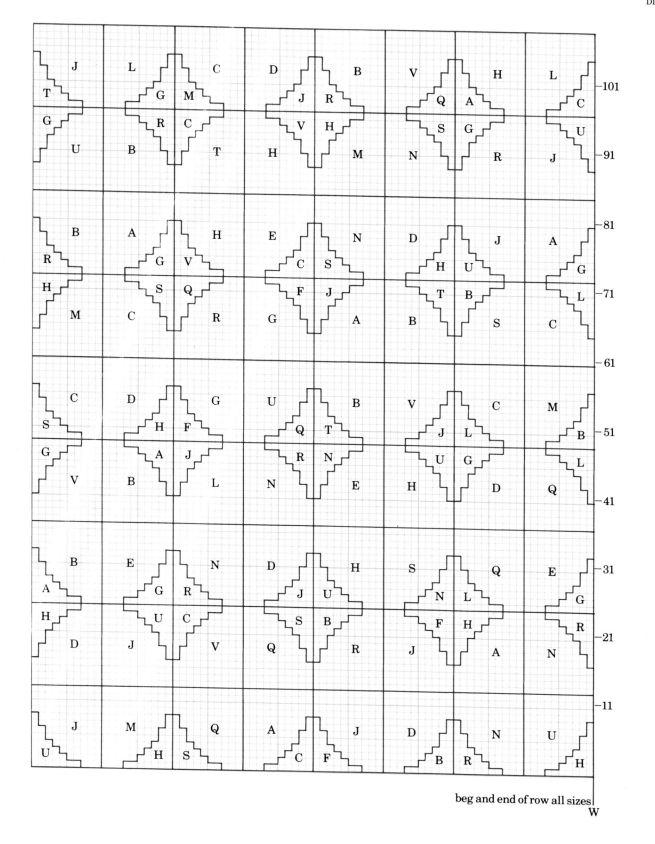

beg and end of row all sizes
W

SIZES

To fit 2[4,6]yrs or 53[56,61]cm/21[22,24]in chest.
Figures for larger sizes are given in square brackets; where there is only one set of figures, it applies to all sizes.

FINISHED MEASUREMENTS

Waist 56[60,64]cm/22½[24,25½]in
Length 25.5[29,32.5]cm/10[11½,13]in
Width at lower edge 112[120,128]cm/44¾[48,51¼]in

TENSION(GAUGE)

25 sts and 33 rows to 10cm/4in over patt on 3¼mm (US size 3) needles.
Check your tension(gauge) before beginning.

NOTES

The circular needles are used backwards and forwards in rows.
When working in patt from Chart (pages 182-183), read odd rows (K) from right to left from W to Z then from W to X[Y,Z] and even rows (P) from left to right from X[Y,Z] to W then from Z to W.

SKIRT

Using smaller needle and A, cast on 280[300,320] sts.
Beg with a K row work 5 rows in st st to form hem in stripes of 4 rows A, 1 row U.
Change to larger needle.
Picot edge row (ws) With U, P1, (P2 tog, yrn) to last st, P1.
Next row With U, K to end.
Next row With C, P to end.
Cont in patt as foll:
Beg with a K row and working in st st throughout cont in patt from Chart, beginning and ending rows as indicated. Cont until 84[96,108] rows in all have been worked in patt.

Waistband

Dec row (rs) With C, K1, (K3 tog, K1) to last 3 sts, K3 tog. 140[150,160] sts.
Cont in patt as foll:
1st row (ws) P (2A, 2B) to last 0[2,0] sts, 0[2,0]A.
2nd row K 0[2,0]A, (2B, 2A) to end.
3rd row P (2B, 2A) to last 0[2,0] sts, 0[2,0]B.
4th row K 0[2,0]B, (2A, 2B) to end.
5th and 6th rows As first and 2nd rows.
7th row With C, P to end.
8th row With U, K to end.
Picot edge row (ws) With U, P1, (P2 tog, yrn) to last st, P1.
10th row With U, K to end.
Change to smaller needle.
With A, beg with a P row work 8 rows in st st to form hem. Cast(bind) off *loosely*.

STRAPS

Using smaller needle and A, cast on 140[152,164] sts.
1st row (rs) K4, cast(bind) off 2 sts, K to end.
2nd row P to end, casting on 2 sts over the 2 cast(bound) off.
3rd row K to end.
4th row P to end.
5th row With U, K to end.
Change to larger needle.
Picot edge row (ws) With U, P1, (P2 tog, yrn) to last st, P1.
7th row With U, K to end.
8th row With C, P to end.
9th row K 2A, 2B, with A, cast(bind) off 2 sts, (2B, 2A) to last 2 sts, 2B.
10th row P (2B, 2A) 33[36,39] times, 2B, with A, cast on 2 sts, 2B, 2A.
11th row K 22C, do not break off C, (2A, 2B) to last 2 sts, 2A.
Divide for front end as foll:
12th row P (2A, 2B) to last 24 sts, 2A, 22U.
Cont on last 22 sts only in U as foll:
Picot edge row (rs) K1, (K2 tog, yfwd) to last st, K1.
Change to smaller needle.
Next row P to end.
Next row K to end. Cast(bind) off.
Using smaller needle and U, cast on 22 sts.
Next row K to end.
Change to larger needle.
Picot edge row (ws) P1, (P2 tog, yrn) to last st, P1.
Next row K to end.
Join these 22 sts to main knitting as foll:
12th row With ws of main knitting facing and using C (already attached), P these 22 sts. 140[152,164] sts.
13th and 14th rows As 9th and 10th rows.
15th row With C, K to end.
16th row With U, P to end.
Picot edge row (rs) With U, K1, (K2 tog, yfwd) to last st, K1.
Change to smaller needle.
18th row With U, P to end.

RIGHT *The Child's Circle Square Skirt with the Adult's Circle Square Sleeveless Sweater as the background.*

BELOW *Circle Square among the lively pinks and reds of a Moroccan village.*

PREVIOUS PAGE *A Child's Circle Square Button Shoulder Sweater with the Adult's Tweedy Diagonal Box Stripe Crewneck Sweater, page 56, worn as a cheeky dress. The dark-haired boy is wearing the Adult's Circle Square Crewneck Sweater, also seen as the background; both adults' sweaters are available in kit form.*

BELOW *The Adult's Circle Square Crewneck Sweater and a Child's Circle Square Button Shoulder Sweater.*

With A, beg with a K row work 3 rows in st st.
<u>22nd row</u> With A, P to last 6 sts, cast (bind) off 2 sts, P to end.
<u>23rd row</u> Cast(bind) off, AT THE SAME TIME casting on 2 sts by the thumb method over the 2 cast(bound) off.
Make a 2nd strap in the same way.

FINISHING

Press work lightly on ws according to instructions on bands, turning up hems at picot edge. Using an edge to edge st, join centre back seam of skirt. Sl st hem at lower edge lightly on ws. Sl st hem at waist lightly on ws, leaving a small opening for elastic. Measure the waist of the child and cut elastic 7cm/2¾in longer, thread through waistband and overlap by about 5cm/2in, join to form a circle. Join opening. Sl st hems at inside edges of short sections of straps lightly on ws. Sl st main hems of straps lightly on ws. Sew round double buttonholes. Mark waistband at back 7cm/2¾in either side of seam and sew on straps to inside of waistband, matching centre of strap to markers. Sew on buttons 5cm/2in and 9cm/3½in either side of centre front on waistband. Cross straps at centre back if preferred, then fasten to buttons at front. Press seams lightly on ws.

ADULT'S CIRCLE SQUARE CREWNECK SWEATER

MATERIALS

General yarn weight used – chunky (bulky)
2 strands of yarn are used together throughout.
Rowan *Lightweight DK* (25g/1oz hanks) in the foll 8 colours:
  A (88) pale airforce – 3[4] hanks
  B (52) steel blue – 2[2] hanks
  C (65) dark airforce – 2[2] hanks
  D (53) sea blue – 2[2] hanks
  E (82) camel – 2[3] hanks
  F (61) dark grey – 3[4] hanks
  H (60) silver – 4[4] hanks
  J (616) donkey – 2[3] hanks
Rowan *Light Tweed* (25g/1oz hanks) in the foll 6 colours:
  L (210) charcoal – 1[2] hanks
  M (203) pebble – 2[2] hanks
  N (221) pacific – 1[1] hank
  Q (223) atlantic – 2[2] hanks
  R (222) lakeland – 2[3] hanks
  S (205) autumn – 2[2] hanks
Rowan *Fine Cotton Chenille* (50g/1¾oz balls) in the foll 2 colours:
  T (378) shark – 1[1] ball
  U (380) mole – 1[1] ball
Rowan *Grainy Silks* (50g/1¾oz hanks) in the foll 4 colours:
  V (810) petrol – 1[1] hank
  W (804) slate – 1[1] hank
  X (801) flint – 1[1] hank
  Y (809) twine – 1[1] hank
Rowan *Silkstones* (50g/1¾oz hanks) in the foll 4 colours:
  Z (833) marble – 1[1] hank
  a (825) dried rose – 1[1] hank
  b (832) blue mist – 1[1] hank
  d (828) teal – 1[1] hank
One pair each 4mm (US size 6) and 5mm (US size 8) knitting needles *or size to obtain correct tension (gauge)*

SIZES

To fit 91-102[107-117]cm/36-40[42-46]in chest.
Figures for larger size are given in square brackets; where there is only one set of figures, it applies to both sizes.
For finished measurements see diagram (page 190).

TENSION(GAUGE)

18.5 sts and 25 rows to 10cm/4in over patt on 5mm (US size 8) needles.
Check your tension(gauge) before beginning.

NOTES

When working in patt from Chart (pages 190-191), read odd rows (K) from right to left and even rows (P) from left to right.

BACK

Using smaller needles and DD, cast on 84[92] sts.
Work 17 rows in K2, P2 rib in stripes as foll:
2 rows WW, 1 row aa, 1 row LL, 2 rows AA, 1 row QQ, 1 row EE, 2 rows TW, 1 row LL, 1 row YY, 1 row SU, 1 row RR, 1 row BB, 2 rows WW.
<u>Inc row</u> (ws) With WW, rib 5, make 1, * rib 5[3], make 1; rep from * to last 4[6] sts, rib to end. 100[120] sts.

Change to larger needles and cont in patt as foll: Beg with a K row and working in st st throughout cont in patt from Chart, beginning and ending rows as indicated until 140[152] rows in all have been worked in patt, so ending with a ws row.

Shoulder and Neck Shaping

Keeping patt correct, cast(bind) off 11[14] sts at beg of next 2 rows.

Next row Cast(bind) off 11[14] sts, patt 18[21] including st already on needle, cast (bind) off 20[22] sts, patt to end.

Cont on last set of sts only for left back:

Cast(bind) off 11[14] sts at beg of next row, then 7 sts at beg of foll row. Cast(bind) off rem 11[14] sts. Return to sts which were left; with ws facing rejoin yarns to neck edge, cast(bind) off 7 sts and patt to end. Cast(bind) off rem 11[14] sts.

FRONT

Work as given for Back until 120[132] rows in all have been worked in patt.

Neck Shaping

Next row (rs) Patt 46[55], cast(bind) off 8 [10] sts, patt to end.

Cont on last set of sts only for right front:

Next row Patt to end.

Keeping patt correct, cast(bind) off 3 sts at beg of next row, 2 sts at beg of foll 3 alt rows, then one st at beg of foll 4 alt rows. 33[42] sts.

Work 4 rows without shaping.

Shoulder Shaping

Cast(bind) off 11[14] sts at beg of next and foll alt row. Work 1 row without shaping, then cast(bind) off rem 11[14] sts.

Return to sts which were left; with ws facing rejoin yarns to neck edge, cast(bind) off 3 sts and patt to end.

Complete to match first side, reversing all shaping.

SLEEVES

Using smaller needles and DD, cast on 44[48] sts and work 17 rows in striped rib as for Back.

Inc row (ws) With WW, rib 5[2], make 1, * rib 3[4], make 1; rep from * to last 6[2] sts, rib to end. 56[60] sts.

Change to larger needles and cont in patt as foll: Beg with a K row and working in st st throughout cont in patt from Chart, beginning and ending rows as indicated AND AT THE SAME TIME, inc one st at each end of the 6th[5th] and every foll 5th[4th] row, working inc sts into patt until there are 100[116] sts. Cont without shaping until 120 rows in all have been worked in patt, so ending with a ws row.

Cast(bind) off *loosely*.

Make a 2nd sleeve in the same way.

FINISHING

Press work lightly on ws according to instructions on bands, omitting ribbing.

Using backstitch, join left shoulder seam.

NECKBAND

Using smaller needles and WW and with rs facing, pick up and K 38[40] sts around back neck and 62[64] sts around front neck. 100[104] sts.

Work 7 rows in K2, P2 rib in stripes as foll:

1 rows SY, 1 row AA, 1 row LL, 1 row aa, 2 rows WW, 1 row DD.

Using DD, cast(bind) off *loosely* in rib.

Using backstitch on main knitting and an edge to edge st on rib, join right shoulder and neckband seam. Press seams. Mark back and front at side edge 27[31.5]cm/10¾[12½] in down from shoulder seam. Using backstitch, join cast-(bound-)off edge of sleeves to back and front between markers, matching centre of top of sleeve to shoulder seam. Press all seams. Using backstitch on main knitting and an edge to edge st on rib, join side and sleeve seams. Press seams.

ABOVE *The Adult's Circle Square Crewneck Sweater. Those a bit shy of strong colours can wear this classic neutral colouring most comfortably.*

189

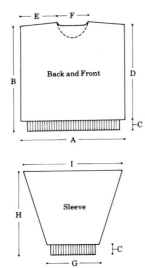

Back and Front

Sleeve

ADULT'S CIRCLE SQUARE
CREWNECK SWEATER
A = 54[65]cm/21½[26]in
B = 62.5[67.5]cm/25[26¾]in
C = 6.5cm/2½in
D = 56[61]cm/22½[24¼]in
E = 18[23]cm/7[9]in
F = 18[19]cm/7½[8]in
G = 30.5[32.5]cm/12[13]in
H = 54.5cm/21¾in
I = 54[63]cm/21½[25]in

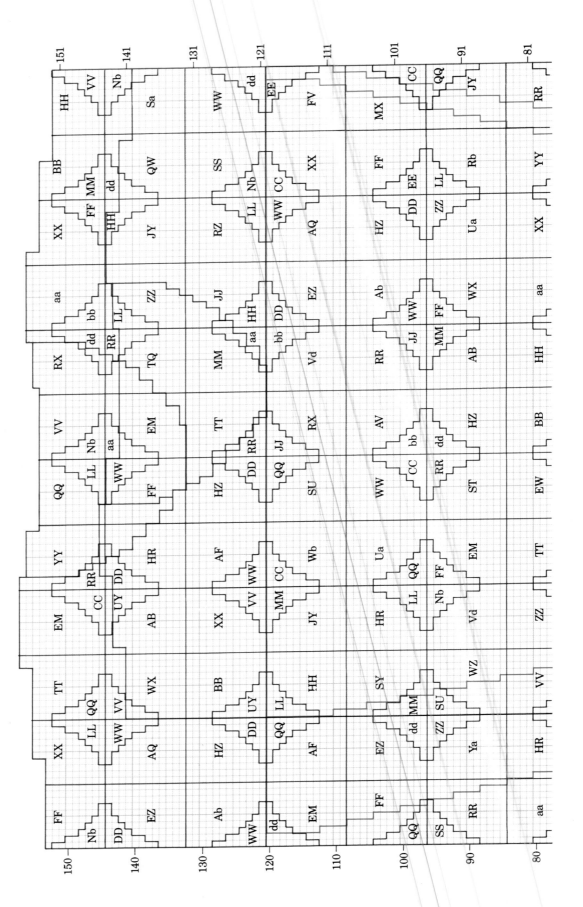

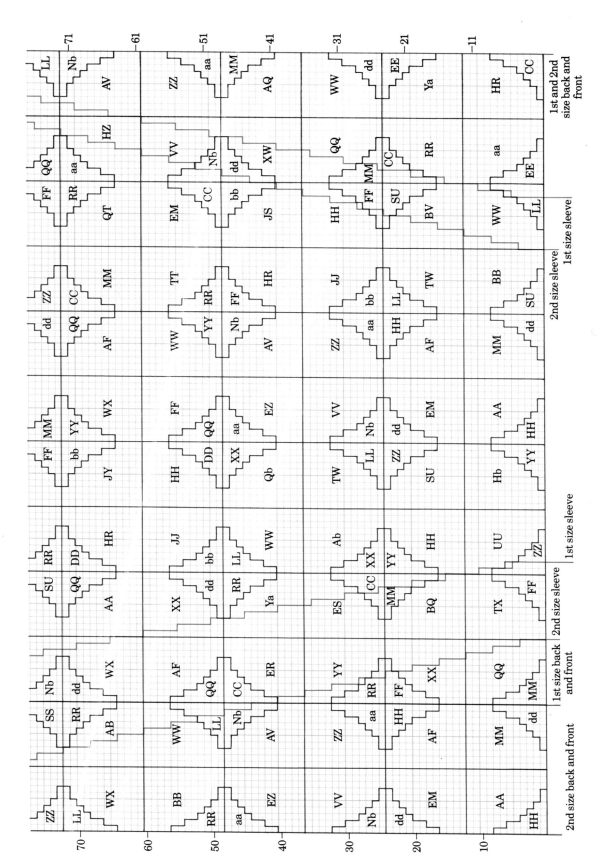

OVERLEAF *The Adult's Circle Square Crewneck Sweater, a Child's Circle Square Button Shoulder Sweater and the Adult's Tweedy Diagonal Box Stripe Crewneck Sweater, page 56, also available in kit form.*

BASIC TECHNIQUES

YARNS

The first thing you need to do when working in the way that Kaffe and I do is to forget any preconceived ideas about mixing different fibres, textures or dye lots. If you find the perfect colour and it happens to be the wrong fibre, so be it! Provided the design is such that only small areas of each yarn are used, no disasters will befall you. You can also get away with using quite different thicknesses of yarn in small areas when the need arises. However, if you find this disturbing, you can always run two fine yarns together to make a thicker one, or even split one yarn into two strands.

As for dye lots, it is a rare thing for me to worry about these nowadays. If you run out of yarn, and have to use another dye lot, look on it as a virtue, a way of enriching your work. Very few people will realize that the subtlety and richness of your design is thanks to the fact that you ran out of some yarn before you got to the sleeves!

Don't throw away any leftovers – you never know when they may be needed. I have kept all my odd bits for the last 10 or 12 years and now have all my yarns in baskets, one for each colour, in my workroom. They look attractive and inspire new colourways as I sit knitting and glance across the baskets out of the corner of my eye.

Always remember, the more colours, the merrier. You will never get a rich look to your work unless you use lots of colours – not five or six, but 25 or 26, or more. You have to work as if you were a painter. When a painter wants a slightly different shade, colours are mixed together on a palette. This isn't possible when working with yarn (except by running two yarns together), so you have to have a vast collection of colours to choose from in the first place.

Go to the sales and buy up old balls. Visit wool shops and buy a ball or two of anything that takes your fancy. If you have a design already in your mind's eye, go to your local yarn shop and collect enough shades to get you started. Once you get knitting, you will soon see which shades give you the effect you want. I often stuff the ball band into the centre of the ball so that I can replace it if I want to.

QUANTITIES

In the patterns, we have specified the amount and type of yarn for each colour. You will have to buy the minimum of each, usually 25g (1oz), and you may find that you have some over when the garment is finished. Try to see this as a bonus – you can make something else with the scraps you save.

If you don't want to use the specified yarn, or find it difficult to buy (Rowan stockists page 197), the equivalent thickness is given. Where specific colours are not given, the overall quantity and thickness of yarn is stated. In either case, do be sure to work a tension (gauge) square as the smallest difference in the yarn can wildly affect the size of the finished garment. The weights are approximate because they depend on the type of yarn you choose, for example, cotton is heavier than silk.

CHOOSING YARNS

I try to use natural fibres as much as possible. Those parents amongst you will throw up your hands in horror at the thought of all that hand-washing, but I feel that natural fibres are much better, especially for small children. Cotton is particularly suitable and I have tried to use it as much as possible in this book.

An increasing number of woollen yarns are being treated so that they can be machine washed; these are worth looking out for, especially for children. Although all the yarns used in this book are made from natural fibres, I am not averse to the odd bit of synthetic fibre if it happens to be the perfect colour or texture; for example, a woollen yarn with some nylon in it is useful on the edge of a rib or hem where it is going to get heavy wear. I suspect that as the garments in this book are fairly time consuming to make, they are unlikely to be used every day, but please don't let the thought of all that handwashing put you off. Use whichever yarn is most suitable for your lifestyle and don't feel hampered by rules.

YARN KITS

For those of you who prefer to copy our designs exactly, we have produced some yarn kits which contain the patterns and yarns in the colours and quantities required for that design. This is easier and cheaper than buying all the yarns separately, especially where there are small quantities of many different yarns involved (see pages 197-198 for list of patterns available as kits, and addresses of suppliers).

TENSION (GAUGE)

It is vital to match your tension (gauge) to that given for the pattern if you want the garment to come out the size indicated in the measurement diagram. I know this seems frustrating and boring but the time spent doing a tension (gauge) swatch is never wasted. The instructions give the tension (gauge) over the pattern for each garment. This means that you must work a swatch using the appropriate yarns and a section of the chart exactly as you would on the actual garment, casting on about 10 stitches more and working a few rows more than those given for 10cm (4in). When you have worked your sample square, press it (see overleaf) and leave it to settle for a short while, then measure it carefully, without cheating! If your tension (gauge) is different from that given in the pattern, change needle sizes and try another sample. You may find that the original swatch is as near as you can get. Nothing is more depressing than spending weeks making a garment only to find that it is a perfect fit for the family teddy! If you are designing something yourself, the swatches can be used as tension (gauge) squares provided you don't change the yarns when you make the garment. Keep all your little swatches and squares, crochet around each one and sew them together to make a blanket.

SIZES

Choose a size given in the pattern and then check that the finished measurements on the measurement diagram given for your chosen size are the right ones for your child. Children's arms may be short for their age, or their chests are chubby and the length from neck to hip is standard. Girls and boys are usually different sizes at the same age. It is vital that you check the size you want to knit;

children are severe critics and will refuse to be seen in a sweater with sleeves that hang below their knuckles.

You may need to adjust the pattern to accommodate this. The best way is to use your common sense. If your child has long arms for his or her age, add on the necessary length to the rib at the wrist or include a border between the rib and the beginning of the chart. Remember that if you make the body wider on a garment with straight armholes, the sleeves will be longer and may need to be readjusted.

HANDLING MANY COLOURS

Although many of these designs look complicated and have many yarns in them, they can often be quite easy to work provided you know how to handle the yarns. The main problems seem to concern tangling, joining in the colours and what to twist around what in order to avoid holes.

There are manageable tangles and what Kaffe calls rat's nests, which should be avoided at all costs. To achieve this you have to decide which yarns to work in balls and which to work in short lengths. Personally I like to avoid knots as much as possible, so I tend to keep balls hanging on when Kaffe would have long since cut them off and been happily tying knots for hours. So try to work in a way that is appropriate to your turn of mind. Obviously if the design has two colours in a row, keep the balls on, but if it has a lot of small areas, work with separate pieces of yarn. You can soon work out roughly how long a length is needed to complete these areas. We have given some suggestions at the beginning of each chapter as to how best to cope. If you do end up in a hopeless mess, it is worth untangling the whole thing so you can enjoy a few rows of angst-free knitting before it gets out of hand again.

It is fundamental to your enjoyment of this kind of knitting that you learn to knit in your ends rather than having to sew them all in afterwards. When joining in a new colour at the beginning of a row, leave an end of about 5cm (2in), or more if you are working on large needles, of both the old and the new yarn. Hold these ends together while you work a couple of stitches, then lay both ends over the yarn in use and work a third stitch, thus catching them down (1). Now insert the needle into the next stitch, and with your non-knitting hand, bring the ends up over the point of the working needle and work the next stitch. Now lay the ends

1

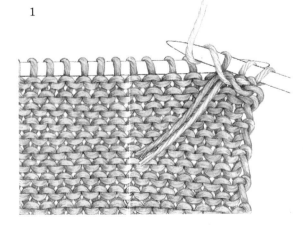

down over the working yarn and work the next stitch. Continue to take the ends up and down over the working yarn (2), leaving about 1cm (½in) on

the wrong side of the work. If you cut the yarn too close, it will come through on the right side.

The same technique can be used in the middle of

2

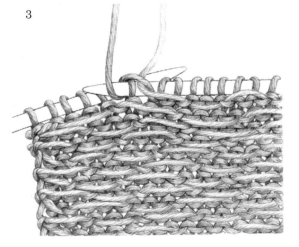

the row but be sure to twist the new yarn around the yarn just worked to avoid holes before continuing as above. If you do tie a knot, use a reef knot and work one of the two ends in on the current row and the other in the opposite direction on the following row.

As most of you will know by now, there are two distinct methods of working with more than one yarn in a row: intarsia and fairisle or weaving in. We call it 'knitting in'. The intarsia method is mostly used where there are lots of different colours in a row. Instead of being carried across the back, these yarns are simply worked in their place and left hanging at the back until the next row, and then the next colour is worked and so on across the row. The important thing to remember in order to avoid holes is to twist each yarn around the one next to it as you go from one yarn to the next. With this method it is possible to work vertical stripes or lines of many different colours with totally flat, neat joins between them (3).

When using this method to work diagonal stripes or any design where the colour moves from left to right on subsequent rows, always catch the

3

yarn into the back of the work one stitch further over than where you will need it on the next row. For example, on a diagonal stripe that moves over one stitch on every row, catch the yarn in two stitches further over so that on the next row it will be hanging in the correct position (4 – overleaf).

The fairisle or knitting in method is appropriate

where a yarn is being used repeatedly across the row. It is probably best not to work more than

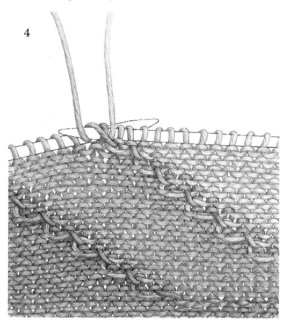

4

three colours in one row like this or the work becomes very thick. The yarn or yarns being carried across the back should be caught into the wrong side of the work about every third stitch when not in use, and this should be done in different places on subsequent rows wherever possible (like staggering bricks in a wall) to avoid the yarns grinning through onto the right side (5).

It is important that this knitting in is done at a relaxed and even tension (gauge) or the knitting will pucker. This comes with practice, so don't give

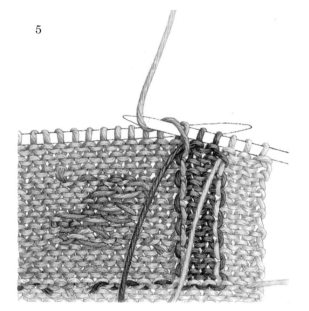

5

up if you find it difficult at first. Most people tend to pull the yarn too tight so try to think 'loose' while you're working.

CIRCULAR NEEDLES
I use circular needles (twin pins) to the exclusion of all other knitting needles. The weight of the work falls onto my lap and I can get needles long enough to hold hundreds of stitches. We have only specified circular needles where they are abso-

lutely necessary, but I strongly recommend them to anyone who has never tried them – you will never look back.

FINISHING
I feel the garments are often ruined by bad finishing. You can spend months knitting something, then spoil it by sewing it up badly or not pressing it properly; so here are a few hints.

Picking up stitches
This subject seems to cause more heartache than any other in the knitting field. In these patterns we have, as far as possible, given a guide as to how to pick up the stitches for buttonbands, cuffs etc. These are only approximate, but should make the job a bit easier. However, if you are designing something yourself and want to pick up stitches for buttonbands for instance, first consider how these bands are to be knitted. Are they plain, patterned, ribbed or moss stitch? Knit a small sample and check the tension (gauge). Measure the length of the garment from neck to lower edge, then calculate how many stitches at this tension (gauge) will be needed. Also consider at this point how the pattern (if there is one) fits into this number of stitches and where the buttons will come. You may need to add or subtract a stitch or two to make the pattern fit. Count the number of rows from neck to lower edge of the main knitting – say 100 – and if you need 90 stitches for your front bands, you will need to pick up one stitch for nine out of every 10 rows up the front of the garment. This gives you the general idea.

Always pick up stitches around the neck in a colour that tends to disappear into the main knitting so as to avoid showing up any imperfections.

Hems
Wherever possible, work hems on smaller needles than the main knitting. Use a plain yarn so that the hem lies as flat as possible and always press well. Be careful to cast (bind) off loosely, especially at the front edges of a garment, so that the cast-off (bound-off) edge doesn't pull the main knitting out of shape. It should be the tension (gauge) of the sewing when you catch (tack) down the hem on the wrong side of the garment that dictates the way the front edges hang.

Pressing
I have to admit to being fanatical about pressing. You may notice how often this is referred to in each pattern. It seems to be something that most people find nerve wracking. My own method is unorthodox but works for me. If you do try it, proceed with caution and not at all unless you have a powerful steam iron with an extra steam button. I simply lay the pieces of work upside down on an ironing board, which is covered with several layers of towelling, and with the iron on somewhere between wool and cotton (depending on the composition of the yarn), and the most steam possible, I press, being careful not to distort the knitting, lifting the iron rather than pushing it across the work and omitting ribs.

For those who find this heretical, use a damp cloth over the knitting but do make sure you know what is going on underneath. You can buy special transparent cloths made with this in mind. If you prefer to block your work and find this method satisfactory for you, keep doing it. Do whatever is best for you.

Press seams and hems when you have sewn up

the garment – always omitting ribbing. The only garments I do not press are those with any kind of stitch pattern, such as cable.

Sewing up
We have specified in each pattern the method of sewing up to be used, either backstitch or an edge-to-edge seam, which is almost invisible. In either case, a tapestry needle and a fairly fine, strong yarn should be used (not necessarily yarn from the knitting if this is too thick), in a colour that will fade as much as possible into the knitting.

An edge-to-edge seam is worked with the wrong side of the work facing you. Take up the end of a row on one piece and the end of the corresponding row on the other piece. Then pull the sewing thread fairly tight so that it almost disappears. Don't allow the seam to pucker.

Whichever method you choose, pay attention to the pattern, checking every four or five stitches to see that it matches wherever possible.

Buttons
Choosing buttons for a garment is always great fun. Because knitting is usually quite thick, there has to be some sort of shank on the buttons. For those buttons without shanks, you must make one when you sew on the button by inserting a matchstick or knitting needle between the button and the knitting while you fix it in place. Remove the matchstick and wind the sewing thread several times around to form the shank.

YARN AND KIT INFORMATION

YARN SUPPLIERS
Nearly all the patterns in this book specify Rowan yarns with types and colours for the illustrated design. Rowan yarns can be obtained either from yarn shops (see below) in the usual way or in the form of yarn kits for selected patterns. For details of stockists and mail order sources of yarns and kits, write or contact the following distributors:

United Kingdom
Rowan Yarns, Green Lane Mill, Holmfirth,
West Yorkshire, England, HD7 1RW.
Tel: (0484) 681881

USA
The Westminster Trading Corporation*,
5 Northern Boulevard, Amherst,
New Hampshire 03031, USA.
Tel: (603) 886 5041

Handcraft from Europe,
PO Box 372, 1201 Bridgeway,
Sausalito, CA 94965, USA.

Australia
Sunspun Enterprises Pty Ltd*,
191 Canterbury Road, Canterbury,
Victoria 3126.
Tel: (03) 830 1609

Belgium
Ma Campagne,
rue du Village 4,
Septon 5482, Durbuy.
Tel: (086) 213451

Canada
Estelle Designs and Sales Ltd*,
38 Continental Place, Scarborough,
Ontario M1R 2T4.
Tel: (416) 298 9922

Cyprus
Colourworks, 12 Parnithos Street,
Nicosia.
Tel: (047) 2933

Denmark
Mosekonens Vaerksted,
Mosevej 13, L1 Binderup,
9600 AARS.
Tel: (08) 656065

Finland
Stockmann,
PO Box 220, SF-00101 Helsinki.
Tel: (0) 12151

Holland
Henk & Henrietta Beukers, Dorpsstraat 9,
5327 Ar Hurwenen.
Tel: (04182) 1764

Italy
La Compagnia del Cotone, Via Mazzini 44,
10123 Torino.
Tel: (011) 878381

Japan
Diakeito Co. Ltd, 1-5-23 Nakatsu Oyodo-Ku,
Osaka 531.
Tel: (06) 371 5653

New Zealand
Creative Fashion Centre, PO Box 45083,
Epuni Railway, Lower Hutt.
Tel: (04) 674 085

Norway
Eureka, PO Box 357, 1401 Ski.
Tel: (0987) 1909

Sweden
Wincent, Luntmakargatan 56,
113 58 Stockholm.
Tel: (08) 32 70 60

West Germany
Textilwerkstatt, Friedenstrasse 5,
3000 Hanover 1.
Tel: (0511) 818001

YARN SHOPS
Creativity,
45 New Oxford Street, London WC1.
Tel: (01) 240 2945

Colourway,
112A Westbourne Grove, London W2.
Tel: (01) 229 1432

Liberty,
Regent Street, London W1.
Tel: (01) 734 1234

Ries Wools,
242 High Holborn, London WC1.
Tel: (01) 242 7721

Shepherd's Purse and Meadow,
2 John Street, Bath.
Tel: (0225) 310790

Bobbins,
Wesley Hall, Church Street, Whitby,
North Yorkshire.
Tel: (0947) 600585

Up Country,
12 Towngate, Holmfirth, West Yorshire.
Tel: (0484) 687803

Rowan / Oxford,
102 Gloucester Green,
Oxford, Oxfordshire.
Tel: (0865) 79366

Harlequin,
65 Thistle Street,
Aberdeen, Scotland.
Tel: (0224) 635716

Needlecraft Ltd,
27-28 Dawson Street, Dublin, Eire.
Tel: (0001) 772493

Siop Jen,
36-38 Castle Arcade, Cardiff, Wales.
Tel: (0222) 342933

Ritzynitz,
37 Bond Street, Brighton, East Sussex.
Tel: (0273) 28860

KNITTERS

If you would like a design knitted up, contact the following for further information.

Beatrice Bellini,
74 Pimlico Road, London SW1W 8LS.
Tel: (01) 730 2630

Jenny Francis,
36-38 Castle Arcade, Cardiff, Wales.
Tel: (0222) 342933

YARN KITS

The following kits are available from Rowan Yarns stockists and distributors worldwide.

Adult's Tumbling Blocks Sweater *page 44*
Adult's Bright Diagonal Box Stripe Crewneck Sweater *page 53*
Child's Diagonal Box Stripe Sweater *page 61*
Child's Comb Dress *page 85*
Baby's Flags Jumpsuit *page 135*
Baby's Harlequin Button Shoulder Sweater *page 150*
Child's Turkish Lattice Button Shoulder Sweater *page 156*
Adult's Turkish Lattice Sleeveless Sweater *page 164*
Adult's Split Diamond Crewneck Sweater *page 172*
Child's Split Diamond Button Shoulder Sweater *page 174*
Adult's Red Diamond Crewneck Sweater *page 178*
Adult's Circle Square Crewneck Sweater *page 188*

The following kits are available from Ehrman, 21-22 Vicarage Gate, London W8 4AA and from Rowan distributors marked with an * in the list of distributors.

Adult's Squares Jacket *page 22*
Adult's Tweedy Diagonal Box Stripe Crewneck Sweater *page 56*
Adult's Diagonal Stripe Shawl Collar Sweater *page 61*
Adult's Brushstrokes Crewneck Sweater *page 71*
Adult's Tulip Shirt Collar Sweater *page 117*
Adult's Pink Brocade Sweater *page 123*
Child's Harlequin Turtleneck Sweater *page 147*
Adult's Turkish Lattice Scoopneck Sweater *page 158*
Adult's Circle Square Sleeveless Sweater *page 180*

ABBREVIATIONS

alt	*alternate(ly)*		P	*purl*
approx	*approximately*		patt	*pattern*
beg	*begin(ning)*		psso	*pass slipped stitch over*
cm	*centimetre(s)*		rem	*remain(s)(ing)*
cont	*continu(e)(ing)*		rep	*repeat(s)*
dec	*decreas(e)(ing)*		rs	*right side of work*
foll	*follow(s)(ing)*		sl	*slip*
g	*gram(s)*		st(s)	*stitch(es)*
in	*inch(es)*		st st	*stocking stitch (stockinette stitch)*
inc	*increase(e)(ing)*			
K	*knit*		tbl	*through back of loop(s)*
make 1	*pick up loop lying between last stitch worked and next stitch on left hand needle and work into back of it*		tog	*together*
			ws	*wrong side of work*
			yfwd	*yarn forward (yarn over)*
			yrn	*yarn round needle (yarn over)*
mm	*millimetre(s)*		yrs	*years*
oz	*ounce(s)*			

INDEX

ACKNOWLEDGEMENTS

More than usual, this book is a collective effort. Our models in Florida, New England, California, New Mexico, Morocco and Britain were hunted down or stopped in the street by Steve and some inspired talent scouts. Our grateful thanks go therefore to June Bridgewater, Jane Newdick, Craig Biondi, John Torson, Margaritte McBey, Robert Serofi, The American School in Tangier and Mohamed Sahraoui. To our tireless and attractive models, a huge thank you for making our garments come alive. For beautiful knitting and help with the patterns, thank you to Maria Brannan, Caroline Day, Kay Kettles, Francesca Nurse, Julliana Yeo. For co-ordinating patterns and developing kits, thanks to Sue Roberts, Marilyn Wilson, Charyn Jones, Sally Harding and the team at Rowan yarns. Thanks also to Cherriwyn Magill for the design. For encouragement and moral support, thanks to Jamie, Richard and Sarah Wallace.

Editor Charyn Jones
Art Editor Cherriwyn Magill
Designer Elaine Hewson
Pattern writer Sue Roberts
Pattern checker Marilyn Wilson
Charts Dennis Hawkins
Additional artwork Sally Holmes, John Hutchinson

Text and designs copyright © 1989 Kaffe Fassett and Zoë Hunt
Photographs copyright © 1989 Steve Lovi

Published in the United States of America by Clarkson N. Potter, Inc., and distributed by Crown Publishers Inc., 201 East 50th Street, New York, New York 10022
Published in Great Britain by Century Hutchinson Ltd.
CLARKSON N. POTTER, POTTER and colophon are trademarks of Clarkson N. Potter, Inc.
Manufactured in Spain
Library of Congress Cataloging-in-Publication Data
Fassett, Kaffe.
[Family Album]
family album / By Kaffe Fassett and Zoë Hunt.
P.   cm.
1. Knitting—Patterns.   I. Hunt, Zoë.   II. Title.   III. Title: Family Album.
TT825.F37   1989
746.9'2—dc20   89-3955
ISBN 0-517-57385-7

10 9 8 7 6 5 4 3 2 1
First Edition